REVOLUTION
PRICING

# PRICE FOR
# GROWTH

A Revolutionary Step-by-Step Approach
To Massively Increase the Value of Your Company
By Leveraging Focused Pricing Strategies

*Specifically Tailored for Repeat-Customer Businesses*

## JEFF ROBINSON

Published by:

Revolution Pricing LLC, Houston, Texas, United States of America

RevolutionPricing.com

For additional information related to this book, please visit the book's website at:

PriceForGrowth.com

ISBN 978-1-7368225-1-7

Credits

Editing: J.D. Ho

Print Design: Bhagchand

Authored, Edited, and Published in the United States of America

Printed in China for International Distribution

To my wife and best friend, Michelle.

Thank you for believing in me and standing by me through all the good times and the bad times. You've given me more than you will ever know.


And to my three wonderful daughters: Whitney, Jessie, and Sydney.

You've given me the privilege of seeing the world through younger eyes, and you've always encouraged me to look out for the underdogs.


And to my mother, Kathy Robinson.

You've always been my biggest cheerleader. Even when I thought I was pretty average, you thought I was great.


And to my large extended family.

You've always been a great support net throughout my whole life.

# Contents

# In Memoriam

## A Tribute to Michael Davis

Many people in the pricing industry had the privilege of knowing Michael Davis. And many would say he had an important impact on their lives. I was lucky enough to count myself among his friends. Unfortunately, we lost Michael in December 2019.

I had the good fortune to work with both Michael and his sweet wife, Kala, at PROS, starting in 2005 and 2007 respectively. Immediately, people gravitated to  them because of their values of care, respect, diligence, honesty, and teamwork. These values were reflected in all of Michael's work. As customers got to know Michael, they always wanted him involved in their projects because they knew they could trust him, and he wouldn't let them fail. Michael was super intelligent. I noticed he seemed to pick up on ideas faster than others, and he quickly rose to the top of whatever team he was working on. Many of his customers sought to hire him because of his integrity, work ethic, and leadership. After PROS, Michael shared his talents and leadership working with Tyco Electronics, GE Oil & Gas, Covia, and Stanley Black & Decker.

Michael's friends describe him as passionate, driven, always smiling, positive, strong, smart, funny, a good friend no matter the time between chats, trustworthy, and just a great guy to be around, both personally and professionally. Those who know Michael well know he was a great family man. It was always clear to us that family was the most important thing to him at all times.

Michael and Kala have been raising three beautiful daughters: Sydney, Payton, and Raegan. It's hard to look at any of them without seeing Michael in their features and characteristics.

Michael, thank you for the life you led and the wonderful values you shared with us. We will miss you.

*Five percent of the profits from the sale of this book will go to a college fund for Michael and Kala's children.*

# Acknowledgements

So many people deserve to be acknowledged for helping me get here.

First of all, I'd like to acknowledge some of the key thought leaders, some of whom are referred to as the "Godfathers of Pricing" in the relatively small community of pricing experts and practitioners. But I learned and benefited tremendously from the discussions and writings of Dan Nimer, Tom Nagle, Reed Holden, Mike Marn, Herman Simon, and Craig Zawada.

I'd also like to recognize Eric Mitchell, the founder of The Professional Pricing Society, which is currently the largest professional organization for pricing on the planet. Today, his son Kevin is leading what his father started, advancing pricing knowledge and expertise around the globe.

I must also acknowledge several other key individuals who spent years with me working through ideas and putting them into practice to challenge them and perfect them, including (in alphabetical order): Gary Alexander, Navin Aswal, Rohan Bairat, Neil Biehn, Erik Bleyl, Steve Bondi, Andy Boyd, Christine Byun, Rob Christenson, Roxy Cramer, Ajay Damani, Jacqui Davis, Michael Davis, Bhavit Desai, Bill Dudziak, Sean Ferguson, Doug Fuehne, Steve Goldstein, Ed Gonzalez, Tom Gorin, MG Gurbaxani, Chuck Hinkle, Phil Holladay, Anshu Jalora, Sunil John, Matt Johnson, Royce Kallesen, Vernon Lennon, Stephan Liozu, Ashish Malhotra, Augustin Manchon, Kevin McCraw, Oscar Moreno, Joanna Papakonstantinou, Todd Pate, Harold Peck, Adriana Rapolla, Wilbur Reid, Rob Reiner, Tony Ruggiero, John Salch, Patrick Scheidau, Walt Sepaniac, Justin Silver, Martin Simoncic, Alex Smith, Mark Stevens, Charles Sweeney, Ted Valkov, Ulrich von Beck, Geoff Webb, David White, Steve Wilkins, Wagner Williiams, and many others I don't have room to name individually.

I would like to thank key people who gave me opportunities to grow my career and expand my skill set under their leadership, including Ivan Boyd, Mark Lamp, Greg Smith, Bert Winemiller, Charlie Murphy, Ron Woestemeyer, Andres Reiner, Tom Dziersk, and Erik Bleyl.

I would also like to thank J.D. Ho, my editor, for her excellent work on this book. She magically turned broken noodles into spaghetti.

And to many others I haven't named who have helped me along the way, I say Thank You!

# About the Author

Jeff Robinson has spent over 20 years of his career designing, marketing, selling, implementing, and consulting in the field of pricing. He has worked with over 100 companies across 15 different industries to help them solve their highest priority pricing challenges. He has authored several blogs, articles, white papers, presentations, and training materials, and he has presented at pricing and industry conferences on the subject of pricing and pricing strategy. He has held several executive leadership positions, leading product management, data science and innovation, consulting services, business development, and sales and marketing. His real-world experience is built on the foundation of a strong education with a bachelor's degree in Economics from Brigham Young University and an MBA from Rice University.

His current LinkedIn profile can be found at:

https://www.linkedin.com/in/jeffrobinson4/

And his Author website can be found at:

https://jeffrobinson.com/

# Introduction

What if you could double the value of your company in less than a year just by using the right focused pricing strategy?

Is this scenario even possible? How would you know?

What if we've been wrong about profit-focused pricing strategies? What if our efforts to grow margins were actually hurting our ability to maximize long-term profit growth? **What if we've been missing out on the most powerful ways to use pricing to maximize the value of the company?**

For the last two decades, companies have been told that a 1% increase in price will, on average, translate to an 11% increase in profits. During that time, an entire pricing solution industry has exploded, fueled by the quest to help companies achieve that extra 1%, in hopes of achieving that extra profit that's been "left on the table."

Many of the short-term results have shown promise. A multitude of companies have invested millions of dollars in pricing solutions, and many of them have reported price improvements as high as 2%–3% or more, easily exceeding the quest for the extra 1%. But unfortunately, these reported benefits are seldom able to continue for more than two to three years.

Why?

From my observations, the typical pattern might start with a multi-month sales engagement to elevate expectations and paint the picture of how one's pricing solution is "the answer" to all their pricing needs. This is typically followed by a multi-month implementation effort to get the solution operational and capable of delivering prices that might make a difference. Many companies reach this point and, if they are among the lucky majority, start to see some impressive results. They may see one or two years of significant benefits … maybe a little more. But then something eventually changes. Doubt creeps in. Executives wonder if their pricing solution is really working as designed. Minds start questioning why the margins on the financial statements don't seem to be growing at anywhere close to the rate that was expected or promised. Vocal champions may try to defend the value of the solution, insisting that things would be much worse without it … even though they may also start to let doubts and questions creep in. Eventually all the momentum is gone. People start looking for other types of solutions to help them achieve the more sustainable profit growth they still believe to be possible.

The old solution is abandoned. What might have previously generated over 1000% ROI …now collecting dust, along with all the other IT projects whose relevance has passed.

This scenario is very demotivating for both customers and solution providers. With so many solution providers moving to SaaS (Software as a Service) models, it can be quite detrimental to have subscriptions cut short because of misaligned expectations and a shortage of legitimate margin expansion opportunities after just a few years.

While these scenarios may include measurable successes along the way, they're not producing sustainable and repeatable profit growth year after year into the future.

And companies that are using those pricing strategies are NOT doubling the value of their respective companies as a result of those strategies.

Yet there are companies who ARE doubling their value, multiple times, over the same timeframe between 2000 and 2020. Companies like Amazon, Apple, Netflix, Alibaba, and Domino's Pizza, just to name a few, and hundreds more. All of these companies have doubled their value multiple times since January 1, 2000. Many of them did it multiple times in periods of two years or less. None of those companies were implementing margin-expansion pricing strategies. They were implementing growth pricing strategies…because they wanted to grow.

The reality is, most companies are using the wrong pricing strategies—pricing for margin when they want to be growing—and missing out on opportunities to grow the value of their companies.

Without a comprehensive framework for identifying the opportunities that can have the biggest impact on growing the value of the company, it's too easy to default to profit-based pricing strategies and to miss the bigger picture.

That's why, after twenty years of designing, building, selling, and implementing pricing solutions (that have now reached hundreds of companies whose revenues total over $1 trillion), I developed the **five sacred metrics of pricing success** and a comprehensive framework for identifying impact and deploying pricing strategies to have maximum impact on company value.

After reading this book, you will see how using this framework, along with the accompanying tools, will allow you to easily identify which pricing strategies will give you the best chance to double the value of your company in a relatively short period of time.

In the decades leading up to this book, it's become crystal clear that too many companies are neglecting some of the most important principles of pricing, most notably how pricing affects customer attitudes and behaviors, both in the short term and over time. And this neglect is costing companies the long-term sustainable growth they desire.

Furthermore, this lack of understanding and clarity around pricing has caused executives to question their faith in well-meaning pricing people, resulting in clouds of doubt over the effectiveness of pricing strategies and solutions in general. And in all this confusion and complexity, people have stopped trusting the very people who can help.

This vacuum of clarity creates the perfect breeding ground for pricing myths and bad ideas, which can easily be spread across the organization by well-intentioned stakeholders who just want to help. Unfortunately, without a common, sustainable framework to rely on, these otherwise intelligent individuals just end up making things worse.

Yes. Pricing is complex. But the fundamentals are really quite simple. And despite the many attempts I've witnessed over the years, you just can't outsmart the fundamentals. I've seen people try. It never ends well.

While most people have all the basic bits of knowledge necessary for creating successful pricing strategies, what's missing is a framework to bring all this knowledge into a cohesive structure for making decisions. That's what I'm giving you in this book—a revolutionary, step-by-step approach to create the best pricing strategies to maximize the value of your company.

The concepts and principles shared in this book will help clarify much of the confusion that currently exists around pricing. Once you've read what I have to share, I'm confident that you will also understand why so many pricing solutions have not succeeded in a more sustainable, mainstream fashion and why companies need to adopt a different perspective in order to finally leverage pricing to maximize company value.

This is my passion. This is why I'm writing this book—to offer up a new framework for making pricing decisions that will make your business much more successful. The path to this success begins with a focus on customer relationships—how to improve them and how to grow them. This is the win–win outcome that makes the world a better place. After all, customer value is at the heart of any strategy for long-term business success.

## The Benefits of Reading This Book

By reading this book, the most impactful benefit you will receive is knowledge—knowledge that will likely change your life. Knowledge is how you will win.

If you read this book and follow its principles, you will see how you can make massive improvements to the value of your company in a relatively short period of time. It's not unreasonable to think you might be able to double the value of your company in less than a year. After all, the value of your company is really just the present value of all the future profits your company will generate over its life. There is tremendous leverage in changing your trajectory of growth. You will see, from the **five sacred metrics of pricing success**, that there are many ways to increase the present value of your future profits beyond just increasing the value of your present profits. Even though most pricing solutions have been developed to help companies selectively increase prices for higher overall margins, this book will uncover many other pricing opportunities that can drive more sustainable profit growth and immense company value. I expect you will start making positive changes immediately after reading this book.

So, here is my value promise to you if you are willing to invest in reading this book:

**New Knowledge:** You will accumulate new knowledge about pricing that will help you make much better and more efficient decisions throughout your career. You will make your investment back tenfold just by reducing the time it takes to make decisions. Previously difficult decisions will become almost automatic. After all, you'll get information in this book that is typically sold in training workshops costing $1,500 or more.

**New Metrics:** You'll learn about the **five sacred metrics for pricing success**, and why they're so important when it comes to impacting the value of your company. You will see which pricing metrics matter most in your business, and you will understand how to use them to interpret what's happened and how to best respond.

**New Decision Process:** You will get a new step-by-step approach for planning and executing pricing strategies. I will give you the template. You can use it as is, or you can adapt it to your own business. Either way, you will have a repeatable process for making high-value decisions.

**Avoidance of High-Cost Mistakes**: You will learn about potential decisions that can harm your business, so you can avoid them. You will become more sensitive to whole categories of decisions that should automatically raise red flags in your mind. You'll become more aware of risks that can hurt your growth.

You'll learn about several pricing myths and misconceptions that often lead companies to make bad decisions that work against company objectives.

**Money-Saving Advice**: Your new knowledge and perspective will help you avoid hiring solution providers who might otherwise distract you with "shiny objects," while preventing you from accomplishing your most important objectives. At the end of this book, you should be telling solution providers what your solution needs to do—not just taking the solution provider's recommendations.

**Resource Downloads:** If you register your book on the website PriceForGrowth.com, you will get access to downloadable examples, tools, and slides to help you communicate inside your own organization.

**A More Expansive Mindset**: I am a big believer in the "growth mindset." All of the principles I cover in this book stress the adoption of a growth mindset—a way of thinking which can change your ability to imagine and find solutions to life's most impactful challenges. If you take nothing else away from this book, you will benefit from adopting more of the growth mindset into your life.

In short, I am writing this book to help you and your company be more successful by focusing on the specific pricing metrics and opportunities that have the biggest impact on growing the value of your company. You will gain a new frame of reference for making pricing-related decisions. With this new perspective, I am confident that your decisions will inevitably lead to a massive increase in the value of your company.

## This Book's Target Audience: Repeat Customer Businesses

While many of the principles and lessons in this book are applicable for any company, this book is specifically targeted to companies who sell to repeat customers. This includes most B2B (business-to-business) companies and some B2C (business-to-consumer) companies. If you track your customers, and you aspire to sell to them on a repeat basis, this book is for you.

If you are a CFO, CEO, COO, VP of Pricing, VP of Growth, VP of Sales, or any manager or executive who has responsibility for company growth and/or pricing, this book is for you. Reading and understanding this book will help you ensure that your pricing strategies are working for you and not against you. The stakes are too high, and the knowledge in this book is too valuable to ignore.

I hope you enjoy the journey we're about to take.

PART 1

# Foundations

*One must have first of all a solid foundation*

—Sri Aurobindo

Foundations

## CHAPTER 1

# Redefining the Pricing Journey

*Every product and service sold since the beginning of time has had a price assigned to it. Setting that price is among the most crucial, most profit-sensitive decisions that companies make. Ironically, very few companies price well.*

—*The Price Advantage* © 2004, Marn, Roegner, Zawada

This quote above is one of my all-time favorites regarding the power and impact of pricing. After reading *The Price Advantage* in 2004, I was further convinced that the world of pricing was full of opportunity. And I doubled down on my decision to focus my career on helping companies get the most out of their pricing decisions. Pricing was everywhere…on every product…on every transaction. Every dollar of revenue transacted in the world's vast economies has had a price attached to it.

Yes, pricing was everywhere. Pricing expertise was not. This meant opportunity!

As one might expect, the pricing solution industry has exploded over the last twenty years. Today there are large and small software companies devoted to pricing. There are literally hundreds of consulting firms that collectively employ thousands of consultants focused on improving pricing across many of the world's most forward-thinking companies. Several thought-provoking books have been written by a variety of authors on the topic of pricing, each adding to the collective knowledge of pricing best practices. For ages, companies have been building their own custom pricing solutions, and this practice has only accelerated over the last few years. For better or for worse, the business world has been flooded with pricing solutions.

Ironically, despite the massive attention pricing has received over the last two decades, it seems that, collectively, companies have not made much progress in solving "the pricing problem" or achieving the promise of sustainable profit growth through better pricing.

Although many companies have invested in software and consulting solutions to improve their pricing capabilities, most of those companies are still trying to solve the same problems they were seeking to solve many years ago. Even companies who publicly claimed that their pricing solutions were at one time generating incremental profits of 150–300 basis points (or sometimes even more) have, in subsequent years, let those same pricing solutions lose momentum, struggle for legitimacy, and eventually become abandoned. It's not uncommon to see many of the same companies back in the market, looking for a new pricing solution, claiming their old solution was not delivering the results they were expecting.

But I think the biggest indictment of most profit-focused pricing solutions is the lack of long-term sustained growth in profit margins on public company financial statements. If pricing solutions were really delivering 150–300 basis points of incremental margins year after year, you would expect companies to be adding 1500 to 3000 basis points (15% to 30%) after 10 years of benefits from these solutions. But the public financial statements of these companies do not show this. What you see instead is that margins are mostly flat year over year with very few exceptions. In some cases, where companies show impressive short-term margin improvements, the long-term observations almost always reveal that the improvements have either stalled or, more commonly, regressed back to original profit levels.

For the most part, the billions of dollars invested in pricing software and consulting solutions over the years have not produced the sustained profit growth that was promised or expected. Companies are still looking for that silver bullet solution that will finally deliver results in a sustainable fashion, year after year.

Pricing opportunities have not gone away. Pricing still has considerable leverage on profitability, probably more than any other single variable, and yet it remains one of the last frontiers still left unconquered.

## Why Aren't Pricing Solutions Delivering Long-Term, Sustainable Profit Growth?

If pricing is so important to the success or failure of a company, as I and many others continue to believe, then why do so many pricing problems still exist?

Why are so many questionable pricing strategies and decisions implemented by some of the world's most well-known companies? Why, despite the availability of so many pricing software and consulting solutions, do so many companies continue to struggle with pricing?

I've asked this question many times to both consultants and employees of pricing software companies: "Why are pricing solutions failing to deliver sustainable profit growth over the long term?" And I've received many thoughtful answers which typically blame the problem on things like lack of executive commitment, lack of sales adoption, or pricing becoming a political battle between Finance and Sales.

I've asked the question of customers and former customers: "Why did your pricing solution lose momentum and essentially become abandoned?" Again, I received thoughtful answers which typically blamed the problem on the software being too difficult to use, trouble with getting the right data updated in the system, lack of enforcement by executives, lack of a good way to measure ROI, and sometimes the claim that the solution simply didn't live up to its promised capabilities (overpromising and underdelivering).

The question of why most pricing solutions fail to deliver sustainable long-term profit growth is critically important to both the solution providers and the companies who might use them in hopes of maximizing the value of their companies. How can we have any trust in a solution if we can't understand why it works or, in this case, why it fails to deliver results over a long, sustained timeframe?

It is a question that troubled me for years, until the answer finally clicked into place. The answer is the substance of this whole book, but I will give you a teaser.

**Why are the majority of today's pricing solutions failing to deliver long-term, sustainable profit growth?** In short, the answer is because most solutions focus on only one aspect of pricing (typically margin improvement), where a one-time correction may be needed. And once that correction is achieved, further corrective effort does not lead to improvement. As my good friend Harold Peck once said many years ago, "Raising prices is not a sustainable source of profit growth."

Why do these types of solutions get so much attention in the market? Because companies want to see rapid return on their investments, and the easiest way to show rapid returns is to implement select price increases to show increased margins. The problem is that it's not usually possible to continue to grow margins every year over a sustained period of time.

Without a comprehensive framework that ties pricing actions to the metrics that drive real growth in all present and future profits (including customer acquisition, growth, and retention), pricing solutions will lose their potency as their targeted corrective actions stall out. Most pricing solutions based on selectively raising prices for expanded margins tend to ignore these other critical customer relationship metrics and the risks imposed upon them when prices are increased.

That's the short answer. You will discover the full, comprehensive answer as you read through the rest of this book.

The framework I will share with you brings pricing objectives and business objectives together through a collection of **five "sacred" metrics.** These metrics will bring clarity to the size and impact of opportunities and how they translate to the growth of the value of your company, not just for the short term, but for the long term. And you will be able to see the connection between today's pricing decisions and all future profit flows. Even though it's based on common-sense logic, the approach itself is quite revolutionary, and it should transform the way you think about pricing.

## Building onto the Progress of the World's Pricing Pioneers

Every generation has its own pioneers that build advancements based on the knowledge and expertise of those who came before. I have tremendous respect for the many people who have made contributions and advancements in the world of pricing over the last few decades. There are many intelligent individuals who have developed inventive solutions and pioneering ideas—ideas which have greatly improved our collective understanding of pricing. Along with many others, I owe a debt of gratitude to the truly outstanding pricing experts I've had the opportunity to work with and learn from over the last 20 years.

The intent of my observations is not to take away from any of the progress that has been made so far. Instead, my intent is to build on that progress in order to create better solutions for the industry.

From my own conversations with many of these pricing pioneers whom I respect a great deal, they have also been disappointed with the lack of sustainability of the many pricing solutions that have been implemented and then abandoned over the years. This is something that has troubled me and many of my industry friends for a long time.

In the chapters that follow, I will share with you my observations about why so many pricing solutions have failed to live up to their promise of sustained profit growth. With this knowledge, you will learn a new prescribed approach for solving the "pricing problem" in a way that ultimately avoids many of the internal conflicts that have prevented sustainable success in the past.

In the end, you will see that pricing solutions have been limited in their effectiveness and their ability to produce sustainable success because they've been focused on the wrong metrics (or only a subset of the right metrics), and they've struggled with the naturally conflicting objectives of margin expansion and sales growth.

## Growth-Focused vs. Profit-Focused Companies

One of the things that absolutely baffles me is why high-growth-aspiring companies prefer to act like profit-harvesting companies in how they approach their own pricing strategies.

The famous Boston Consulting Group (BCG) company classification model describes four different types of companies, as follows:

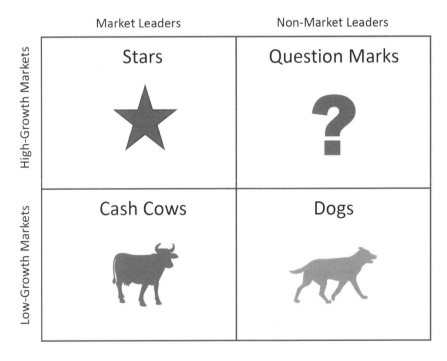

- **Stars**: market leaders in high-growth markets
- **Cash Cows**: market leaders in low-growth markets
- **Question Marks**: non-market-leaders in high-growth markets
- **Dogs**: non-market-leaders in low-growth markets

The implication of this classification is that **Stars** are great investment candidates; **Question Marks** need work; **Cash Cows** can yield profits but are not good investments; and **Dogs** should be avoided at all costs.

From a growth strategy perspective, **Stars** and **Question Marks** should theoretically focus on growth, either to protect their own market leadership as Stars, or to attempt to overtake Stars. Not focusing on growth could lead to a massive, missed opportunity to either become a Star or stay a Star. In high-growth markets, winners are determined based on who wins the market-share battle. For this reason, you would expect both Stars and Question Marks to be highly focused on growth and growth strategies.

Conversely, Cash Cows and Dogs have little opportunity for growth because they are in low-growth markets, and they're more likely to be focused on harvesting profits. Cash Cows, as market leaders, have a larger opportunity to "milk" profits because of their larger market shares and their ability to leverage economies of scale.

For Dogs, it's not so straightforward. Either way, their prospects are not great. And it's not always clear whether they should prioritize growth or profit harvesting. There are cases where Dogs have the opportunity to disrupt a mature, non-growing market and steal share to try to gain a leadership position. So, it is possible that some Dogs may focus on growth in hopes of carving themselves a leadership position in their low-growth markets.

How would you classify your company? Are you a **Star**? Are you a **Question Mark**? If you said yes to either, you probably should be focused on growth strategies. If you are a **Dog**, you could be focused on either profit harvesting or growth. If your company is a **Cash Cow**, it's both likely and justifiable that your company would be focused primarily on profit-harvesting strategies. In that case, the rest of this book may not be ideally suited for you (but you can still learn and benefit from it).

## Growth Pricing Strategies vs. Profit-Harvesting Pricing Strategies

There is a significant difference between **growth pricing strategies** and **profit-harvesting pricing strategies.** The primary difference is the objective metric. In profit harvesting, the objective metric is typically profit margin percentage. Growth pricing strategies focus on the objective metrics of revenues, customers, and sales growth. Growth pricing strategies tend to focus on incentivizing the acceleration of customer acquisition, expanding revenues per customer, and reducing customer churn. And, in fact, growth strategies can often be harmed by attempting to increase profit margins.

If your company is a growth-focused company, ask the tough question: Is your company appropriately pursuing growth-focused pricing strategies? Or do your company's pricing strategies seem to be focused mostly on expanding margins? I have seen too many growth-focused companies erroneously focus their pricing efforts on expanding margins, while their competitors focus on gobbling up market share.

## Growth Companies Need Growth-Focused Pricing Strategies!

Chasing profits when you are fighting a market share battle is a fool's errand. You can pocket dividends, but at what cost?

Unfortunately, the cost may be a long-term leadership position that could otherwise have lasted for decades. Most companies that focus on profit expansion too early seem to forget that growth and market leadership lead to sustainably lower costs from economies of scale. Growth opens the door to higher margins without increasing prices. By prioritizing profit margins too soon, companies might be sacrificing the ability to have extraordinary profits in the future.

**CAUTION:** Beware of Frankenstein strategies that claim to combine both growth and profit into some sort of super-strategy. This is a fallacy. While it is possible to grow both revenues and profits, there is no strategy that simultaneously maximizes profit margins and maximizes growth. Such a strategy is not a super-strategy. It is a tug-o-war strategy. If you are growing margins, you are most likely not maximizing your growth opportunities. The only exception would be if you are growing so fast that you are actually able to decrease costs due to economies of scale. But that is not the output of a margin-expanding price strategy—it's a bonus outcome of a growth strategy.

So how do you know whether your company should be fighting for growth or fighting for profits?

The reality is that most companies have aspirations for growth and should, therefore, be using growth-focused pricing strategies, not margin-expansion pricing strategies. Here is a quick litmus test you can use to make a rapid determination. If you can answer yes to most of the following questions, you are a growth-focused company, and you should be implementing growth-focused pricing strategies:

1. Does your company desire to grow annually at a rate of 20% or more?

2. Is your company's market growing by more than 10% per year?

3. Does your company want to improve its share of the market?

4. Are there credible competitors attempting to take market share away from your company?

If you can answer yes to most of those questions, it is pretty clear that your company should be focused on growth-focused pricing strategies. That means pricing strategies should be focused on things like new customer acquisition, existing customer revenue expansion, and minimizing customer churn.

On the other hand, if you have people in your company who believe your pricing should be more focused on margin expansion, it is likely that you would be answering yes to most of these questions:

1. Is your company's market growing at less than 5% per year?

2. Is your company's market already saturated with solutions?

3. Does your company have little concern for its market share position?

4. Is it very unlikely that customers will switch to different providers due to moderate price increases or decreases?

If you answered yes to most of these questions, then it is likely your company is either a Cash Cow or a Dog, and a margin-expansion strategy is probably the right way to go. Margin-expansion strategies are strategies to raise prices, and thereby expand margins, even at the expense of losing a few customers, provided the margin gains are large enough to offset the customer losses. The key reality for these companies is that their markets aren't growing, and competitors are fighting each other for a share of what's left.

The good news is that most companies are solidly in the growth category. That means chances are high that your company is also a growth-focused company. And so, to help your company achieve success in its growth objectives, you should ensure that your company's pricing strategies are growth-focused rather than profit-focused. That means margin percentage should NOT be your primary objective metric in optimizing your pricing decisions. Instead, your primary objective metric should be market share, overall revenue growth rate, and the present value of all future profits.

## The World Is Changing—Customers Matter More

Today we are at a tipping point in the evolution of commerce; the old approaches to pricing simply won't be effective anymore. Not only are customers getting smarter, but their values are changing. Companies must adapt to succeed.

Successful pricing strategies need to reflect a practical understanding of customer behavior, along with the needs, desires, and priorities that drive that behavior. At the end of the day, customers are people. Even inside large organizations, purchasing decisions are ultimately made by people. And people have needs and desires. They have goals and aspirations. They have feelings. They have curious minds that can think and learn.

The most successful pricing strategies are ultimately based on what's good for the customer. Businesses live or die based on their ability to successfully attract customers and fill their needs.

Every business transaction has a value proposition, where ideally both buyer and seller benefit from the exchange. Successful and sustainable pricing strategies must reflect this understanding. Good pricing practices keep profitable customers coming back year after year. This means you will need pricing metrics that look far beyond the present transaction opportunity in order to measure how well pricing helps to increase and sustain customer loyalty. This is the only way companies can be competitive and successful in the post-digital-transformation era, where customers are moving more of their purchases to self-service, online channels versus the traditional buying and selling channels of the past.

## A New Approach

In the chapters that follow, I will share with you a new philosophical approach to creating effective pricing strategies. To do this, I will use "case parables" to illustrate some key themes. These are fictitious stories based on real situations I've experienced in my career. I use these stories to illustrate points without revealing the names of specific individuals or companies. (*Any relation to actual people is strictly coincidental.*)

Once those key points are established, I will share with you a step-by-step approach for using focused pricing strategies to maximize the value of your company. That step-by-step approach will be combined with key metrics, which will help you gauge progress along the way.

While I am confident that you will find immense value in the concepts and framework I have to share, I hope you will take these ideas and build upon them to make them even better. Apply a growth mindset to everything you do, and you will experience unlimited possibilities for solving any problem you wish to conquer.

## Key Questions We Will Address

The journey through this book will include checkpoints for considering some important questions about pricing, including the following:

- How does pricing affect the value of a company?
- When are margin expansion strategies appropriate to maximize company value? And when are they not appropriate?
- What are the risks that result from pushing prices too close to the edge of a customer's willingness to pay?
- How is the digital revolution changing customer behaviors and expectations?
- Is price transparency helpful or hurtful?
- How should the concept of elasticity factor into pricing strategies?
- Is it possible to optimize prices without the ability to forecast demand?
- How can pricing have the greatest impact on sustainable profit growth?
- What is the best way to measure pricing success?
- How should pricing strategies for new customers be different than pricing strategies for existing customers?
- How do pricing strategies affect churn—the loss of loyal customers?
- How does one's mindset affect pricing decisions?
- Should companies apply different pricing strategies for different products? If so, how?
- Does price negotiation improve the customer experience?
- What are the most common obstacles to implementing and maintaining successful pricing strategies?
- How does customer lifecycle factor into pricing strategy design?

If these questions are important to you, then this book is sure to provide thought-provoking content worthy of your consideration.

## For the Advanced Reader

If you are well versed in pricing strategy and overall pricing knowledge, you may be wondering where this book is going. Perhaps you want to know, before investing lots of time reading, whether the content of this book is something you are likely to disagree with.

I assure you that this book will be well worth your time to read and digest. Some may suspect that pricing for "growth" might be a disguised way to imply that I will simply be recommending that companies lower their prices to get more sales volume, thereby killing margins and potentially triggering an industry-wide price war.

That's not what this book is, and it's not what I will be recommending.

To put your mind at ease, I will tell you the "punch line" of what I will be recommending right here, but I encourage you to read the whole book to understand the rationale for the recommendations. Stopping here would be like reading the description of the entree off the menu, and then going home before the meal is served.

## The Summary of What I Will Be Recommending in This Book

This book is about a step-by-step process and conceptual framework for determining the best near-term opportunities for maximizing long-term profit growth, specifically defined as the present value of all future profits. This framework will allow you to use specific tools to understand which near-term pricing objectives will have the biggest impact on the metrics used to calculate the present value of all future profits. Once this knowledge is attained, you will be supplied with a menu of specific types of focused pricing strategies to help you make the identified improvements to the respective metrics that lead to the highest growth of present and future expected profits, which will determine how investors will ultimately value your company.

My recommendation will be to leverage this framework to identify the most impactful opportunities for your company to grow its value and to implement the appropriate focused pricing strategies to achieve that growth. Furthermore, I will be recommending the discontinuation of pricing practices that can have a negative effect on your valuable customer relationships.

While there may be nothing wrong with using select price increases to grow margins, this book will offer a framework to determine whether those select price increases might actually be doing more damage to future profits by putting current or future customer relationships at risk. Furthermore, how you communicate with customers regarding pricing actions can significantly impact their perception of your fairness as a supplier and the fairness of your pricing practices. The reality is that most companies will need to implement price increases. That is not what's up for debate. But when, why, and by how much are questions that should be answered with a solid understanding of how those decisions will affect your customer relationships and the future profit streams they might otherwise provide.

The world is moving quickly to e-commerce, and negotiated pricing is going away. Millennials are quickly becoming the dominant generation in charge of the majority of all purchase decisions, and Generation Z is right behind them. These new generations of customers will not accept the old ways of doing business because they have more choices than any previous generation. This book will provide the conceptual framework for how companies must price in the new reality of digital commerce in order to attract and grow the customer relationships that will power the growing streams of future profits.

## Chapter Summary

Despite the explosive growth of the pricing solutions industry, many companies are still struggling to find ways to use pricing to drive sustainable profit growth. Most margin-based pricing solutions lose momentum after achieving one or two years of successful results. Understanding why this happens is critical to charting a better path forward.

Growth-focused pricing strategies and profit-focused pricing strategies are both different and largely incompatible at their respective foundations. Most companies are growth-focused vs. profit-focused in the context of the famous BCG company classification model. Yet many of these growth-focused companies choose, for some reason, to implement profit-focused pricing strategies instead of growth-focused pricing strategies. This is a major problem which produces a logical inconsistency and a no-win situation. In order to be successful, growth companies need to implement growth-based pricing strategies.

Growth-based pricing strategies focus on new customer acquisition, existing customer retention, and existing customer revenue growth in order to drive sustainable, long-term profit growth, which ultimately drives up the value of the company. This means customer relationships matter more. At the same time, customer needs, attitudes, and behaviors are changing as the world evolves to digital commerce and as Millennials become the dominant generation of buyers. Customer buying experience is becoming more important than ever before, and this has major implications for how companies make and communicate pricing decisions.

This book offers a new and revolutionary approach to pricing which will help companies drive more sustainable profit growth, addressing both the challenges of the past and the challenges of today's evolving digital-enabled customers. The concepts and ideas in this book are certain to transform the way you think about pricing in the context of maximizing the value of your company. In the end, the purpose of this book is to show you how to make a dramatic impact on the value of your company by altering the ways you make pricing decisions, starting with the metrics you should use to prioritize potential pricing actions.

———————————

*Next chapter preview: The first case parable shows how two seemingly identical companies implemented two different pricing strategies, one profit-focused and one growth-focused, to achieve different outcomes over a five-year period. This illustrates and amplifies why it's so important for growth-focused companies to implement growth-focused pricing strategies.*

## CHAPTER 2

# The Tale of Two Companies

## Case Parable 1: CommonCo Vs. GrowthCo

*The following case parable illustrates why short-term margin-maximizing pricing techniques can be counterproductive for growth-focused companies. We look at two similar companies, both with outstanding leaders who were able to produce excellent results over a five-year stretch. But they employed slightly different pricing strategies. And those pricing strategies led to quite different destinations at the end of the five years.*

At the end of a long day, Joe sat back in his chair, took in a deep breath, and reflected on his five-year run as CFO of CommonCo, a leading manufacturer of industrial gloves. Out of the corner of his eye, the cover of a magazine on his desk slowly came into focus. Grinning with a sense of pride, he leaned over to pick it up. There he was, posing next to his wife and kids, on the cover of *Success* magazine. The headline: ***How Joe Durban's Five-Year Run Helped CommonCo Nearly Double Profits While Growing Sales to $100 Million.***

The headline said it all. For five years, he had pushed for higher margins, insisting all the time that their products were priced too low, based on the value they provided for their customers. Now, he could sit back and reflect on the success they shared as a company. The magazine article was nice. But the real validation was in the 91% increase (13.8% CAGR) in profits and the continued revenue growth, which had averaged 5% per year over the last five years.

CommonCo manufactured and distributed innovative, synthetic leather gloves, which had the feel of soft leather, but the durability of steel. They were very popular in industrial and construction settings because of their comfort and durability. They had many repeat buyers because their gloves tended to be purchased for high-intensity use. While most competitors' gloves had to be replaced monthly, CommonCo's customers typically went 90 days between purchases.

After hitting record sales of $100 million, Joe was extremely proud of the company's results because they had achieved this record while simultaneously increasing their per-unit profit margins by 50% over that same five-year period.

Like most CFOs, Joe was very profit-focused. Every year, he urged his pricing and sales leaders to focus on continuously pushing up profits by raising prices and reducing discounting. They were able to achieve average price increases of 0.8% each year, which increased overall profit percentage from 8% to 12%, now the highest in the industry.

Their net sales growth of 5% annually translated to a compounded growth rate of 27.6% over five years, as shown in the chart below:

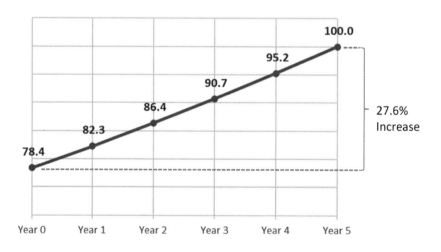

**CommonCo Total Sales**
in $ millions

Of course, Joe was more proud of the growth in profits from $6.3 million to $12 million today, as shown in the chart below:

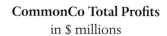

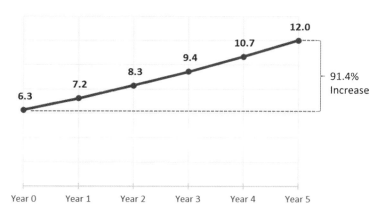

**CommonCo Total Profits**
in $ millions

Companies in CommonCo's industry were typically valued by banks and investors using a profit multiple. This means their valuation was calculated by multiplying their profits—typically EBITDA (earnings before interest, taxes, depreciation, and amortization)—by a factor or multiple. In CommonCo's industry that multiple varied between 3X and 12X, depending on the company's growth rate and profit risk. Since CommonCo was growing revenues at approximately 5% per year, most investors were using the profit multiple of 5X, or 5 times the company's profits of $12 million. This gave the company a valuation of $60 million, an increase of $28.7M or 91.7% since Joe had joined the company five years earlier. This increase in company value is depicted in the chart below:

**CommonCo Total Company Value**
in $ millions

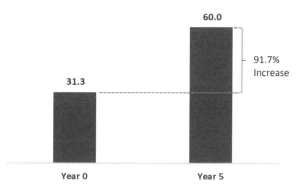

As CFO, Joe had a 10% ownership in the company. In just five years, he had made $2.9 million from the appreciation in company value.

## A Looming Concern

Although all the metrics looked good on the surface, Joe worried a little about some of his other business metrics. Even though they were growing at a net growth rate of 5% per year, that 5% was made up of a **new customer revenue acquisition rate** of 20% per year, offset against a **customer revenue churn rate** of 15%. Churn rate was the calculation of the amount of revenues from customers who had bought in the previous year, but did not buy in the most recent year. In other words, CommonCo was losing approximately 15% of its customers every single year, which was slightly higher than the average for the industry. But this was not really visible because the sales team was bringing in new business equal to 20% of the previous year's revenue. Most people just saw the net growth rate of 5% per year.

Joe believed that his company's churn rate of 15% was due to a combination of the minor price increases and some occasional, but rare, service failures.

Joe expected there would be trade-offs between higher prices and lack of customer retention, but he rationalized that the company was better off keeping the more profitable customers and letting the competition have the more price sensitive customers.

All in all, annual profit dollars had grown by 91.4% over the previous five years, and Joe was very pleased with the results.

## GrowthCo and CFO Mary Matos

CommonCo had a competitor named GrowthCo, which also manufactured and distributed similar synthetic gloves of identical quality. Oddly enough, both companies looked nearly identical five years ago. Both did $78.3 million in revenues and $6.3 million in profits, and both had an 8% profit percentage.

But GrowthCo's CFO, Mary Matos, was driven by a different set of values than CommonCo's CFO. Her strategies reflected a heightened sensitivity and concern for customer growth and retention—acquiring and holding on to her customers—even if it meant sacrificing some profit margins in the short term. Mary was fanatical about making sure GrowthCo was able to acquire new customers at a relatively high rate, even if it required additional price incentives that could eat into average profit margins.

## Mary's Reflections after Her Own Five-Year Run

The flight attendant tapped Mary on the shoulder again to see if she wanted a drink before takeoff. She nodded yes. Exhausted from a day full of meetings with potential investors, Mary reflected on her journey over the last five years and how her pricing strategies had enabled industry-leading growth in company revenues, profits, and valuation. Five years ago, the company was valued at $31.3 million. Now, she had a letter from her investors, which valued the company at $143.4 million, a $112 million increase.

This was validation. Her instincts were right. This would mean financial rewards and new opportunities for growth for everyone on her team. And it wouldn't be long before the company would be achieving their goal of going public, which would give employees the ability to cash out on their new stock options. Her work was about to pay off handsomely.

## Mary's Pricing Strategies

As CFO of a relatively small company, Mary also played the role of Chief Pricing Officer. Mary implemented a pricing strategy that gave new customers a 15% discount on the first $500 of orders placed, as an incentive for new customers to try the product and experience GrowthCo's service. Mary believed that the fair market price for existing customers was probably in the range of 9%–10% profit margins, but her pricing strategy with the introductory trial discounts and periodic loyalty discounts kept the profit percentage right around 8% every year. Mary was also fanatical about making sure all of her customers received excellent service and never got overcharged.

The result of Mary's pricing strategy was a **net growth rate** of 18%, more than three times higher than the industry average of 5%. She had achieved the 18% net growth rate by combining a 26% **new revenue acquisition rate** (new revenue from new customers as a percentage of previous year's total revenues) with an **existing customer revenue churn rate** of only 8%:

$$26\% - 8\% = 18\%$$

After five years of 18% net revenue growth, GrowthCo's revenues had increased by 128.8% to \$179.3 million, up from only \$78.4 million five years earlier, as shown in the chart below:

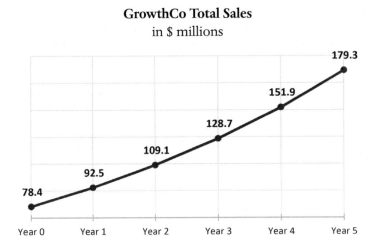

**GrowthCo Total Sales**
in \$ millions

And their profits had grown from \$6.3 million to \$14.3 million—also 128.8% growth, shown below:

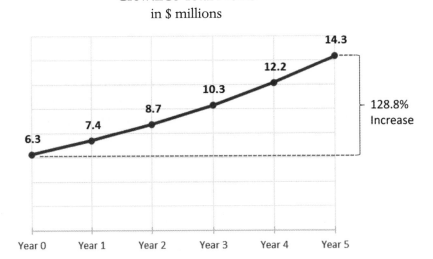

**GrowthCo Total Profits**
in \$ millions

## Comparing the Two Companies

Somewhat ironically, GrowthCo's per-unit profit margins never exceeded 8%, but their total profits were now 19.5% higher than CommonCo's, despite the fact that CommonCo had driven per-unit profit margins up to 12%.

This is shown in the chart below:

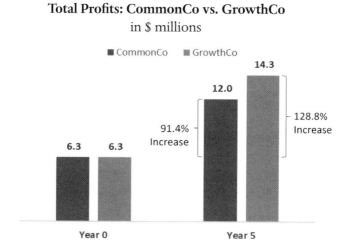

**Total Profits: CommonCo vs. GrowthCo**
in $ millions

In fact, if you compare the two companies, GrowthCo outperformed CommonCo on almost every metric except net profit margin percentage. After five years, GrowthCo's revenues had increased by 128.8% to $179.3M, now 79% higher than CommonCo's revenues, as shown in the chart below:

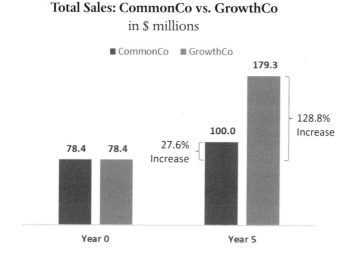

**Total Sales: CommonCo vs. GrowthCo**
in $ millions

But here's the kicker. Because GrowthCo was growing at the high rate of 18% (vs. CommonCo's 5%), GrowthCo's investors and bankers were using a profit multiple of 10X instead of 5X to determine the value of the company. And so, while GrowthCo's profits were only 19.5% higher than CommonCo's, their company valuation was 139% higher, at $143.4 million vs. only $60 million for CommonCo.

A comparison of company valuation growth is shown in the chart below:

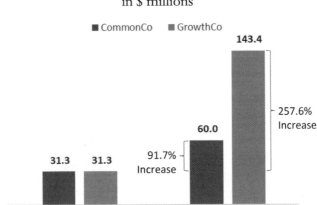

**Total Company Valuation: CommonCo vs. GrowthCo**
in $ millions

Like Joe, Mary had a 10% ownership in her company, GrowthCo. And by increasing the value of her company by $112.1 million (from $31.3 million to $143.4 million), the value of her personal ownership increased by $11.2 million.

Remember Joe was doing great by increasing his wealth by $2.9 million. But Mary did 286% better by increasing her wealth by $11.2 million. Why? Because she focused her pricing strategies on growth and retention instead of margin expansion.

Despite the fact that Joe's company, CommonCo, achieved a 50% improvement in profit-margin percentage, Mary massively outperformed Joe from a total profit perspective, and even more so from a company valuation and personal wealth perspective.

## Under the Surface: CommonCo's Profit Risk

In addition to what we see in the revenue and profit numbers, there are other issues brewing underneath the surface, which we should take note of.

First of all, by driving prices up by four percentage points, Joe was making CommonCo's customers pay significantly higher prices than the customers of GrowthCo and other suppliers in their industry. This puts CommonCo's profits at risk because customers are more likely to either leave or demand lower prices.

Second, Joe's strategy of raising prices is not sustainable. Because he has pushed up the price levels for both new and existing customers, price is starting to become an issue, and it is becoming less likely that customers will tolerate any further price increases. If Joe were to continue to raise prices by 0.8% per year, it is likely that his already high churn rate would start to get even higher. Further price increases would not only be unsustainable, but they might trigger a tipping point of accelerated customer churn, leading to a mass exodus of customers.

If you step back and look at what Joe's pricing strategy has accomplished, it has really done little more than take value out of the customers' pockets and put it in CommonCo's pocket. It has weakened customer relationships by reducing the customer value proposition, asking them to pay a higher price for no extra value. So far, this strategy has resulted in an annual revenue churn rate of 15%, which will be likely to grow if CommonCo continues to raise prices. And at the new higher price levels, it will also be more difficult for CommonCo to win new customers in the future, so they should also expect the 20% new revenue acquisition rate to drop dramatically.

Joe has delivered attractive profit growth numbers so far, but what's not so apparent in the numbers is the fact that he has loaded up the business with immense risk—the precursor to poor performance.

Mary, on the other hand, has made increasing growth and reducing churn a primary focus of her financial strategy. She has been rewarded with higher customer acquisition rates and significantly lower churn. This bodes well for her ability to continue her strategies into the future and to see repeatable positive results.

## Key Lesson: Customer Growth Trumps Profit Harvesting

While Joe has put his customer relationships at risk, Mary has strengthened her customer relationships with consistency and trust, and she has delivered on her strategy of offering high value at a fair price.

This story is valuable because it illustrates how companies can miss opportunities for longer lasting profit growth by focusing on short-term profit gains—specifically the kind of profit gains achieved by simply raising prices and hoping the majority of customers won't mind. This is called profit harvesting because it is the act of extracting more money out of the customers' pockets without necessarily delivering any additional value to them.

Sometimes profit harvesting is justified, especially when customers are buying at unnecessarily low prices—perhaps prices that were offered earlier in order to get the customers to switch from another vendor. But from the customer's perspective, if you raise prices without offering more value, you're just taking money out of their pocket and putting it in your own. Let's call it what it is: It's profit harvesting.

Buyer inertia and switching costs often keep customers buying, even though the value equation has changed. At some point, customers will re-evaluate the value relationship with their providers, and if they feel that the relationship has gotten too expensive, they may abandon it. Unfortunately, most companies won't know how to interpret these delayed customer reactions because they often happen out of sync with the actual price increases.

In the example of CommonCo, we see a company that achieved 50% per-unit profit growth, which most CFOs would drool over. But even though they increased total profits by 91.7%, CommonCo fell short of GrowthCo's 128.8% profit growth. More importantly, CommonCo's 91.7% growth in company value fell dramatically short of GrowthCo's 257.6% increase in company value.

Why?

Because they focused so much on per-unit margin percentage, they failed to achieve a high **net revenue growth rate**, something their investors cared about more than high profit margins. Remember, GrowthCo achieved 18% annual net revenue growth with a pricing strategy that generated zero per-unit profit growth—yet GrowthCo outperformed CommonCo in both overall profit growth and company valuation growth.

## Chapter Summary

The case parable comparison of CommonCo and GrowthCo illustrates many points that reinforce why growth-focused pricing strategies will almost always outperform margin-based pricing strategies, especially for growth-focused companies:

- Even though a company may appear to be doing well, in terms of both revenue growth and profitability, it is possible that it could be doing even better by changing elements of its strategies.

- A myopic focus on profitability and margins can lead to suboptimal results if your main objective is to grow the value of the company.

- Just because it may be common practice to use a profit multiple to value a business doesn't mean growth doesn't matter. Investors will often pay a higher multiple for companies who have better growth. Growth rates always matter.

- Sometimes a company's growth is limited by churn—the loss of revenues from customers who are leaving. CommonCo's sales team was acquiring new customers at an annual rate of 20% of revenues. But because of the 15% churn, their net growth rate was much lower—only 5%.

- Continuously raising prices can add excessive risk to customer relationships and increase the probability of customer churn.

The future of pricing, as we will soon see, is to focus on the growth and strength of customer relationships and to make efforts to reduce preventable churn.

------

*Next chapter preview: Pricing is a unique role that is often wedged in between Finance and Sales, and Pricing often faces the inherently conflicting objectives of margin expansion and sales growth. For this reason, a growth mindset is critical to the success of Pricing and the ultimate success of the company. Pricing should lead this mindset, while at the same time finding the best path to grow the overall company value.*

## CHAPTER 3

# The Growth Mindset and Pricing

*The reasonable man adapts himself to the world; the unreasonable one persists in trying to adapt the world to himself. Therefore, all progress depends on the unreasonable man.*

—George Bernard Shaw

## The Pressure to Think Small

For decades, Pricing has been a profession that has been wedged in between Finance and Sales, charged with protecting margins, but often in a way that goes underappreciated.

And the way the pricing profession has evolved, it now carries mutually conflicting objectives. On one hand, Pricing is the champion of profit margins, measured by how much they are able to increase prices and margins over time. On the other hand, most pricing professionals instinctively understand that sales growth is critical for the company to maximize its value to shareholders. The conflict arises because experienced pricing people understand that raising prices and growing margins are ultimately in conflict with the objective of increasing sales and retaining customers. They are fundamentally different objectives that require fundamentally different strategies.

Of course, there will always be opportunities to raise prices for some customers without sacrificing the customer relationship. But these opportunities mostly exist because customers are paying below-average prices to begin with. Once those opportunities are corrected, the pricer is back to the same conflict.

This inverse relationship between pricing and sales success is ultimately a no-win situation that can result in unnecessary psychological pressures. And even worse, many people in the pricing profession instinctively suspect that between Pricing and Sales, Sales is ultimately more important to the success of the company. This perpetuates the mentality that pricing is a zero-sum game where one party wins only when the other party loses. And if pricing people feel that Sales is the party that ultimately has to win, then it's logical for them to feel like they are set up to fail.

Because it is almost impossible to continuously raise prices and margins, pricing people often find themselves trying to rationalize why, despite the lack of margin gains, they actually do add value to the organization. And sometimes they struggle to justify their results, or sometimes, even their existence. It only gets worse when other executives in the company begin to question the value of the pricing team.

This is a classic no-win situation, which can amplify feelings of insignificance, futility, and even depression. It can make normal people feel small and insignificant. It's wrong, and it needs to change.

## The Scarcity Mindset

The scarcity mindset can be very demotivational. It can channel thoughts in a negative direction and impede a person's cognitive abilities.

In the famous Minnesota Starvation Experiments in 1944, 36 men voluntarily starved themselves so that researchers could learn about the mental and physiological effects of starvation. What was interesting was that hunger made the men mentally obsessed with food. They would talk about food, dream about food, and fantasize about food. Food became the only thing they could think about or focus on. This phenomenon is commonly labeled as **tunnel vision**, which Dictionary.com defines as:

**tunnel vision** (noun): drastically narrowed field of vision, as in looking through a tube, an extremely narrow or prejudiced outlook; narrow-mindedness, also described as a lack of peripheral vision.

Psychologists have concluded that the lack or "scarcity" of something a person needs, whether physical or emotional, can cause the human brain to become overwhelmed and start to malfunction, sometimes in a way that can lead to counterproductive decisions that actually make the situation significantly worse.

The **scarcity mindset** is the cognitive result of lacking something important. It could be the lack of recognition from someone important, like a spouse or a boss, the lack of visible advancement in a career or a relationship, or the lack of financial freedom. Anything that appears to be a no-win situation can create a scarcity mindset.

The bad news is that, because of the way this mindset negatively affects mental performance, it can be easy to start sliding into a downward spiral that makes things so much worse. The symptoms of the scarcity mindset highlight a pattern of thinking that is more inwardly focused on protection rather than outwardly focused on opportunity. Consider the following list of scarcity mindset symptoms:

### Scarcity Mindset Thinking

- thinking the supply of opportunities is limited and shrinking every day as other people get to them first
- thinking life is a zero-sum game where one party wins only when the opposing party loses
- thinking that other people will try to hold you back if it helps them achieve their own successes
- thinking that success is rare and fleeting, with a constant stream of obstacles and difficulties to overcome
- thinking that sharing is risky, and ideas should be protected so others don't "steal" them
- thinking that trying new things increases the risk of failure
- thinking that change is mostly counterproductive
- thinking that personal success is mostly dependent on getting lucky and meeting the right people more than it is dependent on things that are in one's own control.

The scarcity mindset can make things worse because it allows thinking to be dominated by problems and restrictions rather than opportunities and possibilities. When you have tunnel vision, you can't see anything else. Studies have shown that the scarcity mindset can lead to chronic stress that can reduce your mental and cognitive performance over time. This is not a healthy mindset. And it definitely doesn't help increase performance.

## Ultimate Pricing Success Requires a Growth Mindset

The reality is that Pricing is incredibly important. It is an extremely valuable role based on a complex discipline that very few people really understand. If you are in a pricing job, I have immense respect for you. And I am not alone.

The reality is that pricing should not be a zero-sum game with mutually conflicting objectives. Pricing should be leading the charge to achieve sustainable growth. And appropriate price levels and margins should be based on what will best help the company achieve its growth objectives.

Pricing people are the ones who have the information to bring the necessary visibility to the importance of growth. The ultimate indicator of pricing success is measured by what happens to the value of the company. Therefore, growth is critical to the mission of pricing. And this mission can be accomplished only with a **growth mindset**.

Whether you call it the "Growth Mindset," the "Abundance Mindset," or the "Expansive Mindset," it all leads to the same destination—the intellectual and psychological freedom to think in a world of infinite possibilities.

The key quality I've seen in the most successful people I've ever met is that they have and convey a growth mindset. As a result, they are able to do more to make a bigger difference. More importantly they carry a happy, positive attitude, and they inspire others.

Consider the list below that characterizes thinking patterns in the **growth mindset**:

### Growth Mindset Thinking

- Opportunities are abundant and can be found everywhere.
- Possibilities are infinite and unlimited.
- There is more than enough to go around as long as you are willing to find it.
- There is room for everyone to succeed.
- Innovation is multiplicative and "two heads are better than one."
- Every experience is a learning opportunity.
- Change is a vehicle to learning and progress.
- Collaboration leads to win–win outcomes.
- Everything will eventually work out in your favor if you persevere.
- The success of others is connected to your own individual success.

## How to Develop a Growth Mindset

Transforming to a **growth mindset** is actually easy and self-reinforcing. Once you start to change how you think, you will find that it's easier to think that way all the time.

Start with a belief that success is possible; this will motivate you to look for pathways to succeed instead of giving up because a problem seems too difficult.

Shift to a belief that opportunities are everywhere, and there are multiple solutions to every problem. Remind yourself that you can always shift what isn't working.

Make it a priority to learn from every experience. Set aside time every day to learn. Read. Listen to audiobooks. Watch educational YouTube videos. Just learning and getting smarter will change your outlook. Learning will help you be resilient and look at setbacks as opportunities that will ultimately lead you to success. Being open to ideas and opinions from others opens new learning channels.

Earnestly seek to help others succeed in their own goals and desires. Moving from a philosophy of competition to one of collaboration leads to solutions that can make everyone more successful.

Listen to your intuition; your limbic brain is usually correct. But also become aware of the thought patterns that could be sabotaging you. Reprogram beliefs that come from the scarcity mindset. Don't let fear drive your decisions. If you ever feel that fear is affecting your decision-making, go back to the abundance mindset. Step outside yourself. Think about how to help others.

Most of all, NEVER let another person destroy your belief in yourself or your potential. NOBODY has justifiable authority to do that. You are always right to believe in yourself. If you find that others don't believe in you, it's because they are trapped in their own scarcity mindset. Never let them draw you in to that negativity.

## Applying the Growth Mindset to Pricing

There are specific ways you can improve your success in pricing, just by applying the **growth mindset** in a few different areas.

Start by imagining all the ways you can help your company grow. Don't limit this exploration to just pricing-related ideas. Write down your ideas, and share them with an intent to learn, grow, and improve.

Think about pricing actions that would help you and your company learn— learn about your customers, learn about your products and services, learn about your sales and marketing capabilities, learn about your competitors, and learn about yourself. Sometimes just thinking about potential actions will give you the needed perspective to arrive at the best solution.

Imagine the many ways you could give your customers more value. How could you improve their experience with your company? How could you improve the benefits they receive for the price they are paying? Ask these questions to people inside and outside your company.

Think outside the box. What are the "crazy" ideas you have about pricing? About value? About how to improve the lives of your customers? Let your crazy ideas spark discussions that might generate more ideas. Imagine how you might paint a picture of the opportunities in pricing to serve as a backdrop for a discussion with other executives. Pictures can trigger new ideas and thinking. Pictures are powerful ways to communicate. Here's an example that I've used before:

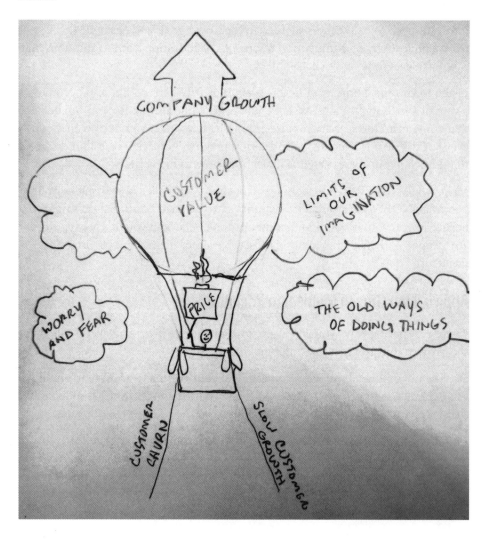

Communicate with others as a way to help them generate their own ideas. Help others understand what you understand. Use your knowledge of pricing to help others see opportunities that aren't otherwise easy to see.

I personally believe that nobody should be in a role where he or she feels personally limited. If you ever find yourself in such a role, I strongly recommend that you either redefine the parameters of that role or move to a different organization. You will find that you have so many positive things to contribute to the world, and the growth mindset will help you achieve both personal success and success in your business pursuits.

### Let My Ideas Lead You to New Ideas

I am about to share with you some important ideas that might change the way you think about the world. This is my goal. But I will not ask you to accept my view of the world.

I ask you to open your mind. Let my ideas spark new ideas for you. Build upon those ideas so that you can achieve success beyond anything you or I could imagine. Don't be constrained by someone else's view of the possible or impossible. In the words of George Bernard Shaw, "All progress depends on the unreasonable man."

## Chapter Summary

In this chapter, we've focused on the importance of having the right mindset in any role with pricing responsibility, highlighting some important ideas:

- In pricing roles, it can be easy to feel limited because of the inherent conflict between margin expansion and sales growth. It's important to be aware of this, so you can take appropriate actions to prevent falling into a scarcity mindset.
- The scarcity mindset occurs because a person feels a lack of something important in their life. If you let it stay, it can negatively affect your ability to think and make decisions, thereby preventing you from reaching your goals.
- The symptoms of the scarcity mindset include inward focus, fear of competition, fear of failure, and reluctance to change. If you detect these symptoms in either your life or the life of a team member, you can easily change the situation just by following some simple steps.
- The best way to kick-start the growth mindset is to convince yourself that any problem is solvable and that opportunities are abundant. Infinite

- possibilities will open up to you as you learn new things and invite new ways of thinking.

- The role of pricing should never be focused solely on improving margins. This leads to cognitive dissonance, unnecessary stress, and misuse of your otherwise powerful mind. The role of pricing should be to determine the right level of margins to best accomplish the growth of company value, which also means pricing should be focused on sales growth. Pricing-focused employees have an obligation to shine a light on the highest-impact opportunities to improve the value of the company, not just for Pricing or Finance, but for everyone who participates in determining company strategies.

- The growth mindset is what allows Pricing to uncover new possibilities and new ways to act on opportunities to grow the value of the company. Because Pricing has the ability to see beyond just the question of margins, they should lead with expansive ideas, collaborative dialogue, and illustrative communication to ensure that everyone is aligned on the best pricing strategies for achieving the company's goals.

- NEVER let another person destroy your belief in yourself or your potential. NOBODY has justifiable authority to do that. You are always right to believe in yourself. Make sure your personal role is set up for success.

In short, the growth mindset should be a prerequisite for all pricing strategy work, both as a defense against the inherent conflicts that can arise in pricing and as a powerful mental toolset for finding and implementing the best pricing strategies for any given situation.

———————————

*Next chapter preview: There are five "sacred" metrics that should be used to manage pricing. This next chapter lays the foundation for these metrics and explains what they are and how they should be used.*

## CHAPTER 4

# The Five Sacred Metrics of Pricing Success

*What gets measured gets managed.*

—Peter Drucker (allegedly)

As we saw in the case parable about CommonCo and GrowthCo, too much focus on near-term margin expansion can be counterproductive to the overriding objective of long-term profit growth and overall company value. The focus, instead, should be on maximizing the strength and longevity of customer relationships because this is what powers long-term profits. We measure this through a metric called **Customer Lifetime Value**—the present value of all future profits from existing customers.

In this chapter, we will discuss the **Five Sacred Metrics of Pricing Success**. Why are they sacred? If you look up the word "sacred" in the Merriam-Webster Dictionary, you will see five listed definitions for the word. The first four definitions have to do with religion or deities. That's not what I'm talking about. Definition number five says:

**sacred**: (5) a: UNASSAILABLE, INVIOLABLE; b: highly valued and important.

That's the definition of "sacred" I mean, and that's why these five metrics are SACRED. They are not liable to doubt, attack, or question. And I will not fault you if you feel a tinge of reverence when you talk about them.

These five metrics combine to calculate the present value of all future profits of present and future customers based on sustainable rates of growth and churn.

In other words, these five metrics combine to calculate the actual **value of the company** as an ongoing concern.

To relieve the suspense, here they are. Later, I will come back to walk through the respective meanings and calculations of each metric.

## The Five Sacred Metrics of Pricing Success

All five sacred metrics of pricing success come together to calculate the value of the company. The illustration of the relationships among these metrics is shown below:

**How the Five Sacred Metrics of Pricing Success
Combine to Calculate Company Value**

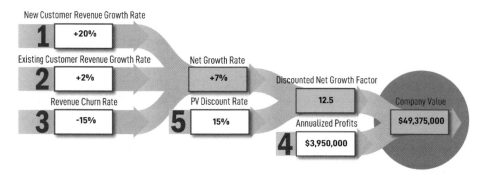

1. **New Customer Revenue Acquisition Rate** (that which is repeatable)
2. **Existing Customer Revenue Expansion Rate** (that which is repeatable)
3. **Customer Revenue Churn Rate** (that which is repeatable)
4. **Annualized Profits** (that which is sustainable)
5. **Present-Value Discount Rate** (a measure of risk)

To calculate the present value of all future profits, we need repeatable growth and churn rates, along with sustainable profits. Because we are applying a present-value discount rate, we care less about what happens 10 or 20 years out because the further-out years are discounted down exponentially. Instead, we care about what is happening now and in the foreseeable future.

In addition, the five sacred metrics will have both forward-looking values and backward-looking values. The backward-looking values are calculated from historical transactions. They are indisputable and inarguable. You simply run the numbers through the calculations, and you have your value. Forward-looking metric values can be different than the backward-looking metrics because they must represent only what is repeatable and sustainable. As long as we believe the backward-looking metrics are good representations of what we can expect in the future, we can use those calculated values. If not, we will need to make adjustments.

We want visibility on these five sacred metrics because these are the metrics that directly affect company value, and that's where we want our improvement focus. Improvements in any one of these metrics will increase the value of the company. There's a school of thought that if you force a metric to be visible, people will almost automatically act to improve it. True or not, that's what we want to accomplish here. Visibility and improvement.

In addition, it's important to keep our eyes on what we don't want to harm as we try to improve other parts of the business. Increasing profits is a great way to increase the value of your company. It's one of the five sacred metrics. But you want to make sure that, in your efforts to increase profits, you don't unintentionally harm your growth or retention rates.

## An Overview of the Five Sacred Metrics

In reality, there are hundreds of important pricing metrics. But we care about these five sacred metrics the most because they are directly impacted by pricing, and they directly determine the value of the business. This is a quick overview of each of these metrics.

**Metric #1 - New Customer Revenue Acquisition Rate**: This is a measure of revenue from new customers, as a percentage of the previous year's total revenues. It tells you how much your new customer acquisitions are impacting your total revenues and your overall net growth rate. The way to calculate this metric is to add up all the revenue from new customers over a one-year period, and then divide this number by the total previous year's revenues. As an example, if the total revenue from new customers this year was $16 million, and last year's revenues totaled $160 million, then the **new customer revenue acquisition rate** for this year would be 10%.

$$\$16M \div \$160M = \textbf{10\%}$$

For most companies, **new customer** is defined as a customer who didn't make a purchase in the previous year. However, as we will see with most of these metrics, the timing will vary based on the natural timing of the business (i.e., how often customers typically buy). We want to be sure that our growth and churn rates represent what is repeatable because they will form the basis for calculating future growth. Whatever we believe is repeatable (with a justifiable rationale) is what we will use for our forward-looking metric values.

**Metric #2 - Existing Customer Revenue Expansion Rate**: This is a measure of how fast you are growing revenues from your existing customers, whether from increasing customer wallet share or perhaps just from the organic growth of existing customer needs. It is calculated by grouping all the purchases of customers who purchased in the most recent two years and adding up the purchases of both years. Then you divide the purchases in the most recent year by the purchases in the previous year and subtract 1 to determine the expansion (or contraction) rate. As an example, if the group of customers that purchased in both of the previous two years purchased $105 million in the most recent year, and only $100 million in the prior year, the existing customer revenue expansion rate would be 5%.

$$105 \div 100 = 1.05$$

$$1.05 - 1 = \textbf{0.05 or 5\%}$$

How we use this metric will be determined by whether we believe the 5% expansion is repeatable year after year. If the reason for the expansion is that newer customers have a pattern of purchasing a lower amount in their first year, and then purchasing a higher amount in their subsequent years, then there would be reason to believe that this is a repeatable growth pattern. Conversely, if the expansion (or contraction) rate is more attributable to random fluctuations in customer purchases, it is not likely to be repeatable year after year. This would bear itself out if the average of multiple years of the metric is closer to zero than it is to any single year's metric. In this case, it would be more appropriate to either use the long-term average or 0% as our forward-looking metric. Later in the book, we will show how to determine if this metric is repeatable or random.

One additional caution: If your **existing customer revenue expansion rate (ECRER)** is the product of price increases, the forward-looking metric should only be representative of repeatable price increases. For example, let's say you increase prices annually due to inflation, and the last few years' inflation has been about 2%, and you measure your ECRER at 2%. Since the inflation and the equivalent annual price increase are both likely to continue into the future, then the 2% ECRER is the right forward-looking metric.

However, if you calculate a 3% ECRER, and it is 100% attributable to a risky, one-time price increase averaging 3%, which is not likely to repeat in the future, then the forward-looking metric should not be the same as the backward-looking metric. In this case, the forward-looking ECRER should be 0%.

**Metric #3 - Customer Revenue Churn Rate:** This is the metric that helps us understand the percentage of revenues lost each year due to customers discontinuing their purchases. The most common way to calculate this metric is to add up all the purchases from customers who purchased in the last two years, but did not purchase anything in the most recent year. If there were 200 customers who purchased in the last two years, but they did not make a purchase in the most recent year, and the total of their purchases two years ago was $8 million, then you would calculate the churn rate by dividing the $8 million by the total revenues from two years ago. Assuming total revenues from two years ago were $160 million, then the calculation for **customer revenue churn rate (CRCR)** would be 5%.

$$\text{\$8 million} \div \text{\$160 million} = \textbf{0.05 or 5\%}$$

Again, our forward-looking metric should only include what we believe is repeatable into the future.

### A Summary Growth Metric: Net Repeatable Revenue Growth Rate

**Net Repeatable Revenue Growth Rate:** If you add up the previous three metrics, you will have the **Net Repeatable Revenue Growth Rate (NRRGR)**. Of course, the customer revenue churn rate should be represented by a negative number. If you assume all of our examples above are repeatable, then the forward-looking NRRGR would be 10%, calculated as follows:

$$10\% + 5\% + (\text{-}5\%) = \textbf{10\%}$$

| New Customer Revenue Acquisition Rate | + | Existing Customer Revenue Expansion Rate | + | Customer Revenue Churn Rate | = | Net Repeatable Revenue Growth Rate |
|---|---|---|---|---|---|---|

**Metric #4 - Annualized Profits:** These are simply the profits generated by the most recent year's sales. What we care most about here is repeatability and stability. We want to make sure that there are no unexpected changes to costs or market prices as we look into the future. We use the term annualized because we want this number to represent the same time period as the annual growth and churn rates.

As an example, if last year's profits were $10 million, but the costs included a $5-million-dollar warehouse expense, which is not likely to be repeated, then the number we would use for our forward-looking annualized profits would add back the $5 million warehousing expense to the $10 million profits because we would not expect to see that cost again in the future. In this case, the forward-looking annualized profits value would be $15 million.

For the purpose of company valuation, **annualized profits** typically refers to the **EBITDA** (earnings before interest, taxes, depreciation, and amortization) of a company, or sometimes free cash flow. But for pricing decision making, it's often helpful to exclude fixed costs and SG&A (unless those costs happen to scale in line with additional sales). It's easier to use Operating Profits for the purpose of valuing a particular line of business. For simplification purposes, in this book we will just use annualized profits to mean generic profits from the sale of goods and services without getting bogged down in details.

There may be a time when you want to calculate annualized profits from data that includes more or less than exactly 12 months. This is sometimes appropriate when the data from a particular time period is deemed more representative of future expectations. Perhaps you made a change 7 months ago, and you believe that your last 7 months of profits are more representative of the future than any other data. To annualize the data, you would just take the 7-month totals, divide by 7, and then multiply by 12.

**WARNING**: **Annualized profits** is where most companies and pricing solution providers tend to exclusively focus, mostly because it is the easiest way to show quick benefits. People have become so demanding of immediate results and payback that they are reluctant to invest in complex solutions they don't entirely understand unless they can see immediate impact on their financial statements. Generally, the easiest way to see immediate results is to raise prices because customers typically react to price increases in delayed fashion. For this reason, companies can show short-term gains in both margin percentage and overall profit dollars fairly quickly. Even though increasing prices might ultimately add unwanted risk to customer relationships, most customer defections don't occur immediately after a small price increase. Companies should be aware of what's happening here, and they should understand that this type of benefit measure is not always a good way to justify the **return on investment** (**ROI**) of a pricing solution. Unfortunately, exclusive focus on annualized profits, as we've seen in the preceding pricing parable, can often lead to poor strategy decisions— decisions that can even destroy instead of improving the value of the company. It is vitally important to look at pricing success through the lens of all **five sacred metrics**.

**Metric #5 – Present-Value Discount Rate:** This is the financial discount rate that is used to value future profits. It is similar to an interest rate. This rate is highly correlated with risk. In fact, this metric is ultimately a measure of both risk and the time value of money. As future profits become riskier, the **present-value discount rate** (**PVDR**) will commensurately increase, and the value of future expected profits will commensurately decrease. For our purposes in this book, we will usually just assume this number as a constant. However, it is important to remember that, in the real world, your pricing decisions can have a significant impact on the value of the present-value discount rate. Any pricing decision that adds risk to future profits should theoretically result in a higher **discount rate**. As you become more advanced in your strategies, you will need to reflect in your calculations how you expect pricing to affect this important metric.

If you are a public company, or you have a good idea of how investors value your company today, you can calculate an implied present-value discount rate using the other four sacred metrics and a **company value calculator**, such as the one available at this book's website, PriceForGrowth.com.

However, it is usually fine to use an estimated discount rate in order to calculate the impact of pricing strategies on company value. If you don't have a good idea what your **present-value discount rate** should be, a good rule of thumb is to take the greater of 10% or your annual growth rate plus 8%. So if your **annual growth rate** is 7%, a good starting point estimate for your present-value discount rate is 15% (7% + 8% = 15%). This may need to be adjusted higher if you are contemplating significant changes to your overall growth rate.

Sometimes companies can come up with pricing strategies that will actually reduce the "risk" of future cash flows and merit a slightly lower discount rate in those future years. This tends to happen as companies get larger and have more entrenched loyalty among their customers. And any strategy that adds risk to the expected results could also require a higher discount rate to compensate for it. Higher discount rates lead to lower company value, and lower discount rates lead to higher company values.

Since raising prices is usually a risky proposition that becomes less repeatable the more you do it, any strategy that relies principally on price increases should come with a higher present-value discount rate, which will show a more realistic effect on the value of the company. In some cases, it can reveal a dampened positive effect. In other cases, it can reveal a negative effect on the value of the company.

Ultimately, how your pricing strategies impact the present-value discount rate should be considered in order to fully evaluate their impact.

## Another Key Summary Metric: Discounted Net Growth Factor (DNGF)

**Discounted Net Growth Factor:** This key summary metric combines the net repeatable growth rate with the **present-value discount rate** to produce what is essentially a profit multiple.

If you multiply the **discounted net growth factor** (**DNGF**) by the annualized profits, you get the theoretical company value:

$$\text{Discounted Net Growth Factor} \times \text{Annualized Profits} = \text{Theoretical Company Value}$$

We will talk about how to calculate the discounted net growth factor later in the book. For now, we want to recognize that it is an important summary metric used to calculate the theoretical value of the company.

## The Sacred Pricing Metric Dashboard

The Sacred Pricing Metric Dashboard is a framework for measuring pricing results in terms of their impact on the five sacred pricing metrics. It will allow you to directly measure the impact of pricing strategies on the theoretical value of the company. After all, company value is the primary objective metric you want to maximize through your pricing decisions. In order to accomplish this, you should communicate in the language of the **five sacred pricing metrics**. This will make it easier to get beyond the myopic focus on profit margins and, instead, point attention to the other metrics that have a significant impact on growing the value of the company. For this reason, I recommend creating a standard dashboard or report that includes all **five sacred metrics**, along with the **company value metric**, such as the example shown below:

## The Sacred Pricing Metric Dashboard

| | Baseline | Year 1 | Year 2 | Year 3 | Today | Company Value Increase |
|---|---|---|---|---|---|---|
| **1** New Customer Revenue Acquisition Rate | 16.4% | 16.9% | 17.5% | 17.8% | 18.3% | **+65.4%** |
| **2** Existing Customer Revenue Expansion Rate | 1.1% | 1.1% | 1.3% | 1.3% | 1.5% | **+13.8%** |
| **3** Existing Customer Revenue Churn Rate | 8.9% | 8.9% | 8.5% | 8.4% | 8.0% | **+31.0%** |
| Net Repeatable Revenue Growth Rate | 8.6% | 9.1% | 10.3% | 10.7% | 11.8% | **+110.2%** |
| **4** Annualized Profits | $2,680,625 | $2,911,159 | $3,176,074 | $3,503,210 | $3,878,053 | **+44.7%** |
| **5** Present Value Discount Rate | 16% | 16% | 16% | 16% | 16% | **0%** |
| Discounted Net Growth Factor | 13.5 | 14.5 | 17.5 | 18.9 | 23.8 | **+110.2%** |
| Company Value | $36,224,662 | $42,190,707 | $55,720,600 | $66,098,299 | $92,334,602 | **+154.9%** |

This particular dashboard is extremely useful because:

- It shows the values for each of the five sacred pricing metrics, starting with the initial baseline, and proceeding along the time periods that lead up to the present.

- It shows how changes in each of the five sacred pricing metrics have contributed to the overall change in company value over time. For example, this chart shows that the improvements in new customer revenue acquisition rate roughly account for a 65.4% increase in company value.

- It shows how each metric is trending in order to highlight areas of recent improvement and areas of needed focus.

- It shows how the **net repeatable revenue growth rate** (**NRRGR**) translates to the **discounted net growth factor** (**DNGF**) and how the **DNGF** multiplied by **annualized profits** (**AP**) translates to the overall company value.

- It shows how the theoretical value of the company has changed year by year, from the initial baseline through the present day.

It's important that you find a way to carry this dashboard with you into planning meetings on pricing strategy, so you can explain why it's important to "invest" in growing revenues and reducing churn.

This particular dashboard example shows how an improvement of 3.2% in **net repeatable revenue growth rate (NRRGR)** translated to a 110.2% increase ($56 million) in the theoretical value of the company. Given the order of magnitude of this huge impact on company value, it becomes much easier to justify another potential investment to try to improve net revenue growth rate by another 2%. Being able to visualize how the five sacred metrics of pricing success are performing and impacting company value makes it much easier to have productive, data-centered discussions on pricing strategy vs. the emotional discussions that seem to pop up in the absence of data and metrics.

It is also interesting to note that while **annualized profits** increased by 44.7%, and therefore increased the value of the company by 44.7%, none of the profit growth came from margin expansion. One hundred percent of the growth in profits was due to growth in revenues. You can see this because the increase in profit percentage tracks with the exact value of previous year's net repeatable revenue growth rate, leaving no room for either margin erosion or margin expansion. This dashboard shows an incredible story of company value growth fueled by net sales growth.

For the purposes of managing better pricing outcomes, it is more productive to focus on the objective measure of **theoretical company value**, which is simply a calculation of the present value of all future profits using a standard discount rate. The theoretical value of the company should move in correlated fashion with the actual market value of the company (although sometimes in delayed fashion) because both are ultimately based on the same inputs. And for this purpose, all the inputs you need are found in the five sacred metrics.

## How Much Does Net Growth Rate Matter?

The net growth rate is extremely important because of its compounding effect. Let's say you have a company that is generating $100,000 of profits per year. If you use the traditional Gordon Growth Valuation Model for a growing perpetuity, it's easy to see how sensitive the value of the company is to changes in the net growth rate. For reference, the Gordon Growth Valuation Model calculates the present value of a growing stream of profits by dividing the profits by the present-value discount rate (r) minus the growth rate (g), as shown below:

$$PV = \frac{Profits}{r - g}$$

The chart below shows the value of a company, using the Gordon growing perpetuity model above, based on a discount rate (r) of 10%, a starting profit value of $100K, and various net growth rates.

**The Present Value of a $100K Growing Annuity by Growth Rate**
In $ millions

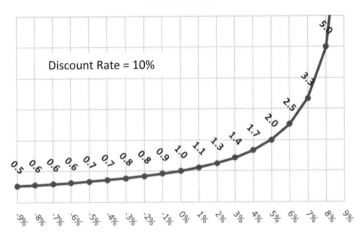

Because of the compounding effects, incrementally higher net growth rates produce exponentially higher valuations of future profits. For example, looking at the chart above, a perpetual stream of $100K in profits, growing at 4%, is valued at $1.7 million. However, if you increase that growth rate by just 2% to a 6% net growth rate, the valuation increases to $2.5 million. That last 2% was worth $800K in value. But if you increase the growth rate just 1% more to a 7% net growth rate, the value increases by another $800K to $3.3 million. Another way to look at it is that if you double the repeatable net growth rate from 4% to 8%, the value of the company almost triples, going from $1.7 million to $5 million.

There's nothing magical about this. It's just financial compounding and math. But it represents the reality of how value is accumulated.

## Comparative Impact of Different Metrics on Company Value

If you want to maximize your ability to impact company value, you have to understand which individual output metric has the highest leverage on company value. To illustrate this, let's look at an example of an arbitrarily conceived

$100 million company that does $10 million in profits, and currently uses a 10% discount rate. If this company has a net growth rate of 4%, how does a 1% improvement in each of the five sacred metrics translate to an increase in company value? The answers are shown in the chart below:

### The Effect of a 1% Improvement on Company Valuation

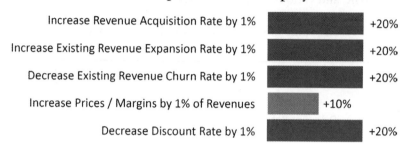

| | |
|---|---|
| Increase Revenue Acquisition Rate by 1% | +20% |
| Increase Existing Revenue Expansion Rate by 1% | +20% |
| Decrease Existing Revenue Churn Rate by 1% | +20% |
| Increase Prices / Margins by 1% of Revenues | +10% |
| Decrease Discount Rate by 1% | +20% |

As is clearly illustrated in this example, a 1% improvement in price (or margin) has a smaller impact on company valuation than a 1% improvement in any of the other sacred metrics. At this point in the book, this should not be a big surprise. But remember, that was just one example. What if we were to look at five different types of company profiles to see what impact a 1% improvement in profits, growth rate, or discount rate would have on the value of the company? (Since new customer growth, existing customer growth, and churn are all represented in the net growth rate, they don't necessarily need to be split out individually for this analysis.) The results are in the following table:

### The Effect of a 1% Improvement on Company Valuation For Various Company Profiles

| Company Profile | Profit Percent | Growth Rate | Discount Rate | Intial Valuation | Profit + 1% | | Growth + 1% | | Disc Rate - 1% | |
|---|---|---|---|---|---|---|---|---|---|---|
| | | | | | Val | % Diff | Val | % Diff | Val | % Diff |
| Medium Growth | 10% | 10% | 15% | 200 | 220 | 10% | 250 | 25% | 250 | 25% |
| High Growth | 5% | 15% | 18% | 167 | 200 | 20% | 250 | 50% | 250 | 50% |
| Low Growth | 16% | 5% | 12% | 229 | 243 | 6% | 267 | 17% | 267 | 17% |
| High Profit | 25% | 8% | 15% | 357 | 371 | 4% | 417 | 17% | 417 | 17% |
| Low Profit | 2% | 8% | 15% | 29 | 43 | 50% | 33 | 17% | 33 | 17% |

This shows the same phenomenon. Except for very low-margin businesses, increasing growth rates seems to have a mathematically greater impact on company valuation than increasing profits. If it takes roughly the same effort to produce a 1% improvement in price and margin as it takes to achieve a 1% improvement in all the other metrics, then your efforts would get the worst **return on investment (ROI)** by focusing on margins. You would be better off focusing on improving growth or reducing churn by 1% than focusing on margins.

But that's not how life works. It would be rare to find a situation where you could achieve a 1% improvement in every sacred metric with identical efforts. Sometimes it is easier to reduce churn by 1% than it is to increase prices by 1%. What we usually find is that improvement is either easier or harder depending on how far away you are from the target benchmark. For example, if the industry average churn rate is 10%, but your company is churning at a rate of 30%, it should be easier to get a 1% improvement than if your company were only churning 5%. Going from 30% churn to 29% churn should be easier than going from 5% churn to 4% churn.

Long story short, we will need to look at both relative impact and relative opportunity—how easy or likely it will be to improve a particular metric.

If your profit percentage is only 1%, then a 1% improvement in pricing and margins will produce a 100% increase in company value.

Later in the book, I will give you the tools to diagnose your own situation, and you can see where the lowest hanging fruit is for your business.

This is how companies can accomplish true price optimization, which actually drives the highest incremental value of the company.

## Potential Valuation Concerns Related to Risks Associated with Future Revenues (Optional)

Clearly, the riskiness of future profit streams will affect the value of the company. This is captured through the fifth sacred metric: **present-value discount rate**. As risks increase, the discount rate should also increase to reflect the lowered values of future profits. This is fairly straightforward. However, as companies start implementing strategies to increase growth rates, it's likely that those changes also will have a material impact on the company's risk profile. Higher growth rates can be inherently more risky than lower growth rates.

If you are interested in understanding more advanced ways to deal with these issues in your company value calculation, I've included a commentary in *Appendix A*.

However, for most comparisons of different pricing scenarios, it's probably fine to assume the same **present-value discount rate**. The only absolute requirement is to ensure that your growth rates never exceed your discount rates. If that ever happens, the easiest way to handle it is probably to just increase the discount rate for all scenarios.

## Theoretical Company Value vs. Actual Company Value

As we've discussed, the five sacred metrics of pricing success are extremely useful in generating a theoretical estimate of company value, which can be estimated by calculating the present value of future profits using the widely accepted Gordon Growth Formula.

Obviously, a theoretical valuation is not necessarily the same as an actual market valuation, which can be determined only by buyers and sellers as transactions take place. For public companies, actual market value is determined by the value of the stock price. For private companies, the actual value can only be estimated until the company, or a part of the company, is sold. Even when companies seek out new investments, the portion of company ownership exchanged for those investments is determined based on the valuation of the company using traditional valuation methods.

Although company valuation is often subjective and can vary depending on the technique being used, it is not uncommon to find different "preferred" techniques in different industries. These techniques can include methods that incorporate valuation multiples like revenue or profit multiples. They can also include the more traditional discounted-cash-flow techniques like the Gordon Growth Formula. Or they can include other more complex techniques such as Economic Value Added (EVA). Different valuation techniques put different weights and emphases on different metrics. If, for example, most companies in your industry are valued at six times revenues, then it would be logical for those companies to focus more on increasing revenues. And pricing strategies should then focus on how to have the biggest impact on increasing revenues.

For the purposes of this book, we obviously want to understand what will help us maximize the actual market value of a company. Since most valuation techniques are at least loosely related to traditional discounted-cash-flow methodology, we will use this methodology for the valuation examples in this book. To do this, I have laid out a default approach, based on the five sacred metrics of pricing success, to be used in conjunction with the Gordon Growth Formula. It is possible that the model I've laid out will generate a company value estimate that is quite different than the actual market value of your company. However, because this valuation technique is based on a widely accepted methodology, it is safe to assume that the metrics that increase the theoretical value will also increase the actual market value, at least directionally, and very likely in similar orders of magnitude. In other words, if you improve metrics that double the theoretical value of your company, you can feel confident that those improvements will also lead to significant increases in the actual market value of your company.

When we get to the optimization section based on maximizing company value, we will use the five sacred metrics valuation methodology. But we can also tailor the approach to emphasize the metrics that are deemed most important by investors in your specific industry.

A final word on company valuation in the context of the Boston Consulting Group Business Matrix (Stars, Question Marks, Cash Cows, and Dogs): This model cares about two things—market leadership and industry growth, both of which are very sensitive to overall revenue growth. This model has no concern for company profitability directly. I can say, from my experience, that this model has a high level of acceptance and credibility in the executive suites of companies across industries. Almost all companies aspire to be Stars—high growth and high relative market share. The disproportionate focus on growth is corroborated by this model and many other models used by investors today.

In any case, if your overriding business objective is to maximize the value of the company, then the first point of focus should be on the metrics that have the most impact on that value.

## Chapter Summary

In this chapter, we've covered a lot of ground. We started by defining the **five sacred metrics of pricing success** and illustrating their direct connection to the value of the company. And we pointed out some key lessons:

- In order to create pricing strategies that directly increase the value of the company, it's important to maintain visibility on all **five sacred metrics of pricing success.**

- The **pricing metric dashboard** is a critical communication tool for keeping executive attention on how pricing strategies connect to the five sacred metrics and ultimately the value of the company. It is very important to have and display that information in discussions about pricing strategy to help get people aligned with the most important opportunities.

- The most attractive opportunities to increase the value of the company can be determined by looking at the relative impact of increasing any one of the five sacred metrics, and then determining the apparent ease of accomplishing an increase to each metric. An easy way to determine this is by comparing

- the relative value of each metric to its respective minimum, maximum, and theoretical target value.

- The discount rate used to value future profits can be adjusted to account for different levels of uncertainty over the horizon of future profits. However, this level of sophistication is not generally required to determine good pricing strategies to maximize the value of the company. Higher levels of sophistication will, however, help reconcile actual market value to theoretical company value. (More commentary available in *Appendix A.*)

The most important takeaway from this chapter is that company-value-maximizing pricing strategies can happen only with continuous visibility, attention, and focus on the **five sacred metrics of pricing success**. Companies that strategically prioritize their efforts, based on potential impact and opportunity, have a much better chance of making significant improvements to the overall value of their companies than those who focus randomly on one metric or attempt to improve all five metrics simultaneously.

The **Pricing Metric Dashboard** and the **Comparative Impact Report** are both helpful tools for making decisions and for communicating the rationale of key pricing strategies throughout the organization.

———————

*Next chapter preview:* *A case parable about a new pricing VP and his experience of helping his new employer, ElastiCo, grow profits using pricing analysis and elasticity modeling…until he finds himself in an undesirable situation.*

## CHAPTER 5

# The Story of Leroy Studemont

**Case Parable 2: ElastiCo and Leroy Studemont**

*The following pricing parable looks at a scenario where a new VP of Pricing, Leroy Studemont, with proven skills in pricing analytics and elasticity modeling, puts together consecutive years of margin expansion and profit growth. Those familiar with popular pricing philosophy will notice that his decisions seem to follow defensible, profit-maximizing principles, at least for the short term. But in Year 4 the unexpected happens, and Leroy finds himself in a difficult situation.*

## Leroy Studemont, ElastiCo's New VP of Pricing

As he slowly walked back to his new office, Leroy found himself in deep thought about the company he had just joined. On one hand, this job was a major step up in his career. On the other hand, he knew it had some risk attached to it. Prior to ElastiCo, most of Leroy's jobs had been turnaround situations where he used his knowledge and skills to fix poorly performing businesses.

ElastiCo was different. Unlike Leroy's past employers, ElastiCo was riding a wave of success. As a leading manufacturer of drive belts for machines and engines, they had recently grown their total annual revenues to $120 million, which allowed them to go public on the New York Stock Exchange. Leroy had been hired to make the business perform even better.

Now, after meeting with his new boss, the company's CFO, Leroy realized that expectations were quite high—maybe too high. The CFO had already promised the other executives that Leroy would deliver 2% higher profits in his first year by implementing new pricing strategies.

His CFO was adamant about increasing profit margins in order to prove to their investors that ElastiCo's premium products had the ability to garner higher prices and greater profits. Achieving this would also be seen as an indicator of "excellent financial discipline." Leroy had been chosen because of his proven experience in pricing analytics and elasticity modeling.

At this point, Leroy had no choice. He had accepted the job, and now he had to act quickly in order to show positive profit results in his first year. But Leroy was not intimidated by this challenge. He was extremely confident in his ability to understand the data and quickly focus in on the most achievable opportunities. He was ready to start making a name for himself at ElastiCo.

## Year 1 – The "Prove It" Year

After analyzing ElastiCo's transaction data, Leroy determined that, if his projections were correct, they could raise prices by 2% and grow total profits by 22.4%. Although the 2% price increase would likely result in a 4% decrease in customers and unit sales, the increase in profit margins would more than compensate for the loss. The math was straightforward. Revenues would shrink by 4% due to the loss in customers and unit sales, but then the remaining revenues would grow by 2% due to the price increase, and the overall effect would be a 2.1% decrease in revenues, but a 22.4% increase in profits.

The financial calculations were as follows:

$120 million revenues – 4% customer churn = $115.2 million

$115.2 million + 2% price increase = $117.5 million

| Year | Revenues | Profit % | Profit $ | Year over Year Profit Increase |
|------|----------|----------|----------|-------------------------------|
| Year 0 | $120 million | 8% | $9.6 million | - |
| Year 1 | $117.5 million | 10% | $11.75 million | 22.4% |

The relative unit volumes and unit margins from Leroy's analysis are shown in the chart below:

### ElastiCo Unit Sales vs. Unit Margin

Under Leroy's hypothesis, revenues would shrink by $2.5 million. But profits would actually increase because the price increase would more than offset the unit volume decrease.

### ElastiCo Total Revenues and Total Profits
in $ millions

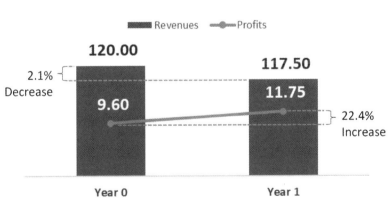

After gaining approval from the CFO, Leroy implemented his plan.

Sure enough, at the end of the year, it turned out that Leroy's analysis was right on. Profits grew by 22.4%, from $9.6 million to $11.75 million, a difference of $2.15 million.

Leroy had passed his first test by producing significant profit growth in his first year. He had proven to his boss and the other executives that he could use pricing as a tool to generate higher profits.

Leroy's boss came by at the end of the year to personally thank him for his work and to deliver the news that Leroy would be getting a significant raise as a result of the profit increase. Leroy couldn't wait to go home and tell his wife the good news. Just like with all his other jobs, Leroy was continuing his track record of success.

## Year 2 – The Continuation

Toward the end of Year 1, as results seemed to be trending in the right direction, Leroy started working on his pricing strategy for Year 2. He conducted a similar analysis and concluded that another 2% price increase would likely result in another 4% decrease in customers and unit volumes. But, again, total profits would likely grow, although this time by only 17.5%. But it did add up to another $2.06 million in total profit dollars, so Leroy assumed his boss would want to go ahead with another price increase. Leroy's analysis of projected unit volumes vs. unit margins is shown in the chart below:

ElastiCo Unit Sales vs. Unit Margin

And the revenue and profit projections from this exact same analysis are shown in this chart below:

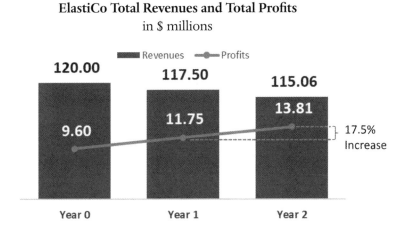

**ElastiCo Total Revenues and Total Profits**
in $ millions

Revenues were projected to fall again, this time from $117.5 million to $115.06 million. As a NYSE-traded company, Leroy worried what investors would think about a second straight year of declining revenues. Could ElastiCo afford to be losing revenues? Although he was sure he could generate more total profits for the company, Leroy expressed concern to his boss that the incremental profits were coming at the expense of revenue growth.

But Leroy's CFO was not interested in any strategy that would slow down profits. He had already promised multiple years of additional profit and margin growth prior to their IPO. He felt that sales were the responsibility of the COO and VP of Sales, and declining revenue was a problem they would have to fix on their own without putting the promised margin growth in jeopardy.

As expected, the CFO endorsed the second straight 2% price increase, and once again it was executed flawlessly.

At the end of the year, just as expected, revenues fell, but profits grew by the expected $2.06 million.

During their earnings announcement at the end of the year, the CFO expressed pride in ElastiCo's ability to increase margins, now for two consecutive years. But, as Leroy had feared, some of the analysts expressed concerns over the declining revenues. Of course, they were reassured by the CFO that the revenue problem would be taken care of by the sales team, and in the meantime, keeping margins strong was a top priority. And regardless of their sales performance, they were growing profits—the most important financial metric for both the company and the investors.

Despite the concerns about the declining revenues, the CFO was confident they were making the right decisions because profits continued to rise. For a second year in a row, Leroy was given an increase in compensation, which was welcomed as another validation that he was delivering what was expected of him. Leroy felt very satisfied that he had taken this job, and he felt like his career was moving in the right direction.

## Year 3 – Finally, a Difficult Pricing Decision

Before Leroy had even finished his analysis for Year 3, the CFO told him he expected another 2% price increase.

But when Leroy finished his analysis, it appeared that another price increase would be more damaging than in the previous years. This time, Leroy's analysis suggested that a 2% price increase would result in a 12% decrease in customers and unit sales. This was three times worse than the previous years' volume decreases.

Leroy understood what was happening. He realized that prices were getting dangerously close to the maximum willingness-to-pay of the customers, and as result, customers would start dropping off at a higher rate. He had suspected this would eventually happen, but suddenly the reality was here. And suddenly he was more worried about the path they were going down. Further price increases would be extremely difficult to pull off. Below is the chart from Leroy's analysis that had him so worried:

ElastiCo Unit Sales vs. Unit Margin

Yet, even with the 12% reduction in unit sales, Leroy's analysis showed profits would grow by another $650K to $14.46 million. Leroy didn't know if his CFO would still want to go forward with a 2% price increase that would make revenues drop by almost $12 million, only to pick up another $650K of profits. It seemed like a big risk for not much reward.

But to Leroy's surprise, the CFO gave the order to execute the price increase. No questions. No discussion. He saw the analysis and said, "Let's do it."

The chart below shows the projected revenues and profits with a third price increase of 2%:

**ElastiCo Total Revenues and Total Profits**
in $ millions

This is what Leroy's CFO was looking at when he said, "Let's do it."

And so, they did it.

At the end of the year, just like before, everything happened as expected. Revenues fell to $103.3 million, but profits increased by $650,000, just as they had planned.

In the earnings call, both analysts and investors took notice of the decrease in revenues—and more importantly, the decrease in the rate of profit growth. They began to question the sustainability of ElastiCo's profit growth strategy. Leroy's CFO continued to reassure investors that they were in the business of selling premium products that should have a premium price in the market, and that they would continue to grow profits through disciplined pricing and good financial management. Separately, their new sales leaders would soon fix the declining revenue problem.

After the earnings call, the CFO did not seem as happy as he had been after the first two years. Leroy received neither the congratulations nor the raise he had received the prior two years. He was starting to feel like he'd painted himself into a corner. Deep down inside, he knew that further price increases were just not going to go well. He'd tried to communicate this concern to his CFO before, but his warnings had fallen on deaf ears. Leroy was told to focus only on pricing and margin improvement and not to worry about sales—that would be taken care of by the newly hired Sales VP. In the eyes of the CFO, the increased customer churn was a failure of the Sales team—not a failure of Pricing, even though Leroy knew differently deep down inside. Despite the uncomfortable ending to the year, the CFO was adamant that prices and profit margins should continue to grow.

Leroy knew what was happening, and he felt helpless to change it.

## Year 4 – Digging a Deeper Hole

The following year, assuming his boss would want to see another price increase, Leroy ran his analysis again. Unfortunately, it showed that another 2% price increase would likely result in a 14% decrease in customers and unit sales, as shown in the chart below:

**ElastiCo Unit Sales vs. Unit Margin**

Although the drop in unit sales would produce another significant decrease in revenues, it would come with a $40K increase in profits—almost nothing. It certainly didn't seem worth the trouble to increase prices again and further put their customer relationships at risk. But at this point, after three years of declining revenue, the CFO felt like it would be moving backwards to try to get some of those revenues back. He felt that increasing margins was their only possible area of potential success, given the analysis. After all, 16% profit margin was almost double the industry average. This would show the investors that Finance and Pricing were strong, even if Sales was failing to generate their customer retention or growth numbers. The CFO did not want to "bail out" the "underperforming" sales team with lower prices or profit margins. If the company moved forward with the 2% price increase as planned, the new VP of Sales would either perform and drive even higher profits, or he would give the company the ammunition needed to get rid of him.

After all, both Leroy and the CFO were compensated based on overall profit dollars and profit margin percentage—not sales and not revenues.

The decision was made to go forward with the 2% price increase.

## Year 4 Results – Worse Than Expected

Unlike the first three years, Year 4 did not go as planned. Instead of losing 14% of their customers and unit volumes, ElastiCo ended up losing 25%. Of course, the CFO blamed the loss of customers on the new Sales VP, but that didn't really matter. The damage was historically monumental. The chart below shows actual unit sales volume and profit margin:

Both unit sales and customers were now 45% lower than when Leroy had joined the company four years earlier. The revenue and profit results are shown in the chart below:

**ElastiCo Total Revenues and Total Profits**
in $ millions

Although unit profit margins grew to 16%, ElastiCo's total profits actually decreased by $1.82 million.

Things were bad—worse than Leroy could have imagined.

The public announcement of these results led to a chain of negative events for all the company's major stakeholders: investors, employees, and customers.

- ElastiCo's stock price dropped by 33% in one day.
- Both Leroy and his CFO were immediately fired.
- ElastiCo's new interim CFO determined the company would immediately need to lay off 10% of their employees because of the 12.6% decrease in profits. Unfortunately, this would quickly have a negative impact on the quality of ElastiCo's products and services, which would cause further customer dissatisfaction.
- ElastiCo's few remaining customers became even more dissatisfied from the lower level of quality after constantly being asked to pay higher prices. Clearly there was more customer churn on the horizon.

In summary, ElastiCo seemed to crumble in a single day.

Leroy worried about the conversation he would soon be having with his wife, who was just a few weeks away from giving birth to their first child.

Could things be any worse?

## Time out – Is This Story Even Realistic?

At this point in the story, you may be thinking there is no company in the world that would be this stupid. You may be asking: Where was the CEO while all this was going on? You may be wondering how any public company could possibly think they could get away with four consecutive years of decreasing revenues, and still hold its value based on higher profit numbers.

You know what? You are absolutely right! This company started to have failure written all over it from the very first year, when they raised prices and started losing revenues. This is not a realistic story. And yet this is how I've seen many CFOs and Pricing leaders make pricing decisions—raising prices to grow profits, but at the expense of customers and revenues. Decisions like this happen all the time.

What's worse is that many pricing solution providers, whether consulting or software, seem to be fine with this approach, as many of their tools are designed to do exactly what Leroy did: get prices up, let go of unprofitable customers, and expand profit margins, even if it means slowing revenues. This is what elasticity-based price optimization has to offer. This is what I've seen over the past 20+ years. I'm telling this story to make a point, and I hope it sinks in. This is what **profit-maximizing pricing strategies** are intended to do. And if this is what companies adopt, they should not be surprised if the results are not sustainable. In Year 1, it's not so obvious. But if you continue the strategy, Year 4 eventually happens. That's what companies have to look forward to in a profit-maximizing pricing strategy.

Now, let's jump back into the story…

## Continuing the Story

Leroy was devastated by the events. Up to this point, his pricing optimization and elasticity models had never failed him. He had always tried to make decisions in the best interest of the company. But now, due to a single error in his demand response forecast, his career was "ruined."

But it wasn't just one single error, was it? Every time ElastiCo increased prices without adding any additional value, they were torquing up the inherent risk of a potentially massive customer exodus. This was four straight years of bad decision-making.

Yes. It's true that Leroy's boss put constant pressure on him to raise prices. But Leroy should have known better. Leroy *did* know better. But he was afraid to push back against his boss so early in his tenure at ElastiCo. And he rationalized his actions based on the belief that his boss would back him for doing what he was told.

At this point, none of that mattered. Both Leroy and his boss were now without jobs. And Leroy's decisions and actions directly led to this outcome.

## A Literal Nightmare

It was at this point that Leroy rolled over and suddenly woke up in a cold sweat. It was still dark outside. He grabbed his phone to look at the time.

It was all just a dream…

The future hadn't been decided yet. There was still time to change—time to choose a different path.

Later that morning, Leroy walked into his office with a very nervous feeling, reflecting on the elaborate dream he'd had the night before, which he now considered an omen—a warning about what could go wrong.

"Are you okay?" Leroy looked up to see his CFO and new boss standing in the doorway. "I was getting curious about how big of a price increase you might recommend this year, so we can get those profits up."

This time Leroy knew better. Despite pressure from his new CFO, he realized that increasing prices could put the company's desired growth at risk.

Leroy was smart. He was great at data analysis and elasticity modeling. But more importantly, he knew that he needed to look beyond profit margins to determine the best pricing strategies. He knew that he (and his bosses) would be successful only if their strategies were visibly connected to the growth of the value of the company. He knew that growing the value of the company was dependent on the growth of revenues and profits. And he knew that the growth of revenues and profits meant that the company would need a constant stream of new customers and a way to minimize the loss of revenues from existing customer churn.

In his data analysis, he found that ElastiCo's prices were already high, relative to the rest of the market, and that any further price increases would likely increase churn and make it more difficult to capture new customers. His analysis also led him to believe that the company could likely grow revenues in line with the market at 6% per year if they didn't raise prices any further.

That became Leroy's pricing strategy—hold prices steady in order to get the growth engine started, while trying to minimize churn at the same time. Despite the pressure from his boss to raise prices, Leroy instead decided to leave prices alone all four years. Using the **five sacred metrics for pricing success**, he was able to convince his CFO that raising prices was too risky for their long-term profit growth. Using the **pricing metric dashboard**, he showed the entire executive team that holding prices at their current levels was the best strategy for expanding company value.

## The Actual Results

With no price increases, the company was able to achieve 6% annual revenue growth every single year for four years. After four years, total annual revenues had grown to $151.5 million, and annual profits had grown to a respectable $12.12 million.

The chart below compares the initial result (from Leroy's dream) with the revised (actual) results.

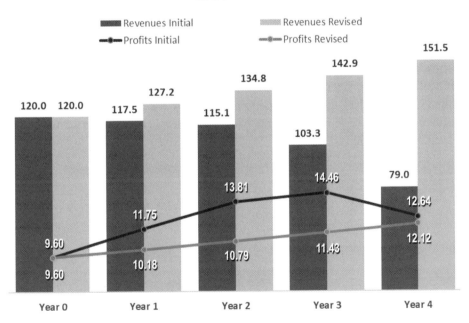

**ElastiCo Revenues & Profits**
In $ millions

In the actual, "revised" world, the company produced four years of consistent revenue and profit growth. Over those four years, the company's stock price doubled. Investors were happy. Most of the customers were happy. And Leroy's bosses were happy.

At the end of the four years, everyone who owned company stock had become a little more wealthy. Leroy's CFO decided to retire due to the increased value of his stock options, and Leroy was promoted to take his place as CFO.

What started out as an ominous nightmare ended up being a remarkably successful four-year run that included very little drama. Just smart people making smart decisions to keep things moving in the right direction.

## Leroy's Secret Pricing Metric: Discounted Net Growth Factor

In order to determine the best pricing strategy for ElastiCo, Leroy used a new metric called **Discounted Net Growth Factor (DNGF)** that he had learned about in a pricing class. This was like a profit multiple that took into account both new customer acquisitions and existing customer revenue churn. It was a metric that reflected the present value of the profits that would be generated by all present and future customers based on existing growth and churn rates. Without going into the specifics of the calculation, it's helpful to know that, after Year 1, in Leroy's actual reality, the value of this DNGF for his zero-price-increase strategy was **24.38X**. Conversely, the value of this metric for the 2%-price-increase strategy in his dream was only **7.14X**. These values were calculated based on extrapolating the Year 1 results out into the foreseeable future. As a gauge of pricing effectiveness, this new "secret" pricing metric showed that Leroy's zero-price-increase strategy was **3.4** times more valuable than his imagined 2%-price-increase strategy. Leroy had a way to quantify the value of each strategy, based on how each would respectively affect future company profitability.

Why is it secret? Because most companies don't know about it or use it.

Without this DNGF metric, it would be difficult to see that the zero-price-increase strategy was clearly the superior strategy. Looking just at the short-term profit outcomes from the two strategies in the table below, it seems like the 2%-price-increase strategy would be better.

| Pricing Strategy | Annualized Net Profits | Total Profit Percent |
|---|---|---|
| 2%-price-increase strategy | $11.75 million | 10% |
| Zero-price-increase strategy | $10.18 million | 8% |

It's easy to see how Leroy and his CFO could be tempted to go with the short-term profit increase strategy. After all, that's how their bonuses were calculated—by whether or not they exceeded an arbitrary profit target. In the absence of other metrics, it seems justifiable to pick the option that results in higher profits.

**But looking one level deeper, it's easy to see that it's the wrong strategy for the company**. The original 2%-price-increase strategy in Leroy's dream considered profit dollars after only one year. It did not consider the compounding effects of customer growth or churn for the subsequent years.

The value of the company is based on the present value of future profits. Leroy's secret metric, the **discounted net growth factor** (DNGF), helps calculate exactly that.

By multiplying the expected **annualized profits** times the **discounted net growth factor**, it's easy to see how each strategy affects the value of the company, as shown in the table below:

| Pricing Strategy | Discounted Net Growth Factor | Annualized Net Profits | Total Company Value |
|---|---|---|---|
| 2%-price increase strategy | 7.14 | $11.75 million | $83.9 million |
| Zero-price-increase strategy | 24.38 | $10.18 million | $248.2 million |

This table is an easy way to show the relative value of each pricing strategy, based on how sales growth will drive the growth of future profits. From this, it is clear that the zero-price-increase strategy was vastly superior. And this is why Leroy was ultimately very successful.

## Chapter Summary

This case parable illustrates some extremely important lessons about pricing strategy and customer behavior. Adhering to these lessons should help you develop the highest-value pricing strategies for your company:

- **Pay attention to all five sacred metrics.** Looking only at near-term profit results as your main metric for making pricing decisions can ultimately put your company in a dangerous position. It's imperative that you also look at how pricing decisions affect customer growth, existing-customer revenue expansion, and customer churn.

- **Annual price increases may not be sustainable sources of profit growth** (depending on what is happening to competitor or market prices). There are limits to how much you can raise prices without putting your customer relationships at risk. Raising prices puts stress on customer relationships, and if you keep applying stress to those relationships, they will eventually crumble.

- **Elasticity curves are not uniform** across the price spectrum. Customers drop off at different rates depending on the magnitude of the price increase. Make

- sure you are accounting for this in any elasticity model you might be tempted to use.

- **Discounted net growth factor** (**DNGF**) is the "secret" pricing metric that combines four of the five sacred pricing metrics into one metric. Using this metric is an easy way to evaluate a pricing strategy, especially when combined with the fifth sacred metric, annualized profits.

These lessons give us a good starting point for driving good pricing strategies. There will be other important lessons as we continue our journey through this book. But these lessons form an important foundation. If you are not currently using these concepts in developing your own pricing strategies, think of this chapter as an opportunity to make improvements that could have a big impact on the value of your company today.

------

*Next chapter preview: The structure of your pricing strategies can either add or remove value from your customer relationships. As a general rule of thumb, consider this: What's good for the customer is ultimately good for the company...*

# PART 2

# Customer Relationships

*There is only one boss. The Customer. And he can fire everyone in the company, from the chairman on down, simply by spending his money somewhere else.*

—Sam Walton

CHAPTER 6

# Losing the Pricing Tug-O-War

*A Customer is the most important visitor on our premises.*
*He is not dependent on us. We are dependent on him.*
*He is not an interruption in our work. He is the purpose of it.*
*He is not an outsider in our business. He is a part of it.*
*We are not doing him a favor by serving him.*
*He is doing us a favor by giving us an opportunity to do so.*

—Gandhiji (Mahatma Gandhi)

Most people agree that long-term business success hinges on the ability to create and deliver value to the customer over and over again. Consistent with that, most people also agree that adversarial customer relationships are bad for business. And so, if most people agree with these two concepts, why do so many companies so often find themselves in battles with customers over price?

In this chapter, you'll learn how seemingly harmless business decisions can cause a domino effect of damage to customer relationships, thereby causing damage to the company's future success. What's unfortunate is that, even though these decisions and their results are quite visible, too many business leaders fail to see what's happening. They fail to see the series of decisions that create a multitude of problems for the health of customer relationships.

I expect this chapter to challenge deeply seated beliefs and habits, and for some of you, it may be difficult to absorb. For this reason, I believe it is important to approach these topics with the **growth mindset**—processing new ideas with an open mind. Consider these topics as starting points upon which you can build. I hope you will find, among the infinite possibilities, a solution pathway that can work for your business.

With this mindset, you'll learn how to take price off the table by eliminating negotiated prices and transitioning to transparent, fair, and rational prices. This transition will help you build customer trust and good will where it might not have been fully possible before.

## The Pricing Tug-O-War and the Ill-Fated Practice of Price Negotiations

The answer to the question above, about why companies so often find themselves engaged in battles with customers over price, is fairly simple. For companies, higher prices lead to higher profits. For this reason, it's desirable to raise prices if you can get away with it. Of course, that's not the way most customers see it. They prefer lower prices. They prefer to keep more of their money if possible. And so, for these reasons, the stage is already set for the **pricing tug-o-war**.

What is the **pricing tug-o-war**?

The best way to answer this question might be to paint a picture through an example scenario: Imagine a company that decides to attempt a price increase. It may even do the responsible thing and notify customers. A customer then receives the notification and decides whether or not the price increase is merited. If the customer decides the price increase is not merited, they may contact the company to say they won't be buying anymore because of the price increase. Or they may say nothing, and just stop buying. When this happens, the company may agonize for a while, and then decide to offer the customer a discount or revert the price back to the previous level. Boom. A price exception is created.

But the story doesn't end there. The company now feels slighted because they had to acquiesce to the customer's will. The customer feels slighted because they had to do extra work and spend extra effort threatening to leave, just to keep the price they had before—or something close to it. Furthermore, now the customer feels less trust for the company, supposing the company will try to increase prices in the future, which means more effort they'll have to spend to fight off future price increases. The company now sees the customer as a "problem customer" because it had to spend extra effort to keep a customer who is now paying a lower ("exception") price than other customers. Now the company has to figure out a better way to raise this customer's price in the future without losing the customer, which creates more work for them, along with the possibility that this customer still might not ever accept any new, higher price.

To sum up, this activity leads to a situation where both parties feel worse off than they were before, plus now they'll have to deal with each other in the future over the issue of price. In addition, both sides feel that trust has diminished, as it becomes more clear that what the company wants and what the customer wants are not aligned. And on top of everything else, now they probably don't like each other as much as they did before. The relationship between the company and the customer has clearly worsened.

This is called the **pricing tug-o-war**. It comes in many shapes and sizes. But it always includes a company trying to increase prices and customers trying to avoid having their prices increased. It's a basic struggle over who will pocket the excess value generated in the business relationship. I call this a "win–lose game" because one side's winning is in direct proportion to the other side's losing. But in some cases, like in the example above, both sides are made worse off, and it can easily be seen as "lose–lose."

From a free-market perspective, there's nothing wrong with the pricing tug-o-war. This is exactly how mutually agreed prices get set and how trades get accomplished—buyers and sellers working in their own interests until one side concedes that the price is good enough to make the trade. In fact, many companies actively promote the pricing tug-o-war by allowing their prices to be negotiated, often based on nothing more than the random discretion of sales representatives.

The problem with the pricing tug-o-war is not that the price isn't mutually agreeable. Technically, it is mutually agreeable, or both sides wouldn't agree to make the trade. The problem is that it leads to unnecessary friction and damage to what could otherwise be a high-value business relationship between a buyer and a seller.

## The Tragedy of Aggravated Price Negotiations

For some companies, the prevailing thinking is that negotiated prices are good because they allow both parties—the company and the customer—to work toward a "mutually agreeable" price through negotiation.

But contrary to what many believe, **negotiated pricing does not improve customer satisfaction**. Negotiated pricing almost always results in a situation where most customers are paying unfair prices, almost by definition, especially when the final negotiated price is based on the random discretion of an individual sales rep. In addition, "negotiated pricing" creates an unnecessary burden for the customer. The minute a customer understands that prices are negotiable, they realize they have an obligation to do more work and go through additional stress to make sure they get the best possible price. After all, the final negotiated price is a product of how much work the customer is willing to put into the negotiation. And even after all the work to negotiate, there will still be some doubt in their mind about whether or not they are overpaying.

Having to negotiate a fair price is an example of unnecessary friction in the buying process. It puts customers and sellers in adversarial positions in a zero-sum game where sellers win only when customers lose, and vice-versa. For some personality types, being forced to negotiate puts them in an uncomfortable position—having to interact with people in an adversarial manner that can jeopardize individual trust and even destroy personal friendships.

And it only gets worse with time, as both sides try to find ways to outsmart each other, and trust continually fades away. It should be no surprise to companies who engage in negotiated pricing when their customers resort to bothersome actions designed to chip away at the company's negotiating position, such as: price complaints, shopping threats, RFPs, and constant commentary on how uncompetitive the prices are. If every aspect of the customer–vendor relationship seems like another chapter in an ongoing price negotiation, why should anyone be surprised when neither party is willing to say anything positive about the other for fear that they might somehow damage their own negotiating position?

Ahead in this chapter, I will show that price negotiations actually work against all of my **seven principles of win–win customer relationships**.

But to close this section, suffice it to say that price negotiations lead to adversarial posturing, diminished trust, extra work, more uncertainty, skepticism regarding fair treatment, and unnecessary friction in the customer buying experience.

## The Irony of Price Negotiations vs. Margins

In a twist of irony, most companies who practice **pricing negotiation tug-o-war** with their customers usually end up with lower profit margins. Why? Because that is where they constantly draw the customer's focus and attention.

On the other hand, companies that find ways to give their customers "fair" but non-negotiable prices typically end up with higher margins. Why? Because they succeed at taking price off the table. Because customers value trust and price integrity, and it's been proven many times that customers are willing to pay more for a "fair" price.

So, here's an easy way to increase margins and save yourself a lot of trouble: **Stop the practice of negotiated prices.**

*DISCLAIMER: To be fair, I freely acknowledge there is a time and place where price negotiations are appropriate. For example, custom projects or one-time sales where there is no existing market expectation of price, and a win–win price must be discovered through a good faith negotiation—where the market is literally a market of one provider and one customer. In this situation, I would expect negotiated pricing because there is no alternative. Or in a one-time purchase, where a repeat-purchase opportunity is not expected, where there's no benefit to creating an environment of ongoing trust in the customer experience, then negotiated pricing might be preferred. But those situations do not describe the typical recurring purchase relationships so common in B2B commerce. In recurring-purchase business relationships, I am asserting that it's almost always better to take the negotiation out of the buying experience. The one exception might be the one or two ultra-large customers that are so big, they can dictate to you what their prices will be. But even in this case, it is possible and recommended to create a standard discount that could be used for any customer who objectively qualifies, even if only one customer could qualify.*

## Negotiated Pricing Must Be Eliminated

The win–lose mentality of the price negotiation tug-o-war is bad for both parties—the companies who enable it and the customers who get drawn into it. Unfortunately, once it's created, it's usually quite difficult to undo.

But make no mistake: for companies to maximize their ability to succeed, it must be undone, with very few exceptions (i.e., one-time customers, custom products, and/or completely custom projects).

Fortunately, it can be undone, and I will show you how. The first step is to start creating win–win relationships between the company and its customers. Instead of the negative aspects of the price negotiation tug-o-war, you will create an environment where you enable the principles of win–win customer relationships.

# The Seven Principles of Win–Win Customer Relationships

Long-term, win–win customer relationships are built on seven key principles or foundations:

1. Trust

2. Consistency

3. Value Sharing

4. Fairness

5. Easy and Frictionless Buying Experience

6. Listening

7. Living up to "The Promise"

Let's review these important principles one by one, so we can understand what they mean and why they are incompatible with both the pricing tug-o-war and negotiated pricing:

1. **Trust**: Trust develops when customers believe your business strategy is aligned with their interests, and it cannot be established in any other way. You demonstrate that your business strategy is aligned with your customers' interests by telling them what you seek to accomplish in your path to success, ensuring that those things are seen as obvious benefits to them as well. For example, long-term customer satisfaction, win–win partnerships, and giving customers more value for their money—these are all mutually beneficial. Communication is the first step. The second step of building trust is never deviating from your stated strategy. Always do what you say you're going to do.

2. **Consistency**: Consistency allows customers to have faith that their expectations will be met. Consistency is one of the most important elements of brand. Whatever you do consistently is what you will be known for, good or bad. But either way, consistency adds value to the customer relationship because it helps customers know what to expect. They can count on you because you treat them the same way all the time. Consistency means minimizing surprises, either good or bad.

3. **Value Sharing**: Value sharing means consistently giving your customers more value than the money they are paying you. It means they end up *much* better off from doing business with you, not just *slightly* better off. There always needs to be extra value for your customers to keep them coming back. If every transaction is priced at the very limits of their maximum willingness to pay, that means they are almost indifferent to doing the transaction—

1. they are equally well off whether they do business with you or not. From a relationship perspective, this is not a good place to be. Win–win is where both the company and the customer get value out of the transaction and have a reason to continue the relationship. Continuously raising prices up to a customer's maximum willingness to pay removes value from the customer relationship and greatly increases the risk of future churn.

2. **Fairness**: Fairness means you treat your customers fairly according to your own standard policies and procedures. It means you have mechanisms in place to ensure that some customers don't unfairly benefit at the expense of others. It means that similar customers pay the same prices. It means that discounts are based on objective criteria—not the random discretion of a salesperson or manager. It means you communicate your policies and prices to your customers in advance to give them a fair chance to make the best decisions for their own benefit. It means you never take advantage of customers. You never overcharge them. You never attempt to sneak a high price past them. Fairness means you look for both parties to benefit from the business relationship.

3. **Easy and Frictionless Buying Experience**: This means just what it says. It means you continually find ways to make it easier for customers to buy from you. It means you look for and remove unnecessary friction in the buying process. It means focusing on core buyer-experience questions: How can you make it easier for customers to find products? How can you make it easier for customers to learn what they need to know about your products? How can you make it easier for customers to find out how other customers feel about the products? Since price negotiation can add friction and defeat the objective of fairness, negotiable prices should be eliminated. On the other hand, price transparency removes friction and improves the overall buying experience.

4. **Listening**: Listening is about inviting comments and questions, showing empathy, and learning about the needs of your customers. It's also about understanding your company's performance in meeting customer needs. This means having open communication channels to listen and hear what your customers have to say. It means showing respect for your customers' voices. It means following up with empathy. But most of all, it means having a process for learning from your customers.

5. **Living up to "The Promise"**: "The Promise" is what your customers expect from you based on how you communicate with them. It goes beyond any explicit promise where you might actually use the word "promise." Living up to the promise means doing what you say you're going to do, for sure. But it means more than that. Living up to the promise means doing what a trusting customer would expect from a responsible business owner—adhering to

1. a standard of good business practices even if you never actually made an explicit promise to do so.

When companies adopt these principles of win–win customer relationships, it's easy to see why the pricing tug-o-war is pointless and counterproductive.

Human intuition tells you that stronger customer relationships lead to greater long-term profits—significantly more than can be attained with weak or adversarial relationships.

The misguided temptation to do things that remove value from customer relationships is nearsighted and generally practiced by people who don't have a long-term outlook. When you see these behaviors or attitudes occurring in your company, it should tell you something about the leaders who tolerate it. You may need to be the leader who changes it.

## Win–Win Customer Relationships and the Growth Mindset

If you find yourself in the midst of a win–lose customer relationship mentality or culture, you have one of two choices: You can try to change the culture and thinking, or you can decide to leave. You won't be doing yourself any favors by staying in a culture of win–lose.

If you choose to try to change the culture and thinking of your organization, CONGRATULATIONS! You can do it, and it will have a positive impact on both you and your company.

The win–lose mentality comes from the **scarcity mindset**. When you see symptoms of the win–lose mentality in your organization, it's very likely that you are facing a cultural problem much bigger than how your company relates with customers. The **scarcity mindset** often permeates across functions and even into personal lives. If this is the case in your company, you may have the opportunity to make a significant impact, not just in the business, but also in the individual lives of the people who work with you. (And as an aside, sometimes this can be more rewarding than any monetary gain.)

The most effective way to help your organization change from the **scarcity mindset** to the **growth mindset** is to begin with yourself and work outwards. You can accomplish this by first adopting the mentality that there are many paths to success. There are many ways to change a culture. We live in a world of infinite possibilities. It's always possible to find a better way.

If necessary, go back to Chapter 3 and review all the ways you can help people transition to the growth mindset. As you focus more on the growth mindset, you will begin to find yourself in the win–win playing space, where all the win–

lose elements seem unnatural and out of place. You will start to see that in order to *get* more value from your customers, you need to *give* them more value. That means giving them more for their money. More product. More service. More value. This needs to become a foundational principle of your company culture and a visible part of your company's strategy for your customers.

It can be done, and you can be the one to catalyze and accomplish it.

## Taking Price off the Table – A Necessary Foundation

There is only one way to change the mentality that allows price to be a variable of contention—take price off the table completely. Customers can never again believe that price can be negotiated with anybody—not the sales rep, not the sales VP, not the CFO, not the CEO, not the Chairman. Nobody. The number of people who have decision authority over price gets reduced to zero.

Zero? Yes. Zero.

That way, everyone gets the same message that prices are no longer negotiable under any circumstances, and you can communicate this new foundational policy to your customers in a way that focuses on the benefits the customer will enjoy from it. For example:

*I'm sorry, Mr. Customer, but our new lower price structure is standardized to ensure that nobody has to worry about paying a higher price than anyone else. This is good for everybody. Now all discounts are standardized based on objective criteria. Customers can get lower prices only if they meet the required volume thresholds for each discount level.*

If the customer asks who has the authority to give a lower price, the answer must be "nobody." If nobody has the authority to change the price, then it makes no sense to spend time worrying about it.

### A Benefit for All Customers vs. Any Single Customer

How do you take pricing off the table? You create a transparent and visible pricing structure, and you make it non-negotiable. You get pricing to the point that you honestly don't care if a customer leaves due to price.

Wait. What? Yes. From now on, if a customer leaves due to price, it's okay.

This may seem counterintuitive. But it's not. The whole purpose of taking price off the table is to improve customer relationships. When you let one customer walk away because they don't get to negotiate their own exception price, you are validating and protecting your relationship with all other customers. You are refusing to let unfairness creep in and injure your relationship with those customers. And any customer who walks away will know that if you are willing to lose a customer due to price, you are committed to your strategy of fairness more than you are committed to short-term revenues and profits. They will know they can trust you.

And because of this, many of those customers who leave will probably be back.

## Zero-Exception Pricing

It's called zero-exception pricing because if any one customer believes an exception is possible, and they don't receive an exception, they will be dissatisfied and believe they are not being treated fairly. This is why it's so important that nobody inside the company believes there can be any exception. If people in your company believe there might be an exception, they might inadvertently communicate this erroneous thought to the customer. The only way any customer can get a lower price is if every customer gets a lower price.

If there is a justifiable discount, it will be available to everyone who objectively qualifies, and it will not be hidden from anyone. It must be completely transparent and visible, so customers can see they are being treated fairly. No secret prices. No secret discounts.

Before you can convince your customers to believe it, you must first convince your company to believe it. This is extremely important. The change must be so permanent and powerful that nobody inside the company believes an exception can ever be possible.

The contention in pricing occurs because customers are allowed to believe they can get lower prices if they work hard enough at it. This belief must change. But it won't go away easily. Customers who have a history of getting their way due to bad behavior will likely have the opinion that if they're not getting what they want, they just need to apply more bad behavior. They might not initially believe you when you tell them they aren't going to get what they want. And that's ok. But you can never cave in—even if it means potentially losing some customers. Without zero-exception pricing, it won't be possible to create the win–win customer relationships that will power your company to a higher valuation.

Zero-exception pricing. That's how you take pricing off the table.

The reward? Better customer relationships, more customer trust due to pricing integrity, and increasing good will from customers based on fair and transparent pricing practices. And ultimately (and somewhat ironically) higher margins.

### Price Integrity: The Path to Transparent, Fair, and Rational Pricing

When you remove the pricing tug-o-war mentality, negotiated pricing, and exception prices, what you should be left with is **price integrity**, which will ultimately enable and ensure transparent, fair, and rational prices—the subject of the next chapter. Price integrity, rationality, fairness, and transparency together provide significant value to your customers. It's been demonstrated across numerous studies that customers will pay more when they can trust the integrity of your prices and when they are relieved from the burden of having to negotiate.

## Chapter Summary

In this chapter, we've covered some important points that are critical and foundational to any good pricing strategy. Although some of these points may be difficult to mentally process if they run counter to years of deep-seated beliefs and habits, the rationale is too compelling to ignore. I ask you to keep an open mind and continue on the journey in this book. Let the growth mindset lead you to new ideas and possibilities. Take what I've shared and add your own ideas to conceptualize an innovative solution that will work for your business.

Let's review what we've covered in this chapter:

- Customer relationships are more valuable to companies over the long run when they are built on win–win principles, not win–lose and, for sure, not lose–lose. In order to achieve company growth goals, it's important to find ways to add value to customer relationships.

- Unfortunately, some pricing-related strategy decisions can create a domino-effect of negative experiences for the customer if you don't specifically plan to prevent them.

- Price negotiations and the tug-o-war mentality inevitably lead to adversarial positioning, unnecessary friction, negative feelings, and loss of trust in the overall customer relationship. For this reason, price negotiations should be eliminated from repeat-purchase businesses.

- Win–win customer relationships are built on the principles of trust, consistency, value sharing, fairness, easy and frictionless buying, listening, and living up to "the promise"—**The Seven Principles of Win-Win Customer Relationships.**

- Win–win relationships are powered by the **growth mindset** because it leads to the discovery of unlimited possibilities for increasing value to customers in affordable and creative ways.

- Win–win relationships require taking price off the table by making prices non-negotiable and by using zero-exception prices that are fair, transparent, and rational.

- Discounts can be possible, but only when they are based on simple and objective criteria with a "fair" and "reasonable" rationale.

So, in one chapter, we've established some important principles of successful pricing and win–win customer relationships. We've destroyed the notion that negotiable pricing creates a positive customer buying experience. And we've established the necessity of having highly visible, transparent, and fair pricing, along with clear, simple, and reasonable discount structures, which must be based on objective and fair criteria.

*We've covered a lot of ground here, but it's foundational for navigating some of the more complex parts of the journey we will cover in the rest of the book.*

---

***Next chapter preview:*** *Price integrity has clear value for customers, especially when combined with price transparency, fairness, and rationality. In the next chapter we'll talk about what all this means and how it translates to pricing strategies.*

## CHAPTER 7

# The Importance of Trustworthy Prices

*Integrity: The choice between what's convenient and what's right.*

— Tony Dungy

Companies like Apple, Tesla, and even CarMax have proven that customers are willing to pay more for products that have price integrity—stable, rational, and non-negotiable prices, which are determined by a disciplined methodology. When customers can trust the price, a burden is removed—a burden of extra work to research, negotiate, or opportunistically time their purchases to ensure they don't overpay for the products or services in question. There is real value in not having to worry about price, and customers are willing to pay more for products that have trustworthy prices. How much more? Research has shown that customers are willing to pay up to 5% more for an instantaneous and efficient buying experience. This is exactly what transparent and trustworthy prices enable.

In this chapter we will cover four interrelated pricing principles that produce trustworthy prices that customers can rely on: **Price Integrity, Price Rationality, Price Fairness,** and **Price Transparency**. When these principles are combined and leveraged in your pricing process, your customers will, over time, begin to trust that your pricing is well thought out and indicative of fair, market-centric pricing. This will shorten their purchase decision process and improve their overall buying experience. This can be an important part of the buyer inertia that keeps them coming back to you over and over again. As they become more entrenched in an improved buying experience, the thought of switching to another vendor will become more distasteful. You will have established, therefore, more customer loyalty.

I will cover each of these principles one by one, but it's important to keep in mind that they should collectively work together to form a better buying experience and improve customer loyalty. As more customers move to digital channels, customer buying experience will likely become a key value differentiator vs. your competitors, making these principles more important than ever.

## Price Integrity

**Price integrity** means your prices are trustworthy, incorruptible, and adherent to a stated strategy or policy determined by a repeatable process that generates consistent and defensible price outputs. It means prices are stable, justifiable, and can be trusted by customers.

Price integrity is more about the process than the actual price; it is a process that ensures prices are trustworthy. It means prices are not "up for discussion" with customers, agents or employees, once they are set. Price integrity is the protection against discretionary pricing decisions by anyone.

Price integrity is what enables price rationality, price fairness, and ultimately price transparency. Because price integrity implies there is a purposeful rationale behind each price, it then indirectly implies that pricing is also "fair" because it would be senseless to have a pricing rationale that is purposefully "unfair." Without price integrity, price outputs are not repeatable, pricing is not defensible, and it's difficult for prices to be stable. Without price integrity, it's difficult to ensure that prices are rational or fair. And if prices are not rational or fair, there is not much benefit to making them transparent.

Customers value prices they can trust, and price integrity is what ensures your prices can be trusted.

## Price Rationality

Price rationality means that prices are intentionally and logically positioned relative to each other in a way that makes sense, according to implied value or customer expectations of value, such as the following examples:

- Products of higher perceived quality are priced higher than products of lower perceived quality.

- Products that are otherwise identical (similar quality and value), except for the color, are all given the same price.
- Larger versions of the same product are priced higher than smaller versions (perhaps because they are more expensive to produce).

When prices violate a customer's perceived sense of relative value, it can cause them to question the trustworthiness of your prices in general, which can then cause a devaluation of the entire customer-vendor relationship. Customers want to believe that prices make sense because, if they don't, then the customer has to do more work to ensure they are not at risk of overpaying for products they buy from that vendor. Furthermore, when they do find a price that's too high (after their extra research efforts), then they have to do even more work to either negotiate the price down or find another vendor.

Price rationality adds value by making prices trustworthy, thereby improving the customer buying experience.

## Price Fairness

Regardless of pricing strategies or practices, almost all customers innately expect prices to be "fair." If prices are not "fair," customers don't have to buy, and as a result, they typically expect that vendors will try to keep prices "fair." Research indicates that approximately 80% of customers will be agreeable to paying a "fair" price, as long as they *believe* it is a "fair" price. (The other 20% are likely to challenge your prices, no matter what, and we'll talk about them later.) And so, this brings us to the core question: What is a "fair" price?

The Oxford Dictionary defines "**fairness**" as follows:

**fairness** (noun): impartial and just treatment or behavior without favoritism or discrimination.

Even though "fairness" seems to have a definable meaning in a general context, when it comes to pricing, "fairness" goes a little deeper than just a lack of "favoritism or discrimination." **Price fairness** implies a little more. From my experience over the last twenty years, it seems that most people expect a "fair" price to exhibit the following properties:

- It is consistent with the value being delivered.
- It is no better or worse than the price everyone else pays.
- It is based on "reasonable" profit margins, and definitely NOT unreasonably high profit margins.

- It is stable and doesn't change very often or by very much when it does change (in the case of market commodities the fair price is defined by a "fair margin" or a "fair premium" on top of a market cost that may fluctuate frequently.)
- It is consistent with advertised prices.
- It is not significantly out of line with other competitive market prices or reasonable expectations of price.

Based on the above criteria, I might define a fair price as follows:

**Fair price**: the highest price a company can charge, which is generally in line with the value delivered to the customer, generally in line with competitive market prices and prices paid by other customers, does not result in unreasonably high profit margins, and is consistent with what the company has previously advertised.

Sometimes fairness has nothing to do with willingness to pay. I may be dying of thirst in the desert, willing to pay tens of thousands of dollars, if necessary, for a drink of water. But I may still think it is unfair to charge $50 for a bottle of water because that would seem to be an unreasonably high profit margin.

Customers value "fair" prices because it leads them to believe they are being treated fairly in other aspects of the business relationship.

## Price Transparency

Price transparency means your prices are visible so all customers can see them. When companies make prices visible and transparent, they are conveying to the world that there are no secrets, and that they plan to honor the same prices for all customers. The easiest way to make prices transparent is to display prices on your website.

Price transparency is a public confession of price integrity, price rationality, and price fairness. It gives customers reassurance that they don't have to worry about price.

### Is Price Transparency a Competitive Disadvantage?

Companies sometimes worry that transparent posting of their prices will put them at a competitive disadvantage because it will make it easier for competitors to undercut their prices. While there is some merit to this concern, its significance is largely overstated. Here are some counterthoughts:

1. It is a fallacy to believe that price transparency is what drives competition to undercut a company's prices. Most of the time, if a competitor is going to try to undercut your prices, they will attempt to do it whether you transparently post your prices or not. While it is true that price transparency may aid in a competitor's precision in their attempts to undercut your prices, that is not necessarily a bad thing. Would you rather have a competitor price 1% below your price or 20% below your price because they don't know where your prices are?

2. For repeat-purchase businesses, most purchases are at the "relationship level" where the price of any individual product doesn't really have that much of an impact on the customer's decision to buy from you. In other words, you don't have to necessarily have the lowest prices to earn your customers' business. You just need to have the best overall value proposition, which should go far beyond the price of an individual product or two.

3. Your customers will appreciate your willingness to post your prices transparently because it makes their buying experiences easier and more efficient. The benefits of instantaneous price transparency often outweigh a 1%–2% price difference. And numerous studies suggest that customers are willing to pay up to 5% more for instantaneous pricing.

Most of the time, when companies are worried about posting their prices online, it's because they have no price integrity, and they're worried about how their existing customers will react to prices that other customers might be receiving. If this describes your company, you may be right, but all the more reason to fix the situation. Eventually customers will require price transparency, so there's no time like the present to start fixing the issues preventing you from going to transparent pricing.

## Price Integrity, Rationality, and Fairness Should Precede Transparency

Price transparency is a great way to show the world that you have prices that are well thought out and that make sense. Unfortunately, if your prices are not well thought out, if they're not rational, if they're not in line with the market, or if they don't make sense, premature price transparency will make sure the world is shown this as well. For this reason, it is important to make sure you first implement price integrity, rationality, and fairness.

Don't wait too long, but take the time you need to get your pricing process where it needs to be first. Define the "fair" prices you will charge your regular customers. Define your focused pricing strategies (which we will cover in depth in chapters 15 through 19). Then you will be ready for pricing transparency.

But remember, transparency is what makes all your good pricing practices visible to your customers, and your customers will get the most value in their relationships with you once your fair and rational prices are easy for them to find on your website. Keep in mind, also, that posting prices online can be a good catalyst for executing a new pricing strategy based on sound pricing principles.

## What about Markdowns?

Many companies have a practice of marking down the prices of products, temporarily, for the purpose of moving excess inventory or trying to stimulate demand for slow-moving products. While the topic of markdown strategy is beyond the scope of this book, I will touch on it briefly to help you ensure you don't jeopardize the benefits of price integrity.

How do markdowns affect price integrity, rationality, fairness, or transparency? Is it possible that, from a customer perspective, markdowns can nullify the positive effects of otherwise stable and trustworthy pricing? In short, as long as a few key criteria are met, it is possible to offer markdowns to customers in a way that improves customer trust and good will and also preserves price integrity:

1. Customers should generally understand that prices of some products will be marked down from time to time for the purpose of achieving a win–win solution to excess or slow-moving inventory by offering short-term discounts to all customers. This should not be a surprise to customers. It's important that customers know how markdowns are designed to benefit them.

2. Customers should receive advance notice that markdowns are coming on a certain date. Advance notice will help prevent a situation where a customer pays full price for a product, and then finds out two days later that they could have saved 30%. Another way to address this problem is a time-based price guarantee, which is the next topic.

3. Offering customers a time-based price guarantee can help give customers the assurance that they won't miss an opportunity to save money. For example, you may have a policy that states, *"We offer a 30-day price guarantee. If we ever offer a lower price for the products you've purchased within 30 days of your purchase, we will automatically send you a refund for the difference."* This will help customers avoid the worry of trying to optimize the timing of their purchases to capture a sale price that may come in the future. And the benefits in customer good will often exceed the cost of the policy. Sometimes, time-based price guarantees also work in retrospect as well, where companies will offer to honor any discounted price for a specific number of days past the end of the promotion, for example: *"We will also*

1. *allow existing customers to get credit for a promotional markdown up to 30 days after the end of the promotion.*" While a time-based price guarantee is not required, it is a great way to keep good will with your customers so that price isn't something they have to worry about. It is the ultimate anti-price-discrimination equalizer, and it's highly recommended as an effective way to protect your loyal customers from missing out on markdown discounts.

In summary, it is possible to maintain price integrity and occasionally offer promotional markdowns, as long as the above considerations are put in place to mitigate potential dissatisfaction from markdown-based price discrimination.

## Standardized Discounts Based on Objective Criteria

Now that we've established the value of making prices fair for everyone in order to build trust and good will with your customers and make their buying experiences more positive, we need to talk about standardized discount structures. It is possible to offer different prices for different types of customers without upsetting the trust and good will built by making prices non-negotiable, fair, and transparent. The key is to make discounts based on standardized and objective eligibility criteria.

Sometimes you have to have the ability to charge different prices for different customers. Some customers expect and deserve discounts based on the volume or type of business they do with your company. Sometimes you need to charge different prices for different customers just to be competitive. This is all fair and reasonable.

Don't worry. You can handle this need for differentiated prices and still maintain price integrity and fair, transparent pricing in a non-negotiable way. By structuring discounts as **standardized programs** with **objective criteria** for eligibility, you will be able to still engender trust and good will with your customers.

This will allow you to handle situations where you need a discount structure to keep your prices in a specific competitive ballpark, perhaps when you have competitors who are liberal with their discretionary discounting. These types of discount structures can also help if you are making the initial transition from an environment of negotiated pricing to an environment of standardized pricing, and you need to maintain some level of price continuity. It is perfectly okay to create standardized discount structures as long as you keep to the following guidelines:

1. **Discounts must be simple and understandable.**

2. **Discounts must be based on objective criteria.**

3. **Discounts must be based on a "fair" and "reasonable" rationale.**

Discount structures can be in the form of on-invoice discounts or post-purchase rebates. I'll explain why later on, but sometimes the post-purchase rebates have more advantages than on-invoice discounts.

For now, let's walk through each guideline individually.

## 1. Discounts Must Be Simple and Understandable

In order to avoid friction in the buying process, it's important to ensure that your discount structures are simple and understandable to your customers. Complex schemas can be confusing and frustrating, making the purchase process more cumbersome. You definitely don't want to add more friction to the buying process. Simple means both simple eligibility criteria and simple incentives. For example, the volume discount structure in the table below has only three levels. The incentives are a simple percent-off list price, and each level's eligibility criteria is easy to understand and calculate.

| If your annualized spend (based on last three months of purchases) is ... | ... you get ... |
|---|---|
| More than $10,000 | 5% off list price |
| More than $25,000 | 7% off list price |
| More than $50,000 | 8% off list price |

Keep in mind that it's not atypical for companies to have multiple standard discount programs that could overlap in eligibility or time. It's important to keep these sorted out to avoid the complexity of compounded discounts. For example, you may have some customers who receive a volume discount, and you may want to offer another discount incentive for customers to try specific new products. Now you have to define how the discounts work together. Does the customer receive both discounts? If so, are the discounts additive or compounding? It's important to be clear and to keep multiple discounts understandable and easy to manage. Simpler is usually better. That means fewer overlapping incentives are preferred, all else equal. Whatever you end up offering, it's important that your customers understand clearly how multiple discount programs will work together. Otherwise, you may be teeing up many unnecessary dissatisfaction triggers.

## 2. Discounts Must Be Based on Objective Criteria

It's critical that your discount structures be based on objective criteria because you don't want any situation where the customer feels they need to argue about eligibility for the discount. For example, if your discounts are based on last year's purchase dollars, that would be considered "objective criteria," and there should be no gray area or confusion—although it's important to be very specific regarding how the eligibility will be calculated or determined. For example, does "last year's purchases" mean purchases over the last 365 days? Or does it mean purchases between January 1 of the previous year and January 1 of the current year? Or is there some other calculation that will be used to determine eligibility. It's not just important to be clear and specific, it's critical. There should be no room for misunderstanding or argument. Without objective clarity, some people might feel obligated to argue over whether or not they qualify for the discount. This is the very thing you are trying to prevent. Pricing cannot be up for discussion. You want no discussion or point of contention because it damages the buying experience and the overall customer relationship. You must take any subjective human decisions out of the process. Otherwise, you risk losing the customer good will you are trying to build.

## 3. Discounts Must Be Based on "Fair" and "Reasonable" Rationale

This is a broad criterion, which could be open to many definitions, so let me explain it. You never want customers to feel like they are being treated unfairly by a discount policy. And you never want to incentivize your customers to behave irrationally in order to become "eligible" for a discount. Discounts will seem fair when customers feel like they have the same opportunity as others if they meet the objective criteria.

However, if the criteria seem random or unjustified, customers will often react negatively. For example, if I created a discount policy that gave anyone with the last name "Smith" 20% off, customers would likely see that as an unfair discount—because there is no clear connection between the criterion and actually deserving the discount. If instead, I create a discount specifying that anyone who's been a customer for more than a year gets an extra 5% off, it would likely be more accepted by customers because it seems like a reward for loyalty, and it's clear that customers who don't meet the criteria could eventually meet it by just being a customer for a little longer.

It's also important to ensure that discount structures don't incentivize customers to behave irrationally. Here's a personal example that violated this principle:

*At one time in my life, I was paying $200 per month for satellite TV service, when I saw a TV commercial where my satellite company was offering that same service to new customers for $99 per month. When I called the satellite company, they told me I was not eligible because I was not a "new customer." Of course, I became angry because I felt, as a loyal customer, I was more deserving than a new customer. And yet, I was being discriminated against because of my loyalty.*

*But that's not where it ended. I then asked the satellite company to tell me their definition of a "new customer" for the purpose of determining eligibility for the promotion, and they told me it was anyone who had not used their service for the past six months. So, guess what I did. I terminated my service and went with a small cable provider for six months, just so I could become eligible for the $99 per month offer. I'm sure this is not what the satellite company wanted. But this is a perfect example of a discount program that did not seem fair to me, the customer, AND it incentivized me, the customer, to act irrationally. I'll just leave it at that.*

It's difficult to specify an exhaustive set of guidelines for making sure offers seem fair to customers, but it is definitely an important consideration to check off before releasing a new incentive program. As a general rule, ask yourself: Would a reasonable third-party individual see a reasonable and rational connection between the discount and the eligibility criteria? Is the new discount fair to existing customers? If you can answer yes to both questions, you're probably okay. If not, you may want to go back to the drawing board.

## Chapter Summary

In this chapter, we've covered the importance of price integrity, price rationality, price fairness, and price transparency in order to create good will with your customers and improve their buying experience. We also talked about temporary markdowns to move excess or slow-moving inventory and what guidelines should be followed to avoid the destruction of good will we built through fair and transparent pricing. And finally, we talked about standardized discount structures that allow for designed price differentiation based on objective eligibility criteria, along with the key guidelines for making them effective.

Key takeaways from this chapter include the following:

- **Customers value price integrity and transparency** because it removes a burden and makes their buying experience more pleasant and efficient, and as a result they are willing to pay more for the same products—on average, as much as 5% more. This alone can be a differentiator that makes customers want to buy from you vs. a competitor.

- **Price integrity** means there is a rationale or reason behind your prices, and you have a repeatable process for determining prices and achieving consistent outputs. Price integrity means your prices are incorruptible, and they can be trusted.

- **Price rationality** means your prices make sense in terms of their relative position to the prices of other related products and services.

- **Price fairness** means the price is generally in line with the value delivered to the customer, is no more or less than what other customers pay, is generally in line with competitive market prices, does not result in unreasonably high profit margins, and is consistent with what the company has previously advertised.

- **Price transparency** means prices are freely visible for all to see, as a demonstration that there are no hidden or secret prices, as everything is out in the open.

- **Markdowns** can be possible without undermining consistent, rational, fair, and transparent prices if they are communicated ahead of time to give customers the chance to alter their purchases to take advantage. But the best way to keep customers from having to worry about price is through a generous time-based price guarantee policy.

- **Standardized discount programs** can coexist without undermining transparent price integrity as long as they are: based on objective eligibility criteria, simple to understand, and based on fair and reasonable rationales that don't incentivize irrational customer behavior that can degrade the customer relationship.

The last two chapters have shown problems that can be created in customer relationships when companies allow the pricing tug-o-war mentality, the practice of price negotiations, and the lack of fair and trustworthy pricing to create unnecessary burdens for customers.

The solution to these problems is to move to standardized, zero-exception pricing that is rational, fair, and transparent along with standardized discount programs based on objective eligibility criteria. Doing this will allow you to "take price off the table," resulting in better customer buying experiences, improved customer relationships, and higher overall margins. This will translate to lower churn and greater predictability of growth and retention rates, some of the most important and sacred pricing metrics leading to increased company value.

*Next chapter preview: A case parable of a new, first-time CEO who joins a company to try to turn around sluggish profit performance, only to find that the whole pricing structure needs a major overhaul.*

## CHAPTER 8

# The Chronicles of Sara's Pricing Overhaul

**Case Parable 3: FriendlyCo and New CEO, Sara Thompson**

*This is the story of FriendlyCo, a $500 million provider of chemicals and plastics for injection-mold manufacturing. After four years of below-average margins and struggling profitability, the board of directors fired the old CEO and brought in an up-and-coming industry leader, Sara Thompson, from one of the company's stronger competitors. Her primary mission as the new CEO was to increase profitability and help the company get back on a growth trajectory.*

## Sara's First Day

Sara had never been a CEO before. As she walked into the conference room for her first executive staff meeting, she was mildly surprised to see all 11 of her top executives already seated and ready to get to work. She briefly paused, took a deep breath, and then took her seat at the head of the table.

As she looked around the room, she realized she hadn't even met half of her new direct reports, who were now all staring at her intently. She had intended to meet with each person one-on-one before the meeting, but schedules had not allowed it, and now it was a moot point. Sara was their new CEO, and she needed to establish her ability to lead.

She cleared her throat, looked again around the table, and then broke the silence: "FriendlyCo is a great company with great people. But our investors aren't happy. They're measuring us by how our key financial metrics compare to our competition. And for a few years, those metrics haven't looked good. I believe we can do better, but today's my first day, and I don't have all the answers yet. Over the next few days, I'd like to spend time getting to know each of you and hearing your thoughts on where we should focus first on our improvement mission. Until then, our time is probably better spent on that, rather than in staff meetings. I look forward to getting to know each of you better over the next few days."

Almost as if it were planned, she immediately stood up, smiled and nodded at the people around the table; then, after a brief pause, she walked out of the room.

## Getting to Know the Company

Sara spent most of her first week on the job in meetings with the sales and pricing teams to try to understand their common practices and policies to determine how pricing decisions were made. Not surprisingly, what she found was somewhat alarming:

- The company had 150 salespeople who all had pricing authority, and whose commissions were calculated based on gross sales revenue.

- Across product lines, Sara found wide price variations—up to 50% or more on most products. This meant that one customer might be paying $600 per unit, while another customer might be paying over $900 for exactly the same product.

- Approximately 20% of the Sales-negotiated transactions were below costs. And at least 70% of prices were below the standard industry average margin of 15%.

- Sara found no correlation between pricing and any of the common criteria she would expect would qualify a customer for a better price, such as volume, loyalty, consistency, or cost to serve. Instead, it seemed like the only determinant of pricing was the customer's willingness or unwillingness to pay higher prices, or worse, the sales rep's willingness to give discounts.

When she asked her Pricing and Sales leaders to explain the company's pricing strategy, the replies were fairly consistent: They wanted to capture as high a price as the customer was willing to pay, and that's why they allowed sales reps the autonomy to set prices. They asked their sales reps to start out quoting "list prices," which were typically based on a 50% gross margin, and then if customers objected to the prices, they would ask the customers what they thought was a fair price, and then they would try to negotiate by splitting the difference until they arrived at a mutually agreed upon price. Sales reps were told not to go below break-even, unless they felt they were at risk of losing the customer, in which case they would consult a manager for special approval.

In one example, a rep quoted a customer a list price of $100. The customer responded that price was ridiculous because most other vendors were selling a similar product at half that price. The sales rep then asked the customer to suggest a fair price. Knowing they were starting a negotiation, the customer offered a low-ball, unrealistic price of $40. The sales rep then counteroffered a price of $70, halfway between $40 and $100, and they went back and forth until they settled on a price of $58.

## How Pricing Practices Affected Attitudes

When Sara asked how their customers felt about their final negotiated prices, her leaders said they thought the customers "should feel fantastic because they were getting 40%–50% off the list price." But upon further reflection, they admitted that their customers never really seemed happy with the prices they had negotiated. "They usually act like they are somehow doing us a favor to agree to prices above what they thought was fair," said one of the sales managers. Somehow the customers seemed to feel adversarial about the whole process, and they seemed more defensive in each subsequent pricing discussion.

When Sara asked how the customers felt about the quality of the products and services, she learned that the customers were reluctant to say anything positive about them, almost like they wanted the right to complain in future price negotiations to get a better price. In fact, most of the customers who had negotiated lower prices seemed grumpy in their interactions with everyone in the company, and they never missed an opportunity to comment on something negative.

Sara then asked how the salespeople felt about the customers. Her leaders confessed that the salespeople generally had a bad attitude about the customers. With respect to the customers who used hard-ball negotiation tactics, the salespeople generally felt a tinge of bitterness. They felt like pawns in a negotiation they had no power to change. In fairness, lower prices meant lower commissions, so besides the stressful work of going back and forth on price, they ended up with lower prices and lower commissions.

On the other hand, the salespeople generally didn't think too highly of the customers who paid full list prices either because they were paying prices that were 25%–30% above market. They believed that if the customers ever found out how much they were paying over regular market prices, they would probably get angry and terminate their relationships with the company.

After these discussions, Sara had heard all she needed to know. FriendlyCo had a massive pricing problem which was causing adversarial and risky relationships with their customers. It was like a ticking time bomb that could go off at any time. Furthermore, it seemed that the negative attitudes were leading to negative interactions that were spiraling downward much too fast for a company that was already suffering from low margins. The company's growth had been stagnant for the last four years, and if Sara didn't make some significant changes, things would only get worse. The situation had to be stopped. So, Sara took a page from her previous company's book, and determined she had to change the pricing strategy.

## The New Pricing Strategy

Sara realized that even though the existing pricing practices were not good for either customers or employees, she would likely receive lots of pushback from both groups if she attempted to make significant changes. In fact, it was very likely that she would lose a few customers in the process, maybe even some of the most important and strategic customers of the previous few years. But she knew that if she could get the company to use a new and better pricing strategy, both the company and its customers would be better off in the long run. And they would be able to replace any customers they lost in the process.

The new pricing strategy would have the following pillars:

- **No More Sales-Negotiated Prices**: All prices would be determined by the Pricing team. Customers would no longer be able to negotiate prices. They would be given take-it-or-leave-it prices, and then they would have to make the decision to buy or not.

- **Price Transparency**: All prices would be posted on the company's website, along with a notice that the company was moving to an everyday-low-price strategy, and the new low prices would be fair for everyone.

- **"Fair Pricing" Commitment**: On the website, and on all quotes, the company would publish their commitment to "fair pricing," which included the following bullet points:

  1. Every customer would pay a fair price, no better or worse than what all other customers were paying.

  2. All prices would be posted on the website, so all customers would have full knowledge of all prices for all products.

  3. Any discount incentives would be based on objective criteria and open to all customers who qualified.

  4. Price changes would happen no more frequently than once every 90 days.

1. The company would seek to keep prices competitive with similar quality products and services in the market.

- **Zero Exceptions**: All pricing changes would go through approval by a pricing committee every 90 days, along with any proposed discount incentives. Beyond that, nobody in the company would have authority to change prices, not even Sara.

- **Market-Relevant Prices**: Since typical margin targets in the industry were 15%, Sara decided the default pricing strategy would be to set list prices to achieve a 20% margin and give them room for standard discounts. So, the starting list price for each product would be cost divided by 80%. If the cost was $60, the list price would be $75. After that, the Pricing team would evaluate any exceptions where the target margin strategy was not in line with market prices and make a recommendation they believed would be fair to most customers.

## A Daunting Transformation Ahead

While many of FriendlyCo's employees were able to see the merit in the newly articulated pricing strategy, most people felt like the change was so drastic it would not be realistically achievable after so many years of ingrained habits and expectations set with customers. Were it not for the fact that Sara had seen a similar strategy work at her previous company, she might have had difficulty believing it was possible herself. She knew she needed a simple and credible transition plan to make the changes without losing too many customers. This transition plan would be built on the following five principles:

1. **Focus on customer experience/no service failures**: For the next 90–180 days, the company would spend extra time with customers to try to deliver a much better customer experience. The intent would be to ensure that customers did not experience any other negatives during the period of price transition, especially unmitigated service failures. Studies showed that most customer defections in the industry were due to service failures, not pricing.

2. **A highly visible and publicized change in pricing strategy**: The new pricing strategy would be highly publicized along with the major benefits to the customers, including: fairness, transparency, stability, etc. This was important because proactivity would allow the company to control the message to make sure it was focused on how the customers would benefit.

3. **Customers would not be made worse off in the short term**: Customers would receive temporary discounts to make sure that the new pricing strategy would not result in significantly higher prices for at least the next 90

1. days. This was important to ensure that customers wouldn't feel the pricing change in their pocketbooks right away. The plan would be to hold prices for 90 days, and then slowly allow prices to inch up where necessary, but in an environment of more stability and buyer inertia.

2. **New prices highly visible**: New pricing would be highly visible to customers on all sales quotes and invoices for the next 180 days, and all major communications would include a link to the public price lists on the website. This would allow customers to see the difference between the prices and discounts they were getting before and the prices they would be paying under the new pricing strategy. Most importantly, this would show that the company was serious about making prices transparent for all customers.

3. **No negotiations, no exceptions**: This was the most critical principle of all. If the company were to make any exception or allow the customer to get the impression that prices were negotiable, it would ruin the entire strategy of "taking price off the table." It was critical that people both inside and outside the company believed that pricing was not up for discussion.

With these five principles, Sara believed the needed transition had a good chance to be successful.

## Preparing for the Transition

To prepare for the transition, the Pricing team first focused on creating a price list based on their future-state strategy. They created "market-relevant" list prices according to the new strategy.

Because previously negotiated discounts were generally based on annual spend, the pricing team created a simple volume-based discount model which offered three tiers of discount, as follows:

| Annualized Spend (based on last three months of purchases) | Discount off List Price |
|---|---|
| $20,000–$50,000/year | 5% off |
| $50,000–$150,000/year | 7.5% off |
| Greater than $150,000/year | 10% off |

These discount tiers were chosen because they overlapped nicely with existing customer prices, leaving very few exceptions.

By comparing the new pricing with existing customer pricing, they found customers generally fell into one of three groups:

**Group 1 (Benefiters):** New prices generally better than previous prices. No problems foreseen.

**Group 2 (Same Ballpark):** New prices were roughly the same as the old prices with some higher and some lower, but generally all within 5% difference between new and old prices.

**Group 3 (Negative Impact):** New prices were generally worse than the existing negotiated prices, but the magnitude was generally 10% or lower, meaning a 10% additional discount would make them better off.

Sara was most concerned about Group 3 because they stood to lose the most, and she considered making the "transitional loyalty discount" available only to those select customers. But after further consideration, she realized that offering it to everyone would help reinforce the idea that nobody would receive preferential treatment, so that's what she decided to do. Furthermore, the simple inconvenience of changing the pricing structures and the actual prices customers would now have to pay was going to be interpreted as at least a slight negative, even if the new prices ended up more favorable to them. So, this incentive would help ease the pain a bit.

## Additional Transitional Loyalty Discount

Sara and her Pricing team were mostly confident that if they could get the customers accustomed to paying the prices in the new price structure for a whole year, the customers would likely form enough habitual buying inertia that they would continue buying the following year. The key was to get them to transition to buying at the new prices.

The team feared that if they offered discounts to offset the difference between the new prices and the old prices, customers would not believe they were really buying at the new prices. Somehow, the team needed to come up with an incentive to make up the difference in the first year, an incentive sufficiently disconnected from the new prices so that customers believed they were paying the new prices.

And so, what FriendlyCo decided to do was to offer a **Transitional Loyalty Rebate Credit** for five quarters, starting with 10% the first quarter, and decreasing the rebate by 2% each quarter. Here's how it would work: At the end of the first quarter, all customers who purchased more than 90% of their average quarterly volume under the new price structure would receive a credit equal to 10% of that quarter's spending. The next quarter, the rebate credit would be 8%. And the next quarter it would be 6%. Then 4%. Then 2%. Customers would receive five quarters of rebates, and all they had to do was exceed 90% of their average quarterly purchase dollar volume. As long as they were spending close to the same each quarter, they would be given the rebate.

Because the rebate credit was a single lump sum at the end of the quarter, it was sufficiently disconnected from the actual product prices that it would allow the customers to get accustomed to the new structure. It was big enough that customers would take it seriously. It was structured so that it would die down over time, as customers became more entrenched in their purchase habits under the new pricing schema. While it did add a little bit of unwanted complexity, it gave sales reps the opportunity to explain that the rebate was being offered in exchange for the inconvenience of transitioning to a new pricing policy.

## The Rollout

It took Sara and her team 90 days to complete the preparations to make the pricing change, including the posting of all the new information on the website. During these 90 days, each sales rep met with their customers to explain the change that was coming. As expected, even though most customers stood to benefit, at least in the short term, there was a lot of complaining, and several customers threatened to leave if they experienced a material price increase. Some customers even cancelled existing orders before the new prices were rolled out. Sara and her leaders made sure to give sales reps the support they needed. For large-volume customers who were disgruntled with the change, Sara offered to meet one-on-one with them to explain the rationale and why the new way would be better for them in the long run.

Finally, the day came, and the new prices and policies went into effect. Everyone was in suspense wondering what would happen. But to their surprise, orders continued to flow in at about the same rate as before. And this repeated day after day throughout the rest of the quarter.

At the end of the first quarter, they compared total sales with the previous quarter's sales. To everyone's delight, sales were up 12% after near zero growth for the previous 16 quarters. Even more surprising, profit margins were up 8%. That's right—800 basis points of incremental margins. Of course, there was a new rebate liability that needed to be factored in. But even that wasn't enough to offset the margin increases.

In the first quarter after the transition, 72% of the customers were eligible for the rebate because they had purchased a greater dollar volume than the previous quarter. That meant roughly a 7.2% hit to margins after the fact. But with the 8% increase in margins before that hit, they still ended up with a 0.8%

profit margin increase over prior quarters, and they accomplished this with 12% quarter-over-quarter sales growth.

Unfortunately, FriendlyCo seemed to have lost 5% of their customers in the first quarter of transition. Although this was anticipated, it was a result nobody wanted to see.

However, they actually ended up gaining business from new customers, and this gain more than offset the losses. It seemed that, previously, several customers had been turned off by the company's overly high published list prices, which were approximately 30%–35% above market prices. Once the new list prices dropped to realistic levels in line with the market, several new customers started buying, and a new source of sales growth was unlocked without any additional sales effort.

The next four quarters were equally impressive in both sales growth and profit margins. The results are shown in the table below:

| Quarter | Sales Growth QoQ | Incremental GM% Growth | Cumulative GM% Growth | Rebate Credit Offset | Net Profit % Growth |
|---------|---------|---------|---------|---------|---------|
| Qtr #1 | +12.0% | +8.0% | +8.0% | -7.2% | +0.8% |
| Qtr #2 | +2.0% | +1.6% | +9.6% | -5.1% | +4.5% |
| Qtr #3 | +3.5% | +1.3% | +10.9% | -3.7% | +7.2% |
| Qtr #4 | +2.3% | +1.2% | +12.1% | -2.2% | +9.9% |
| Qtr #5 | +3.4% | +0.9% | +13.0% | -1.1% | +11.9% |
| Total | +23.2% | +13.0% | +13.0% | - | +13.0% |

Over the entire five-month transition, FriendlyCo grew sales by 23.2% (18.5% annualized growth rate) and grew margins by 13 percentage points, which was a 191% increase over the 6.8% margins the company had been getting when Sara first arrived.

## The Long-Term Results

Over the next couple of years, FriendlyCo maintained 18% annual sales growth rates and held margin percentage steady at approximately 19%. The valuation of the company went through the roof. The stock price increased by 450%.

The **five sacred metrics of pricing success** show how much the theoretical valuation of the company improved from the day Sara arrived ($T_0$) to the completion of the pricing transition, which lasted five quarters (T+5 qtrs).

The data is shown in the table below:

### FriendlyCo Pricing Metric Performance Before and After

| Metric Comparison | Before $(T_0)$ | After (T+5 qtrs) |
|---|---|---|
| Annualized Revenue | $500 million | $616 million |
| New Customer Revenue Acquisition Rate | +6% | +21% |
| Existing Customer Revenue Expansion Rate | 0% | 2% |
| Customer Revenue Churn Rate | -6% | -5% |
| Net Revenue Growth Rate | 0% | 18% |
| Annualized Profits | $34 million | $117 million |
| Present-Value Discount Rate | 20% | 20% |
| Discounted Net Growth Factor | 5X | 50X |
| Company Value | $170 million | $5.8 billion |

The theoretical value of the company increased by 3400%, much more than the 450% increase in the actual stock price. But Sara was confident that if they could continue this performance for another couple of years, the market would continue to reward the company with a much higher stock price. Although Sara was confident in the company's ability to maintain the new performance numbers, the market analysts and investors wanted to see the new numbers continue for more than just five quarters.

In addition to the financial metrics, life was significantly better for FriendlyCo's customers. More customers were happy with the service they received, and they actually left glowing reviews on social media. Sales reps and customers genuinely started to like each other and treat each other with respect. The adversarial customer–sales rep relationships of the past completely vanished. Customers had more honest and productive interactions with the company, which helped FriendlyCo make changes to their service offerings and customer experiences. And these improvements, in turn, resulted in increased customer loyalty. Customer attrition rates fell below 5%. In the end, everyone was better off.

## Chapter Summary

The FriendlyCo parable illustrates some important points that are applicable to many different businesses:

- Negotiated pricing, based on unrealistic list prices and lack of price transparency, can create adversarial and high-risk customer relationships and lead to low levels of customer satisfaction.

- Sometimes drastic changes need to be made to pricing structures and strategies in order to overcome stalled growth and unhappy customers.

- Seemingly impossible changes to pricing and customer policies CAN be accomplished. And when teams are well prepared, it can be done with minimal negative effect.

- The five sacred metrics of pricing success should be the gauge to measure the benefits of new pricing strategies and how they will ultimately affect the value of the company.

- Major changes to pricing strategies and structures MUST include mitigations for inevitable disruptions to customer buying inertia. Often, customers must receive something of extra value to offset the unavoidable negative effects of the change. However, these extra benefits can be short-term benefits that last only until the customers' new habits are formed, and then they can be slowly tapered off.

- Discounts or rewards intended to compensate customers during the period of pricing changes should be sufficiently disconnected, so customers get the experience and feel of the new, permanent pricing and discount policies.

- Removing destructive pricing policies and practices will often unlock potential sources of growth and profitability. This can help offset any negative effects from the change.

Like many companies, FriendlyCo had many dysfunctional customer relationships based on a lack of price integrity and the adversarial nature of the pricing tug-o-war along with the burden of negotiated prices. Although the business had been stagnant for a few years, it was full of customer relationship risk, which ultimately could have caused even bigger problems for the company. The only way to fix the mess was to massively overhaul their pricing strategies and practices.

But most companies in this situation are too reluctant to make the necessary changes because they are worried about the one-time transformation risk. The problem with this thinking is that the one-time transformation risk can be mitigated and managed, whereas the long-term risk to the business of not making the change is potentially fatal. The mitigation to that risk is to make the change to healthier pricing practices.

---

*Next chapter preview:* The new age of Millennials is transforming customer values and expectations. Simultaneously, customers are continuing their migration to digital commerce. How companies adjust to this new generation of customers and their evolving preferences and behaviors can ultimately determine their ability to succeed and thrive in the new commerce environment.

## CHAPTER 9

# The Age of Millennials

*Millennials are more aware of society's many challenges than previous generations and less willing to accept maximizing shareholder value as a sufficient goal for their work.*

—Michael Porter

The current digital revolution is being driven by two forces—the momentum of new technological capabilities and the coming-of-age of a new generation. Both of these forces are critically relevant to the future of commerce. Understanding them is required for companies to succeed in the emerging global marketplace. This chapter is about how the new generation of buyers will shape the requirements for successful pricing strategies in the coming years.

## Millennials – Your New Future Customers

As of 2020, Millennials make up 50% of the global workforce. Experts say that by 2025, Millennials will make up 75% of the global workforce. That means, for the next two decades, most B2B purchases will be decided by…Millennials.

Compared to previous generations, Millennials seem to have different personal values, leading to different considerations in the way they make decisions. A survey of research on the subject of Millennials coalesces around a few key defining attributes of the Millennial generation. Learning about what drives them will help companies create better strategies for attracting and forming relationships with them as repeat customers.

I have found a significant amount of research on the differences between Millennials and previous generations—too many sources to name. That said, I will name a few that I found particularly helpful (in alphabetical order): **Goldman Sachs, *Harvard Business Review, MarketingMag.com.au,* McKinsey Online, Pew Research Center, and *Psychology Today*.**

*Disclaimer: This section contains sweeping generalizations about Millennials. I acknowledge that we are talking about individual human beings with different preferences, attitudes, skills, and characteristics, and that some of the Millennial generation may have different personal characteristics than the ones described below.*

Below are eight different defining characteristics of the Millennial generation, relative to previous generations, based on what I believe is most relevant to the topic of pricing strategies for growth:

1. **Trust, Transparency, and Authenticity**: More than other generations, Millennials value trust and authenticity over product features or hype. They expect transparency in their relationships. They are reluctant to trust salespeople or highly crafted marketing messages filled with buzzwords and industry jargon. Instead, they defer to personal experiences or reviews based on the experiences of others.

2. **Social Connectedness and Collaboration**: Millennials are highly connected on social networks, and they value collaboration with others. They often seek consensus on decisions, and they generally believe a decision that includes everyone's ideas will end up being a better decision than one that includes only one person's ideas. They don't like to be excluded from conversations about their future, and they expect to be consulted on decisions that affect them. They value teamwork. They share their experiences with others. They socialize their buying decisions as well as their own consumption. They talk about what they buy, who they buy it from, how they use it, and how well they like it. They value opportunities to help impact the lives of others. They are sometimes called "Generation We."

3. **Ethical Values and Social Responsibility**: Millennials are generally more socially progressive. They care about the environment, social equality, and diversity. They care deeply about corporate social responsibility, and they prefer to support businesses that visibly care about the same causes they care about. They instinctively challenge the status quo. They are more civic-oriented. They want to change the world for the better. They have very high expectations for their employers and expect them to behave like social institutions rather than entrepreneurial businesses, regardless of size.

1. **Curiosity and Self-Education**: Although Millennials have more formal education than any previous generation, they are adept at critical thinking and solving problems on their own, independent of their level of formal education. They are curious, industrious, and capable of processing decisions based on their own research. They are digitally connected and tech savvy. They embrace innovations and new ideas, and they don't feel anchored to previous generations' beliefs or conventions.

2. **Experientiality and Skepticism**: In contrast to their predecessors in Generation X, Millennials value experiences more than "things." And they value the experiences of others as well. In this vein, they leverage reviews from others to make purchasing decisions. Even though they are optimistic and idealistic, they are naturally skeptical of other people's motivations. They want to be engaged in meaningful work. They value a fun, relaxing, and comfortable work environment. And they care about work–life balance. They are naturally more skeptical of dogma or tradition than previous generations, and consequently, they are willing to challenge any ideas that don't fit their world view.

3. **Impatient and Expectant of Instant Response**: As a result of the instant gratification they've had in many areas of their lives, they generally expect instantaneous responses to online queries and product questions. They expect products and technology to work without problems, and they have very little tolerance for products or technologies that don't work. Although they are generally socially tolerant, they often have intolerance for organizations that promote ideas contrary to their own core values, and they have very little patience for dishonesty, selfishness, or narcissism.

4. **Creative, Entrepreneurial, and Independent**: Millennials don't like being under the control and influence of corporate structures and hierarchies. They have very little loyalty to companies, and they value the freedom to move from opportunity to opportunity. Millennials drove the explosion of the "Gig Economy," and they value the flexibility to earn their living from multiple sources. They value the experiential aspects of career advancement more than they value the monetary rewards, although they clearly expect to be rewarded monetarily in line with others who do similar work. Although they are achievement oriented, they care more about doing meaningful work than they care about maximizing shareholder value.

5. **Frugal, Practical, and Efficient**: Millennials are generally more frugal than the prior generation. They are more attracted to practical and simplified lifestyles than flamboyant overconsumption. This is part of the integral philosophy of not letting money consume their lives. They believe in the concept of ethical spending. They are smart, and they are drawn to efficient

1. solutions to life's challenges. They prefer fast and efficient communication in short bursts, like text messages, tweets, and social media posts, rather than longer emails, phone calls, or meetings. They place importance on tasks and results more than on time spent on work. Millennials are multitaskers. Because of this, they can sometimes be easily distracted. But they are also typically open and adaptive to change.

## So, What Does All This Mean for Pricing Strategies?

It is clear that we are seeing a generational shift in B2B buying behaviors based on both the unique characteristics of Millennials and the broader availability of e-commerce. This market transition opens up opportunities for companies to improve the effectiveness of their pricing strategies to meet the challenges ahead. I suggest companies should consider the following modifications to their pricing strategies, based on the growing influence of Millennials:

1. **Keep Pricing Ethical:** This goes without saying, but you will want to remove any hint of unethical pricing practices. This means avoiding anything that looks like price gouging or excess margins. It means no discrepancies between advertised prices and invoiced prices. And of course, nothing illegal: no price discrimination and no collusion. Millennials are extra sensitive to corporate social responsibility and ethical business behavior. They are connected, and they like to share experiences and opinions, so if they experience anything unethical, it will likely be shared across their many social connections and could end up going viral, as we have seen happen so many times before.

2. **Move to Transparent Pricing**: Millennial buyers place a high value on trust, transparency, and authenticity. They are naturally skeptical of underlying motivations. They will want to do business with companies that share their own personal values, and they will avoid companies who do not. Transparent pricing signals open and authentic willingness to share information across all customers. Millennials will appreciate companies who do not attempt to keep prices secret. Furthermore, Millennials will want to self-educate on products and prices. Making them wait for a price quote from a sales rep will be seen as unnecessary friction in the buying process and a senseless waste of their time.

3. **Keep Pricing Structures Simple**: Millennials will see complexities such as rebates, discounts, price tiers, coupons, and the like as unnecessary friction in the customer buying experience. They may welcome the ability to save some money through a discount or a rebate, but they will expect those opportunities to be extremely simple, easy to understand, and easy to

1. administer. Pricing needs to be fast and easy. It should always be intuitive, and it should always make sense.

2. **Ensure Consistent and Fair Pricing across Customers**: Because Millennials are more connected, they will share their experiences and find out what prices other customers are getting. If they find out that they are paying higher prices than another customer, they may begin to distrust the company, which will have a negative effect on future buying experiences. They already have a propensity to be skeptical, and this one thing could push them over the top.

3. **Avoid Bait and Switch Pricing Practices**: This goes without saying, but I will say it anyway. Millennial buyers will not have patience for companies that waste their time with "bait and switch" promotions or anything that looks similar. They will view such actions as a breach of trust and a disrespectful waste of their time. What is advertised and what is invoiced should not be different. A customer should not have to wait until the end of a 20-minute discussion to learn the price. If you need to increase prices, make sure you communicate to customers ahead of time, so they have time to change their buying decisions if they want to. Sometimes just offering the information ahead of time will produce enough good will that customers will be willing to absorb the price increase without any objection.

4. **Eliminate High-Pressure Sales Tactics**: Millennials are extremely sensitive to being manipulated, and they are likely to withdraw from any experience designed to manipulate them into a decision that is not well thought out. Furthermore, it is in their nature to seek feedback, and even consensus, from others who will be affected by the decision. Never expect them to make a big decision on the spot, and keep in mind that pressuring them to do so will just push them away.

5. **Get Rid of Negotiated Prices**. They will appreciate being informed of a non-negotiable price more than they will appreciate the ability to negotiate a price. Millennials don't need another way to waste time in the buying process.

6. **Keep Customer Communication Channels Open**: Invite feedback and input from your customers. Remember that your millennial customers are socially connected and likely already having conversations with your other customers. It's usually better to uncover potential issues or complaints directly from your customers ahead of time than to wait until rumors and negative experiences affect a larger portion of your customer base. The good news is that Millennials like to share, so if you provide an inviting environment for them to share their experiences with you, they'll likely to take you up on it.

Later in the book, we will discuss specific types of pricing strategies for accomplishing specific objectives. For now, the above themes should give you some general guidelines to consider for any pricing strategy you contemplate in the near future.

## Adapting to the Future Requires Change

In my experience interacting with corporate leaders, I've seen a tendency among many of them to be reluctant to implement significant and widespread change. I've had many conversations with top business leaders who swear that their business is different. While they generally acknowledge that the observations about Millennials are academically interesting, many do not seem to believe those observations are relevant for their business. It's not uncommon to hear business leaders profess that they've been in their industry for twenty or more years, and they've never seen customers who exhibit the characteristics described of Millennials. I've heard many business leaders say things like, "at the end of the day, customers care only about who will give them the lowest price."

I believe this type of attitude is not only misguided, but also dangerous to the future of their business.

Please pause and think about what is happening here. Is it really likely that you will be more successful by NOT adapting to anticipated changes in customer values and expectations?

If this describes you or your boss, the recommendations regarding pricing strategies for Millennials should not be dismissed. Here's why:

- There may be a new definition of success for your company going forward. In some of our earlier chapters we've made the case that margin-maximizing strategies may need to give way to growth-maximizing strategies. This will require maximum reduction of churn, and perhaps the knowledge of millennial-based customer values can be an effective tool in accomplishing just that. At the very least, it will likely be beneficial to ask: "What if...?" What if my customers were to start exhibiting the characteristics of Millennials? What would need to change if that were the case?

- It's possible that your industry hasn't yet begun to experience the inevitable generational changes that will ultimately occur. But it's likely that you will start seeing more of this in the future than you've seen in the past. These changes seem to be happening across all B2B industries, and some competitors will make moves to respond faster than others. If you're not yet seeing these trends in your industry, this may be an opportunity for you to move before your competitors do.

- Even if your business has been successful in the past, it's possible that these new considerations could help you create strategies to become even better. If you have been growing at 20%, perhaps there are new strategies that could enable 30% growth.

The wave of millennial buyers is changing the way companies must compete for business. By getting ahead of this trend and incorporating this knowledge into your pricing strategies, you will position yourself to win against any competitors who react more slowly.

## Chapter Summary

The rise of Millennials, in combination with the ongoing transition to digital commerce, means that your customers are changing. The new generation of millennial customers have different behaviors, expectations, and values than prior customers, and it's advantageous to understand these differences while constructing pricing strategies and go-to-market plans.

Millennial characteristics include:

1. Trust, transparency, and authenticity
2. Social connectedness and collaboration
3. Ethical values and social responsibility
4. Curiosity and self-education
5. Experientiality and skepticism
6. Impatient and expectant of instant response
7. Creative, entrepreneurial, and independent
8. Frugal, practical, and efficient

Pricing strategies should be modified to accommodate these general characteristics of the millennial generation with eight specific considerations:

1. Keep pricing ethical.
2. Move to transparent pricing.
3. Keep pricing structures simple.
4. Ensure consistent and fair pricing across customers.
5. Avoid bait-and-switch pricing practices.
6. Eliminate high-pressure sales techniques.
7. Get rid of negotiated prices.
8. Keep customer communication channels open.

These suggestions should help you be more successful as the millennial generation takes over most B2B purchasing (and B2C purchasing as well) especially if you make adaptive changes more quickly than your competitors.

And even if you haven't yet seen signs of the described millennial characteristics in your business, it is likely things will change. What created success in the past and what will create success in the future are not always the same. More commonly, success comes to those who can most effectively adapt to change.

---

*Next chapter preview: Beyond understanding the general characteristics of your customers that are similar, it is important to also understand how your customers are different. The next chapter covers techniques to better understand and segment your customers for the purpose of exploring opportunities and determining how strategies should be tailored for each respective customer group.*

## CHAPTER 10

# Your Key Customer Categories

*Understanding human needs is half the job of meeting them.*

—Adlai Ewing Stevenson II

In order to understand the most lucrative opportunities for growing the value of your company, it's important to first understand your customers—who they are, how they shop, how frequently they buy from you, and how fast they move through the **natural customer lifecycle**. With this knowledge, you can better understand how you are doing at attracting, retaining, and growing your customer relationships.

Your own customer transaction data can reveal a gold mine of information about your most loyal (and least loyal) customers and what attributes they share. Understanding how and why your customers buy will allow you to target the right strategies at the right customers to maximize your ability to grow. That being said, high-level metrics are useful only to the extent that they help us understand what's happening at the individual customer level. For example, just understanding your annual churn rate is not enough. It's important to also understand which types of customers are churning and what their reasons are for doing so. This type of understanding is enabled as you better understand what types of customers you have along with the attributes of their buying behavior.

It's important to understand, in general, what drives customer loyalty. This understanding will help you interpret what you observe in the transaction data and the important summary metrics.

## The Attributes of Customer Loyalty: Cost Avoidance

Why does **customer loyalty** exist? In most cases, "loyalty" is a misnomer. Loyalty implies that a customer has some sort of underlying commitment to a company. The Oxford Dictionary (lexico.com) defines loyalty as:

**loyalty** (noun): a strong feeling of support or allegiance.

But this is not really what's happening when people talk about customer loyalty. Customers almost always behave in their own self-interest. What may appear to be loyalty is usually nothing more than a collection of benefits sought for the lowest possible cost or inconvenience. And so, "customer loyalty" might be more appropriately named "customer self-interest habits," but since that doesn't really roll off the tongue, I understand why we stick to "customer loyalty."

It's important to think about customer loyalty in terms of customer self-interest because doing so will help form the appropriate context around why it exists and what can affect it. If an otherwise "loyal customer" no longer receives a benefit they had previously received, and it's no longer in the customer's best self-interest to continue in the business relationship, one would expect the customer to exit the relationship. Most of the time, customer loyalty has almost nothing to do with "strong feelings of support or allegiance."

I say "almost" because sometimes a customer's loyalty transcends any direct benefit to the customer and actually does resemble a strong feeling of support or allegiance. Examples that come to mind include Harley Davidson, Apple, Starbucks, and even U.S. political parties. In most of these cases, individuals feel like the brand is closely tied to their identity. If your company is one of these "identity" brands, you are truly fortunate, and you may be able to play by a different set of rules. But for everyone else, **customer loyalty** really means **customer self-interest habits**.

For this reason, discussions about loyalty should really be discussions about how customers are drawn into business relationships where they can avoid costs and attain more benefits than they can doing business somewhere else. In most cases, cost avoidance is a more powerful motivator than benefits, especially when the benefits are uncertain or largely indistinguishable among competitors.

From a cost avoidance perspective, **customer loyalty** is greater when costs can be avoided by consolidating purchases with a single vendor. When a customer has multiple repeat purchases to make, purchasing from a single or small number of vendors can reduce overall **evaluation costs, transaction costs, fulfillment costs,** or **even switching costs**. The most common attribute that drives customers to loyal behavior is the magnitude and regularity of **repeat-**

**purchase needs**. Repeat buyers are likely to exhibit more loyal customer behavior than one-time buyers. The reason for this is the greater opportunity for cost savings, including all the costs listed above, by purchasing from a smaller number of familiar vendors.

So, let's review the five major **attributes of customer loyalty.** Companies that understand these attributes and create strategies around them will almost always have a competitive advantage over companies who don't:

**Repeat-Purchase Needs:** The greater the magnitude and regularity of repeat-purchase needs, the more likely it is that a customer will want to settle into a series of repeated actions (buyer inertia) that makes it easier to make each purchase. When customers need to make lots of repeat purchases, there is a greater opportunity to find cost savings by purchasing from a single vendor. For this reason, the most dominant attribute of customer loyalty is the magnitude and regularity of repeat-purchase needs.

**Evaluation Costs**: This refers to any cost, whether monetary or effort-based, required to evaluate alternative products, services, or vendors to meet a particular need. The size of this cost depends on the answers to a few questions: How easy is it for the customer to evaluate different pricing offers and compare them across vendors? How easy is it for the customer to understand the differences in quality among different products? How much do differences in product or service quality tend to matter to the customer? Customers who don't care about the differences in products or services tend to have lower evaluation costs because evaluation is less necessary for them. Customers who are more technically capable, or who have easier access to information, typically have lower evaluation costs. Customers with low evaluation costs tend to be less loyal.

**Transaction Costs**: This refers to any cost or effort required by customers to get through the purchase process once a decision has been made to buy. Transaction costs may include anything from the initial costs of setting up an account to the process of ordering, purchasing, billing, credit processing, setting up payment terms, tracking orders, etc. Sometimes transaction costs are based on characteristics of the seller, but they can also be a characteristic of a single customer. For example, customers with poor credit may inherently have higher transaction costs than customers with good credit. Customers with procurement departments with multiple levels of bureaucracy may inherently have higher transaction costs than customers with streamlined purchasing capabilities. When transaction costs are high, customers tend to exhibit greater loyalty because they benefit more by consolidating transactions with a single vendor rather than spreading them across multiple vendors. We see examples of this in the many vendor consolidation initiatives that IT and procurement departments have been pushing for the last few decades. It's easier to deal with one vendor than it is to deal with 10 vendors. That being said, providers who offer lower transaction costs are more likely to have an advantage of customer preference vs. providers who have higher transaction costs.

**Fulfillment Costs**: This refers to any cost or effort required by the customer to get purchases delivered, installed, implemented, and accepted. The magnitude of these costs is often determined by the answers to a few questions: How easy is it for the customer to get products and services delivered? How much work goes into inspecting and accepting deliverables? Are some providers at a greater advantage in the area of fulfillment cost, perhaps because they have a service advantage? Do purchases require set-up, assembly, or implementation? Does the customer have to develop specific skills and habits to have orders fulfilled by specific vendors? While fulfillment costs can be product-related or vendor-related, they can also be customer-related. For example, customers who have less product expertise may require higher fulfillment costs. Customers who are geographically isolated can also have higher shipping or fulfillment costs. In an industry where nearly all vendors have similar fulfillment costs, higher fulfillment costs typically translate to greater customer loyalty. However, vendors offering lower fulfillment costs will likely have a competitive advantage over vendors with higher fulfillment costs.

**Switching Cost**: This is the summation of all the costs customers experience when switching between one vendor and another. It can include learning about new products, new shopping and ordering procedures, or new support structures. It can include the cost of retooling systems, entering and managing new sets of data, changing product specs, or informing customers of new products and features. The reality is that in most B2B repeat-purchase situations, switching costs are so powerful that it typically takes an exceptionally large service failure to provoke a change. Therefore, smart companies often try to offer their customers extra benefits that are difficult for competitors to imitate, and which increase switching costs, making it more difficult for customers to change to another vendor.

As a general rule, the more these attributes are prevalent in your industry and with your customers, the more customer loyalty you should expect under regular circumstances. In other words, it should take more than an average inconvenience for your regular customer to want to switch away from their current provider.

## Other Important Customer Attributes

Of course, there could be many other potential characteristics or attributes, such as **size, geography, industry,** or **amount of annual purchases,** which can be used to identify customer loyalty or price sensitivity, thereby aiding in the creation of tailored pricing strategies. Any characteristic that correlates with a customer's likelihood of progressing through the customer lifecycle or becoming a loyal repeat customer should be considered, especially if that data is easy to find in the customer transaction data.

## Question: Is Customer Loyalty a Customer Attribute or a Stage in the Customer Lifecycle?

The question of whether customer loyalty is intrinsic to the customer or simply a stage in the customer lifecycle is a good one. The answer is both. Some intrinsic customer attributes tend to coincide with higher costs of shopping and switching. This reality makes some customers more likely than others to become loyal, regular repeat customers. That would seem to indicate that customer loyalty is a customer attribute. However, it is also evident that customers tend to be less loyal early in a buyer–seller relationship, indicating that loyalty is also a function of customer lifecycle stage. Because customers also tend to be more sensitive to price early in the buying relationship, it's important to adapt pricing strategies based on customer lifecycle maturity. Later in the book we will talk about specific pricing strategies to boost customer acquisition rates. For now, it is important to recognize that customers are generally more price sensitive and less loyal earlier in the customer lifecycle.

# Relationship Buyers (and Other Buyer Types)

Most repeat customers are **relationship buyers** (vs. **product-level buyers** or **cart-level buyers**). This is important to understand because, for **relationship buyers**, the price of an individual product or service almost doesn't matter, as long as it's not flagrantly out of line. **Relationship buyers** expect that overall pricing will generally be in the ballpark of what is "fair," and they will focus on other aspects of the overall relationship, especially those things that help reduce evaluation costs, transaction costs, and fulfillment costs.

Most buyers fall into one of three categories of buyer, depending on the level of granularity at which purchase decisions are made.

**Product-level buyers** make a separate buying decision for each product they buy. If they have three products to buy, they will make three different vendor decisions. What makes them product-level buyers is typically the ease with which they can shop and compare prices at the individual product level and the potential savings they can achieve by buying from several different vendors. This would imply that they generally make relatively large purchases, making it easier to justify additional evaluation or transaction costs by the magnitude of the savings, although this is not always the case. For product-level buyers, the benefits of consolidating purchases with one vendor are not typically large enough to outweigh the cost savings from exploring different vendors for each product purchase. Product-level buyers care about the individual price of each individual product they buy. And they have very little loyalty due to their relatively low evaluation and transaction costs, along with the lack of any material switching costs.

**Cart-level buyers** may shop a few different vendors to see who generally has the most attractive prices, but after they've shopped, they buy most or all of their desired products from the same vendor. For them, shopping is relatively easy, but they don't like the hassle of dealing with many different vendors for similar types of orders, so they generally choose one vendor for all the related products of an individual purchase. Cart-level buyers are definitely price shoppers, so prices matter. But the price of an individual product will not matter as much as the overall price level of all the products in the cart. Sometimes they shop this way because they have support needs that make it more beneficial to buy from a single vendor for a related set of purchases. For cart-level buyers, loyalty is relatively low. Although they may have some preference to buy from familiar vendors, they typically don't care about switching costs.

**Relationship buyers** make up the majority of repeat-purchase customers. They typically don't like to shop for price because it's relatively costly in terms of time and effort, and price is only one aspect of the vendor relationship. Instead, they prefer to find fewer vendors that can serve a high volume of their needs at a "fair" price. They typically build vendor-specific habits for ordering and searching for products they need. This is how they keep transaction costs low— by forming efficient processes around purchasing from a few key vendors. All the work has been done up front, so orders are easy to place. For relationship buyers, switching to another vendor can be very costly because of the entrenched habits, low transaction costs, and specific knowledge of their existing vendor. Relationship buyers don't necessarily have personal relationships with individuals at the chosen vendor, although sometimes they do. But relationship buyers almost always have relationships with other aspects of the vendor's processes and infrastructure. This can include familiarity with the available product selection. It can include the knowledge of how to find products, expedite the purchase process, utilize the support structure, and navigate the communication network. Relationship buyers value the elements of the relationship that contribute to the ease of doing business, including knowledge of what to expect in terms of timing, delays, support, etc. It can include a relationship with a piece of software, a brand, or a history of good experiences. All of these elements can be part of the reason **relationship buyers** stay loyal. And unfortunately, if these relationships are damaged, they become the reasons customers leave.

## How to Identify Relationship Buyers

Anytime you have entrenched buyer inertia and significant switching costs, you have a relationship buyer. That means **repeat purchasers** and **relationship buyers** are generally one and the same. Therefore, the easiest way to determine if you have relationship buyers is to look in your transactions to see if you have **regular repeat buyers**—customers who purchase frequently and regularly. From their purchase behavior, you can infer the many other attributes that are often associated with relationship buyers—the rationale for why they are repeat buyers.

## Why Customers Become Relationship Buyers

**Relationships buyers** get many tangible and intangible benefits from their repeat-purchase relationships. **Relationship buyers** usually develop entrenched buyer inertia to the extent that they would bear significant switching costs if they were to move to another vendor.

*Personal Example: I confess I have a strong buying relationship with Amazon. I am certain that Amazon knows I am a relationship buyer with them. When I need to purchase something, as long as I think it is likely sold on Amazon, I typically go to Amazon and buy it. Most of the time, I don't bother to check other sources on the web. Why do I do this? Because it's easier. There is less friction. My credit cards and purchase history are already there, and I know the return policy. It's just easier than having to learn the terms and conditions of a new website. Evaluation costs, transaction costs, and fulfillment costs are smaller with Amazon than with most other online vendors at this point in time. Switching to another online store would be relatively more costly for me. As long as I believe Amazon's prices are fair, I will probably continue to be an Amazon customer, not because I feel any specific devotion or commitment to them, but because I believe it is in my own self-interest to continue buying from Amazon.*

This is a perfect example of what a **relationship buyer** is.

The good news is that relationship buyers don't tend to switch vendors very often. But if you are trying to win new, loyal customers from your competition, the bad news is, again, that they don't tend to switch vendors very often. Once customers have established entrenched buying habits, for better or for worse, price doesn't seem to have as much impact on purchasing decisions as other factors, like service quality and trust.

## The Natural Velocity of Your Business

One of the most important and first steps in understanding your customers and their behavior is to understand the velocity of your business—the frequency with which typical repeat customers make purchases. Once you understand this important aspect of your business, you will have a benchmark to compare customers and measure abnormal behavior. Although business velocity can be described in terms of a precise average purchase interval, it's generally easier to think in terms of standard business velocities, such as those in the following table:

### Standard Repeat-Purchase Business Velocities

| Business Velocity | Description |
| --- | --- |
| Quarterly | Typical repeat customers buy at least once per quarter |
| Bimonthly | Typical repeat customers buy at least once every two months |
| Monthly | Typical repeat customers buy at least once per month |
| Biweekly | Typical repeat customers buy at least once every two weeks |
| Weekly | Typical repeat customers buy at least once per week |
| Daily | Typical repeat customers buy at least once per day |

Understanding the typical frequency of customer purchases is critical for interpreting customer behavior signals. For example, if you have a customer who hasn't purchased in three weeks, how do you know if you should you be concerned? If your business velocity is monthly, you probably have nothing to worry about. However, if your business velocity is daily, then three weeks without a purchase probably means something is wrong.

A simple way to estimate your business velocity is to count all your purchases by repeat customers in the last year and divide by the number of repeat customers to get average number of annual purchases per repeat customer. Then divide 365 days by that number to get your average purchase interval (in days).

As an example, let's say you have 6,071 repeat customers who have collectively made 75,619 purchases in the last year, the simple (ballpark) calculation of business velocity as follows:

75,619 purchase events ÷ 6,071 customers = 12.5 purchases per customer

365 days ÷ 12.5 purchases = 29.2 avg. days between purchase events

Standard Business Velocity → Monthly

Although the simple approach will get you in the right ballpark, you can get a more precise measure by looking at the actual number of days each customer has been doing business with you. For example, new customers might have been with you for only 80 days, so for them you would divide the number of purchases into 80 instead of 365. If you use this technique for the example above, you might find that the actual average purchase interval across all customers is only 22.5 days, 23% lower than the 29.2-day ballpark calculation. Interestingly, both numbers would classify the business velocity as **monthly**.

More sophisticated tools will do all calculations and produce insightful charts that allow you to understand not only the average purchase interval across all customers, but also the distribution of average purchase intervals across customers, like the example in the following chart:

### Number of Customers by Average Interval Between Purchases

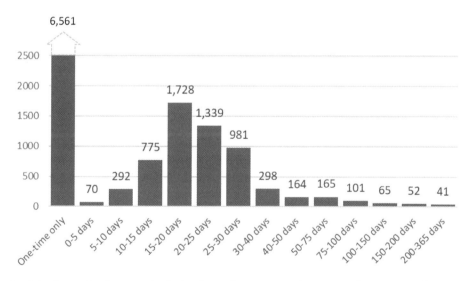

In this chart, the largest single bucket of customers has a purchase interval between 15 and 20 days. But it's easy to see, also, that there are significant volumes of repeat-purchase customers in the range of 10–15 days, 20–25 days, and 25–30 days. The vast majority of repeat-purchase customers would be covered by describing the typical repeat customer purchase interval as ranging between 10 and 30 days. So, again, the velocity of this example business seems to be closest to monthly—meaning customers typically make a purchase at least once per month.

After determining your natural business velocity, you can use this information to define the stages in your customer lifecycle model. Since this example has a business velocity of monthly, I will use a monthly velocity to describe the natural customer lifecycle stages, next.

## The Natural Customer Lifecycle Stages

All customers go through some sort of customer lifecycle. Although there are many different ways to model a customer lifecycle, for the purposes of this book I will put forth a model that will work for most repeat-purchase businesses across different industries. I call this model the **Universal Customer Lifecycle Model for Repeat-Purchase Businesses.** A pictorial representation of this model is shown in the illustration below:

**Universal Customer Lifecycle Model for Repeat-Purchase Businesses**

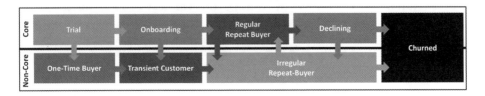

The arrows show the typical flow of how customers can move through the lifecycle model depending on their purchase behavior.

The first five stages are called **core stages** because they include the expected path of "**core**" customers. **Core customers** are customers who are an ideal fit for your business—the ones that you hope will eventually become **regular repeat buyers**.

**Non-core customers** include one-time buyers or irregular repeat buyers who are not on a path to likely become **regular repeat buyers**.

*Note: Typically, you should be able to adapt this customer lifecycle model to your business just by changing the business-velocity-based timing. You can find an example customer lifecycle definition for each standard business velocity at the book website, PriceForGrowth.com.*

## Core Customer Lifecycle Stages

**Trial** (**New**): These are customers who have made a single purchase commitment. They don't yet have any behavioral inertia compelling them to buy more. They are in a fragile state. Whether they intend to buy more from you or not, they are forming impressions about your company. They may even make multiple purchases with your company in the "trial" period (typically 1–2 months) to get a few more data points to evaluate what a customer relationship is like with your company. In some cases, you might have offered these customers a significant incentive to "try out" your products and services, and most importantly, the relationship. It is important to make sure that this trial incentive is seen for what it is, an incentive to try, rather than an indication of what the price levels will be after they are onboarded.

**Onboarding** (**New**): These are customers who have passed the trial period and are starting to make recurring purchases with your company. They will remain in this stage as long as they buy at some minimum frequency during the onboarding period. Because they have begun making repeat purchases, it can be presumed that they have at least a mild intention of continuing to do business with you, as long as everything goes well. And so, the purpose of the onboarding phase is to get the customer to develop a pattern of behavior that results in the habit of buying from you on a regular basis. This is called buyer inertia. In some cases, these customers may still have access to a trial incentive or a separate onboarding incentive, often in the form of a post-onboarding rebate after the customer has completed a certain number of purchases in a specified timeframe. During this onboarding period (typically 2–3 months), it's important for the customer to build behavior patterns that make it easy for them to purchase from you in the future. In addition to monetary incentives, there may be added "hyper-care" to remove friction from the evaluation and buying experience. The objective is to turn the customer into a regular repeat buyer.

**Regular** (**Onboarded**) **Repeat Buyers**: These are customers who have established sufficiently entrenched buying habits that they naturally continue to buy from you on a regular basis. Customers will remain in this stage as long as they continue to make purchases within some minimum frequency. This is the customer lifecycle stage in which most companies want their customers to stay. In this stage, the main focus is to increase the customer's level of loyalty, which you can typically gauge from the loyalty profiles in the next section of this chapter.

**Declining**: These are customers who were at one time **regular repeat buyers** but who have recently slowed down or stopped purchasing for a period of time called the **buffer period**. The buffer period is a defined period of time that is long enough where a substantially lower level of purchasing or lack of purchases likely means something, but not so long that it looks like churn. Typically, for a monthly velocity business, the buffer period is 2–4 months, after which if a customer has made no purchases, that customer is deemed churned. Once customers become **declining** customers, they will transition into **irregular repeat buyers,** if they continue to buy, or **churned** if they don't make any purchases for the duration of the buffer period. Alternatively, they may return to being **regular repeat buyers** if they resume purchases at a regular pace.

**Churned**: These are customers who were once repeat buyers, but who stopped purchasing altogether for the duration of the buffer period and have crossed the **churn threshold** (typically 4–12 months of no purchases). A simple definition of a churned customer is a customer who purchased in the previous year (more than 12 months ago), but not in the current year (the last 12 months). But some companies don't want to wait a whole year to recognize that a customer has moved to the churn category. There is also some debate about whether or not a customer who has only purchased once should be counted in the churn numbers, since they were never a repeat-purchase customer to begin with. These are decisions you can easily make when you set up your own customer lifecycle model.

## Non-Core Customer Lifecycle Stages

**One-Time**: These are customers who purchase only once. Some of them could potentially turn into **repeat customers**, but most of them never will. Typically, one-time purchasers who are still in a trial period would be classified as **trial customers**, until the trial period ends, upon which they would be classified as **one-time customers**, unless—and until—they buy again.

**Transient Repeat Buyers**: These are **repeat customers** who may purchase multiple times in a relatively short period of time, but then stop purchases for a long period of time, appearing as if they do not intend to be a regular repeat buyer. Typically, the period between their first and last purchase is shorter than the trial and onboarding period, so these customers never make it to **regular-repeat-buyer** stage. There are many reasons customers may exhibit transient buying: They have a short-term need for what you sell; they have another regular supplier, and something has gone wrong with that source; or they started with your company as a potential regular provider, and then found another vendor that fit their needs better. Some transient customers buy for a short period each year, like a seasonal customer, potentially with only a seasonal need. But typically, after 12 months of no purchases, these customers will be presumed **churned**.

**Irregular Repeat Buyers**: These are customers who never become regular customers with entrenched repeat buying patterns. Instead, they make sporadic and seemingly random purchases from time to time. Sometimes these customers are loyal customers of the competition. Sometimes they just have sporadic needs, and you may find out that these customers just don't purchase very often from anybody. For those who might be the loyal customers of your competition, there may be a potential opportunity to convert them to regular repeat customers through a conversion incentive (which will be discussed in a future chapter).

These are the primary **customer lifecycle stages** that seem to fit most repeat-purchase businesses. Understanding these stages and what they mean will help you understand the composition of your current and previous customers, along with their revenue and profit potential. Once you have them in place, you can start to see the composition of your customers and your revenues by customer lifecycle stage. The charts below shows how customers are distributed across the various customer lifecycle stages.

**Total Number of Current Year Customers by Customer Lifecycle Stage**

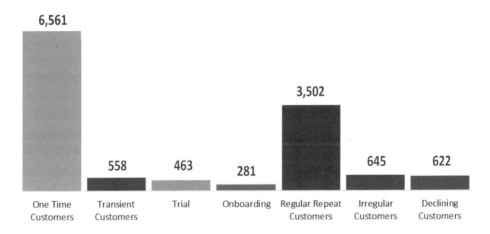

Even though you may have a situation where most of your customers are one-time customers, you should find that most of your revenues and profits are concentrated in your regular-repeat-buyer customers. An example of this is shown in the following chart (taken from the same set of data as the example above):

**Total Current Year Revenue by Customer Lifecycle Stage**

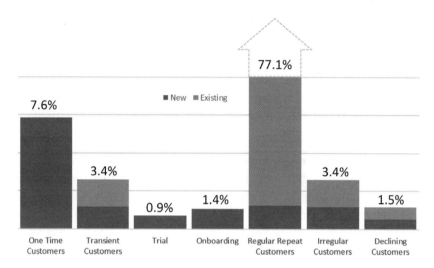

Even though one-time customers make up nearly 52% of the customers, they make up only 7.6% of the revenues. And while regular repeat customers make up just under 28% of the customers, they account for 77.1% of revenues. From this chart, it is clear that the bulk of the business comes from customers who buy regularly. So, this example looks like a very healthy business.

In this snapshot in time, we see 463 trial customers, which doesn't look like a lot, relative to the 3,502 regular-repeat-buyer customers—only about 13%. But when you consider that those trial customers stay in the trial stage for only two months, you would expect the company to cycle through those 463 customers six times in a single year, which would bring the total to 2,778. If the company were able to convert 50% of them to the regular-repeat-buyer stage, that would mean a potential 39% increase to the biggest segment of revenues.

Dividing customers into segments based on their current customer lifecycle stage is a good way to see opportunities for growth.

## The Five Basic Customer-Loyalty Profiles

Almost all repeat-purchase businesses have a mix of loyalty among their customers. The **five basic customer-loyalty profiles** introduced here are helpful for recognizing different types of repeat customers, so you can effectively create strategies for acquiring, retaining, and growing high-value customer relationships. These profiles are defined by customers' needs and their desire to avoid costs associated with evaluation, transaction, fulfillment, and switching costs. In ascending order of value and importance, the **five basic customer-loyalty profiles** are as follows:

**Unprofitable Bottom Feeders (irregular repeat customers)**: These are the customers you generally don't want. They only buy at prices below your profitability threshold. Chasing after these customers doesn't make any sense. If you want to serve these customers, you need to recognize that they have no loyalty and add virtually no value to your company. They probably have exceptionally low evaluation costs, which is sometimes due to indifference when it comes to competing products. Therefore, the best way to do any business with this group is to strip from your offering anything that adds cost and offer them the bare bones offering at a bare bones price. These customers behave as if they have virtually no switching costs, since they are constantly prepared to change vendors, based on whoever is offering the lowest prices. If you are doing things right, there probably won't be many of these customers in your recent sales transactions.

**Opportunistic Customers (irregular repeat customers)**: These customers have no significant buyer inertia, loyalty, or switching costs. They buy from you when your price is relatively attractive. They are shoppers because it is relatively easy for them to shop, and they get a relatively high benefit from shopping, especially on big ticket items. They are different than the **unprofitable bottom feeders** in that they often recognize the major value differences between two competing products. They just prefer to buy when they can get better deals. For opportunistic customers, switching costs, evaluation costs, transaction costs, and fulfillment costs are low relative to the size of the savings on the purchase. That's why you're more likely to see opportunistic customers for large purchases or big-ticket items—their savings are usually more significant. There are two potential strategies for opportunistic customers: (1) Create a stripped-down, low-cost version of your product/service offering that you can sell at a low price (which only works for the customers who don't want premium features), or (2) find a way to stimulate a valuable buyer inertia pattern by adding a service feature they would value and/or introduce switching costs to try to make it more inconvenient for them to buy only occasionally from you. It might be possible to move some of these customers to **regular repeat buyers**.

**Light Inertia Customers (regular repeat buyers)**: These customers have a habit and pattern of behavior which includes buying from you. And while they are not likely to leave due to mild changes in price or mild service disruptions, any significant disruption or price increase (e.g., 5% or greater) would likely result in significant attrition risk. Price typically matters to these customers, but they are looking for efficiency and want to reduce evaluation and bargaining costs by doing most of their business with one vendor. These customers often differ from **heavy inertia customers** in the length of time they have been repeat customers, and it is logical to presume that after more time, they will become **heavy inertia customers**. The logical strategies for this group of customers are: Keep them happy, and don't disrupt their inertia; create benefits that they would lose if they left you (i.e., switching costs). Try to increase their loyalty to see if you can move them into the heavy inertia category.

**Heavy Inertia Customers (regular repeat buyers)**: These customers have entrenched buyer inertia and significant switching costs, and they are not likely to leave unless there is a major disruption or a significant price increase that is not justified or fair. The longer these customers stay with you, the less likely they are to leave. Often, these customers have built businesses around their chosen vendors, so they are not even looking at other vendors seriously. They may do an occasional RFP, just to keep their existing vendors on their toes, but existing vendors are clearly incumbents with incumbent benefits. There is only one strategy for this group: Keep the customer happy, and don't give the customer any reason to look at other vendors. Keep giving them reasons to do business with you. That's the strategy because these are your best core customers. This is the group you want to grow. This is the group that will stay with you even when times get bad, as long as you continue to make it easy for them to do business with you.

**Captive or Die-Hard Customers**: These customers will not leave until your price or service hits some extreme level of unreasonableness because their reasons for buying from you go far beyond price. They are willing to pay high—even "unfair"—prices because they value your products and services and/or the business relationship much more highly than the price of the transactions. Often these customers are buying critical items that might make up a relatively small part of their overall purchase or business—like a high-performance sprocket for a high-performance motorcycle, where the cost of the sprocket is a relatively low percentage of the total motorcycle, but it is critical to the performance and design specifications. If you are lucky, you'll find 5%–10% of your customers in this category, but most of the time the number is not that high. This group typically won't need discounted prices. In fact, they may be willing to pay premiums and surcharges to keep the relationship in place. The logical strategy here is to avoid any type of service failure that could jeopardize the status of the relationship. Discounts will almost never be necessary.

It's important to understand the composition of your repeat-purchase customer base. If your customer base is mostly made up of high-inertia and die-hard customers, then you probably have extremely low risk of churn. Your best opportunities might be found in attracting and onboarding new customers. On the other hand, if most of your customers are in the opportunistic or low-inertia profiles, you may want to focus on opportunities to prevent churn and to increase customer buying inertia and switching costs by solidifying the long-term value proposition of doing business with you.

## Putting It All Together

When you overlay the customer loyalty profiles, you get a multi-dimensional view of your customers, which can help you visually understand how customers move through the customer lifecycle. The customer lifecycle map below is one of these illustrations:

**Customer Lifecycle Map (with Basic Loyalty Profiles)**

Using the customer lifecycle map above, you can see how every customer who has ever done business with you fits in only one box. And you can even trace the exact path the customer took to arrive at their current designation.

## Chapter Summary

In this chapter we've covered some foundational ways to categorize and better understand the composition of your customers, which should help provide context and visibility to pricing strategy opportunities.

"Customer loyalty" is usually a misnomer, as customers typically care much more about their own self-interest than devotion to any particular company. The **attributes of customer loyalty** are typically based on the customer's desire to minimize unnecessary costs and the ability to avoid costs by consolidating purchases with a small number of suppliers. These costs can include evaluation costs, transaction costs, fulfillment costs, and switching costs, and these costs tend to be amplified when customers need to make a greater number of repeat purchases. The more these types of cost are present, the more likely customers are to exhibit characteristics of "customer loyalty."

Most regular repeat buyers are **relationship buyers**, meaning they prefer to find fewer vendors that can provide many of the products and services they require at a fair price. Relationship buyers exhibit very different behaviors vs. product-level buyers or cart-level buyers. While both product-level buyers and cart-level buyers place a lot of importance on finding the lowest prices, relationship buyers assume prices will be in the competitive ballpark and place more importance on minimizing other costs of doing business, like minimizing evaluation, transaction, and fulfillment costs. Relationship buyers seldom switch due to the price of any individual product, as they are more concerned about the holistic aspects of the customer–vendor relationship.

Understanding the velocity of the business—the frequency with which most repeat customers make purchases—can inform the most appropriate customer lifecycle model and allow companies to appropriately interpret changes or gaps in customer purchase behavior.

There is a natural customer lifecycle model for every type of business, especially repeat-buyer businesses. The Universal Customer Lifecycle Model for Repeat-Purchase Businesses is a customer lifecycle model that can be adapted to most companies who sell to repeat-purchase customers. It includes core and non-core customer lifecycle stages.

**Core** customer lifecycle stages include **trial, onboarding, regular repeat buyer, declining,** and **churned. Non-core** customer lifecycle stages include **one-time buyer, transient repeat buyer,** and **irregular repeat buyer.** Using **customer lifecycle stages** as an initial customer segmentation can help you rapidly understand the composition of your customers and revenues, creating visibility on likely strategic growth opportunities. On top of these stages, improved granularity of repeat customers can be achieved by overlaying five basic customer loyalty profile stages, which include **unprofitable bottom feeders, opportunistic customers, light inertia repeat buyers, heavy inertia repeat buyers,** and **captive** or **die-hard customers**. Understanding how your existing customers fit among the different profiles will help you better focus your customer acquisition and retention strategies on customers who have a better potential for longer-term loyalty.

There are many different ways to segment your customers, and it's important to explore and evaluate what types of customer segmentation will allow you to find opportunities and create focused strategies to improve the value of your company via the **five sacred metrics of pricing success**. The standard customer lifecycle stages and standard loyalty profiles introduced in this chapter can create a very fast and meaningful way to segment your customers so that you can better understand the composition of your potential revenue-generation assets—your existing and future customer relationships.

---

*Next chapter preview: The next chapter is a case parable about a new VP of Pricing and Growth who uses some familiar tools to uncover opportunities and drive new strategies to massively improve the company's value.*

## CHAPTER 11

# Hypothesis-Based Pricing Transformation

**Case Parable 4: ChangeCo and New VP Pricing & Growth, Marta McLain**

*The following parable illustrates how a newly hired VP of Pricing & Growth uses the concepts of customer lifecycle progression to identify opportunities and create pricing incentive strategies to impact the value of the company. Through directed focus and hypothesis-based actions, Marta accomplishes what none of her predecessors had even attempted to do. As a result of using the right metrics to evaluate opportunities and measure granular results, she made quite an impact in just under a year's time.*

## ChangeCo's New VP of Pricing and Growth, Marta McClain

With anticipation, newly-hired Marta McClain stood in front of ChangeCo's CEO and CFO to take them through her plan for accomplishing her new mission—to lead the company into a period of accelerated growth through improved pricing and growth strategies. She started the meeting by giving her two bosses each a copy of *Price for Growth*, a new book on how to create focused pricing strategies for achieving growth and maximizing company value. She explained that the book would help the key leaders in the company get aligned with a common understanding of why sustainable growth is so important for increasing the value of the company.

Having recently read the book herself, she found it to be an excellent summary of the many valuable lessons she had acquired over her career in pricing and marketing. When she accepted this job, she decided that the book would be the foundation for planning how to accomplish the most important objectives on their path to success. In fact, she had purchased 24 copies of the book for all the leaders and managers in the company who played important roles in helping the company achieve its growth goals.

To her surprise, both her CEO and CFO agreed to read the book, and they were incredibly supportive of her initiative to get everyone in the company on the same page.

For the next 20 minutes, Marta and her bosses discussed the **five sacred metrics of pricing success** and how she planned to find the highest impact opportunities to improve the company's net growth rate in order to make the biggest possible impact on the value of the company. She was delighted with the amount of support she was receiving as she explained her plans.

After the meeting, Marta was completely energized and ready to get to work.

## ChangeCo: A High-Growth, High-Profit Company

ChangeCo was a $250 million provider of industrial-grade uniforms, safety vests, and construction apparel to manufacturing and construction companies. Over the last three years, ChangeCo had experienced an average annual net revenue growth rate of 11%. Approximately 20% of their revenues came from new customers each year, but their 9% customer churn constrained their annual net growth rate to only 11%. ChangeCo's most impressive financial metric was its healthy profit percentage of 18%, which had been stable for the last three years. Costs and prices had also been stable.

ChangeCo's revenue model was based on a monthly service fee, which included rental, cleaning, and repairing the products so their customers always had clean apparel in good condition and ready for use.

Marta was extremely excited because she knew she would find many improvement opportunities by using tools described in the book. ChangeCo had never before tracked all five sacred metrics of pricing for the purpose of modifying their pricing strategy. From her experience at other companies, Marta knew that just by starting to track the key metrics, they would certainly find many opportunities to make improvements, some of which would require only a few minor changes in order to unlock substantial benefits.

## Laying the Foundation

Having recently read this book, Marta was excited to see how she could apply the principles to her new business.

## Establishing a Customer Lifecycle Model

She immediately analyzed the last three years of transaction data to learn about the natural velocity of their business (monthly) and how often and consistently ChangeCo's customers made purchases. After significant analysis, she and her team laid out a customer lifecycle with the following stages and definitions:

- **trial**: in their first month of trying the service
- **onboarding**: regular spending in months 2 through 4
- **regular**: regular spending after the trial and onboarding periods (after month 4)
- **irregular/transient**: irregular or sporadic spending
- **declining**: previously regular customers who had two consecutive months of reduced spending
- **churned**: regular customers who had no spending or purchasing for three consecutive months or any customer who had not purchased in last 12 months.

## Examining Historical Pricing Practices

Marta quickly learned the history of how ChangeCo had attempted to acquire new customers. Their long-time approach was fairly simple:

- New prospects were offered a 50% off coupon for the first 30 days.
- They didn't have the concept of an "onboarding" period after the first 30 days.
- At the end of the 30 days, customers could get 20% off perpetually if they committed to use the product for the rest of the year. If they didn't stay for the full year, they were sent an invoice for the extra 20% discount they had received but hadn't earned.
- Customers who agreed to continue the service after the first year were allowed to keep their 20% discount perpetually.
- Customers who did not want to commit to long-term service simply paid list prices, which by themselves were pretty competitive in the market.

So, to sum up, customers were incentivized to try the service for 50% off list prices for 30 days, and as long as they were willing to commit to long-term use greater than one year, they got 20% off continued business. Irregular customers paid list prices.

## Historical and Current Results Metrics

Marta was excited to try out some new pricing techniques to see if she could improve the growth and profitability of the customer base because these types of experiments had not been conducted at ChangeCo before.

She started with a report that showed average conversion rates (based on the new lifecycle definitions) from lead to trial, trial to onboarding, onboarding to regular, regular to declining, and declining to churned, shown in the table below:

### ChangeCo Historical Conversion Rates

| From | To | Conversion Rate | Cumulative Rate |
|------|------|------|------|
| Lead | Trial | 20% | 20% |
| Trial | Onboarding | 40% | 8% |
| Onboarding | Regular | 80% | 6.4% |
| Regular | Declining | 12% | .77% |
| Declining | Churned | 75% | .58% |

*All customers who went through trial and didn't end up as regular customers were categorized as irregular/transient customers.*

Without doing any further analysis, Marta could see that the lead-to-trial conversion rates were significantly below industry averages. While the industry averaged 33% lead-to-trial conversion rates, ChangeCo was only converting 20%. She knew that was the first place they should focus. She realized that if she could improve the lead-to-trial conversion rate, it could have a big impact on the number of new customers without the need to necessarily increase the number of leads coming in. So, she decided to start there.

# The First Pricing Strategy Experiment

She wanted to make a dramatic change in the lead-to-trial incentive, so she could learn more about the limits of change and improvement for the company. From the book, Marta remembered the importance of learning from every pricing action and change in strategy, so she decided to try doing something big. In order to understand the possibilities, she decided to do a 90-day promotion, where she would offer the first month for $1 (essentially a 100% discount). She wanted to see how much she could increase the trial rate if she reduced the price of the first month to essentially zero. She was sure to make it clear that this was a one-time promotion that would expire in 90 days (another key lesson from the book was to make sure all new pricing experiments were seen as one-time-only promotions that would expire after a specified timeframe). After meeting with her pricing team and gaining agreement, they proceeded with the new promotional price incentive.

## The Results: Both Good and Bad

As expected, within just a couple of weeks, the company started seeing a major change in the conversion rates. At the end of the 90 days, the results were definitive. The lead-to-trial conversion rate had increased from 20% to 48%, a 140% increase! This was exciting. However, while the **lead-to-trial** rate had increased substantially, the conversion rate from **trial to onboarding** had simultaneously fallen from 40% to just 12%, which unfortunately decreased the overall lead-to-regular conversion rate from 6.4% to only 4.6%, as shown in the table below.

### Initial Experiment Results for $1 First 30 Days Promotion

| From | To | Original Conversion Rate | New Conversion Rate | Original Cumulative Rate | New Cumulative Rate |
|------|----|-----|-----|-----|-----|
| Lead | Trial | 20% | 48% | 20% | 48% |
| Trial | Onboarding | 40% | 12% | 8% | 5.8% |
| Onboarding | Regular | 80% | 80% | 6.4% | 4.6% |

While the new pricing incentive had massively increased the number of trials, somehow the new trial incentive was causing problems after the trial period and worsening the overall new customer acquisition rate. This was definitely something the company didn't want, so they needed to figure out what was happening, and fast.

## The Revised Pricing Strategy Experiment

Marta called her team together to have a brainstorming session on what might be happening and why, so they could make an adjustment to the strategy. After a two-hour discussion, they concluded that they likely weren't getting conversions past trial because the difference between $1 and 80% of list price was too big of a jump—customers weren't getting used to paying real prices during the trial period vs. what they would be asked to regularly pay after the trial period. So, after lengthy discussion, Marta and her team decided to make a change to the promotion. Instead of $1 for the first month, they created a new promotion that would offer a 75% rebate after the first two months. Although not as big an incentive in the first month, it was actually a more significant incentive because it would last for two months instead of one. But by making it a rebate instead of a discount, the team felt that the customers would be more likely to get accustomed to paying regular prices for the service because the rebate wouldn't happen until after the first two months. They also felt that two months of the trial service would allow customers to start forming habits around the new service, so it would be more difficult to switch back to their old provider, as long as the service was good.

They implemented the new promotion within just a couple of weeks after the meeting.

## The Results: Much Better

The results seemed to be more in line with what the team was expecting and hoping for. Not only did they get the **lead-to-regular** conversion rates back to 6.4%, but they also almost doubled that benchmark, achieving 12.2%. The results of the revised pricing strategy experiment are shown in the table below:

**Revised Experiment Results for 75% Rebate Incentive**

| From | To | Original Conversion Rate | New Conversion Rate | Original Cumulative Rate | New Cumulative Rate |
|------|-----|------|------|------|------|
| Lead | Trial | 20% | 38% | 20% | 38% |
| Trial | Onboarding | 40% | 40% | 8% | 15.2% |
| Onboarding | Regular | 80% | 80% | 6.4% | 12.2% |

Lead-to-trial conversions came in at 38%, not quite as good as the 48% achieved by the $1 promotion, but almost twice as good as the original conversion rate of 20%, and they were still able to convert 40% from **trial to onboarding** and convert 80% of **onboardings to regular** customers. This almost doubled the new customer conversion rate from 6.4% to 12.2%. If they could continue this on an annualized basis, they would massively improve their **new customer revenue acquisition rate** (NCRAR) by 90.6%, from 20% to 38.1%. After netting out the 9% revenue churn rate, the **net repeatable revenue growth rate** (NRRGR) grew from 11% to 29.1%, a 165% increase!

## An Early Success to Establish Positive Momentum

Plugging this number into the company value calculator, the 165% increase in **net repeatable revenue growth rate** (NRRGR) resulted in a theoretical company value that was 800% more valuable than when Marta had come on board.

In just over six months, Marta had found a way to massively improve the value of the company. After meeting with all the major executives to explain the changes she had made, along with the new improved growth rate, which appeared to be quite sustainable, her value to the company had been established and validated. The CEO was positive that investors would agree that the new growth rate would easily double or even triple the market value of the company if the company could continue on this path for the rest of the year.

# The Next Improvement Opportunity

But Marta wasn't finished. She believed there were more opportunities to improve the growth rate, specifically in the conversion rate from **trial to onboarding**. She felt that 40% was too low because customer satisfaction surveys indicated that 85% of customers who used the service for at least 30 days actually really liked the service.

Marta and her team hypothesized that the majority of customers weren't continuing after the trial because of the jump in price from effectively 75% off to just 20% off—a 220% price increase. She felt it was too much too soon because the customer hadn't yet developed the purchasing habits to create entrenched buyer inertia. From existing customers who were happy to pay the higher prices, she felt like customers would stick if she could get more of them to make it through the onboarding period of four full months.

## The Revised Trial and Onboarding Promotion

After meeting with her team again, Marta decided she would try a different onboarding approach. She would continue with a 75% rebate for the first month. She would offer a 60% rebate for the second month, a 45% rebate for the third month, a 30% rebate the fourth month, and a 20% rebate every month thereafter, as depicted in the table below:

**ChangeCo 75% Rebate with Declining Monthly Rebate Percentages**

| Timeframe | Rebate (paid at end of each timeframe) |
|---|---|
| Month 1 (trial) | 75% |
| Month 2 (onboarding) | 60% |
| Month 3 (onboarding) | 45% |
| Month 4 (onboarding) | 30% |
| Month 5 and beyond | 20% |

It was a little more complex, but she had 30 days before each different promotion for sales reps to re-explain the offer each month.

The new promotion system was implemented, and the results started to come in, largely improved as expected.

## Results: A Significant Improvement

After 90 days, the team observed a significant overall improvement. Although the lead-to-trial rate dropped slightly from 38% to 36%, the overall results were much better, as shown in the table below:

**Second Revised Experiment Results for 75% Declining Rebate**

| From | To | Original Conversion Rate | New Conversion Rate | Original Cumulative Rate | New Cumulative Rate |
|------|-----|------|------|------|------|
| Lead | Trial | 20% | 36% | 20% | 36% |
| Trial | Onboarding | 40% | 56% | 8% | 20.2% |
| Onboarding | Regular | 80% | 84% | 6.4% | 16.9% |

Although the **lead-to-trial** conversion rates fell just a little, the **trial-to-onboarding** and **onboarding-to-regular** conversion rates were significantly higher. On an annualized basis, the new pricing incentive increased the new-customer revenue acquisition rate by 164.5% from the original 20% to 52.9%. Leaving the churn rate at 9%, the **net repeatable revenue growth rate** (NRRGR) went up from the original 11% to 43.9%, a 299% increase over the original.

## The Impact on Company Value

The impact on the value of the company was unbelievable. Plugging the new NRRGR into the company value calculator showed a new **theoretical company value** of 1500% more than when Marta had been hired, less than one year earlier.

When Marta had first arrived, the company had aspirations of going public within two years at a forecasted initial share price of approximately $10. But now, after these impressive results, both the CFO and CEO were convinced that the company would likely go out at a price closer to $150 per share, as long as the growth rate could be sustained for the next year.

Marta was granted 10,000 more shares of the company as a reward for her excellent work, and they allowed her to grant additional shares to all the members of her team.

# Could Anything Be Done About Churn?

Marta still felt there was opportunity to improve. And she wondered if there was an opportunity to reduce churn below 9%.

She met with her team, but they were skeptical about whether or not they could reduce the churn, which had been at 9% for the last three years. And the metrics showed that 75% of customers who entered the **declining** stage moved to the **churned** stage within just a couple of months.

One team member had the idea that if they could try to rescue customers within 60 days of no purchases, they might have a chance to save a certain percentage of them.

They decided to implement a program called "Operation Rescue," where they would reach out to any **regular-repeat-buyer** who went 45 days without making a purchase. This would entail interviewing the customer to find out the reason they had stopped purchasing, to see if it was service-failure related, competitive-price related, or something else. If the reason was service-failure related, they would log the offending event and then offer one free month of service as a way to make up for the failure. If the reason was a competitive-price related issue, then the customer service representative would attempt to find out what price the competitors were offering, and then offer a special loyalty rebate of an additional 10% plus one free month to try to keep the customer.

If the reason for the customer departure was something else, such as no longer needing the service, they would be labeled as unrecoverable, and the customer service representative would thank the customer for their business and wish them well.

## Implementation and Results of "Operation Rescue"

For the next three months, ChangeCo executed Operation Rescue to see if they could materially reduce churn.

When the results came back, they learned something they didn't expect. For starters, 60% of the companies they contacted simply said they didn't need the service anymore. That meant that 5.4% of the 9% was unrecoverable. Next, they learned that 30% of the people they called had experienced a service failure of significant proportion. These service failures ranged from late deliveries to dirty/unkept clothing. What was more alarming was that most of them said they had been experiencing service failures for more than six months before they decided to change to another company. Marta was floored by this revelation, wondering if many of her other loyal customers might be experiencing the same thing.

The next depressing piece of news was that zero percent of the companies that experienced service failures would take ChangeCo's offer of one free month of service. That meant that price didn't matter at all, and the churned customers were evidently happy with their new uniform service provider. This made Marta even more nervous about the service her existing regular customers were receiving.

The last group, 10 percent of the customers they called, reported they had left because the competitor offered them a lower price. The price they were offered was 1 free month of service to try out the competitor's service. When they were offered 1 free month + an incremental 10% discount, zero customers took the offer. Marta and her team couldn't believe it. They wondered if the service problem was so bad that, even at lower prices, the churned customers preferred the competitors' service. Or was this just an example of customers developing significant buyer inertia with a new vendor and not being willing to bear additional switching costs? Either way, Operation Rescue turned out to be an unexpected failure in terms of reducing the churn rate. However, ChangeCo was successful in capturing important information about their service quality, and they realized they needed to take action right away.

Through the interactions with the churned customers, ChangeCo was able to learn a few other things about how they were perceived in the market:

- Most customers saw ChangeCo as the low-price alternative in the market.
- There was a general perception that the service quality with ChangeCo was going to be slightly worse than other competitors in the industry.
- People believed that if ChangeCo could fix its service issues, they could easily be the most dominant competitor in the market.

## Fixing the Service Quality Issues

Marta very quickly shared her observations with the rest of the executive team, highlighting her concern that if the service issues weren't significantly improved, they could end up losing many of their newly acquired customers. The CEO, upon hearing this information, got personally involved in the initiative to drastically improve service quality. And he made it the number one corporate priority for the next year.

One year later, after significant effort, the quality of the service had substantially increased.

Marta was happy to report that, as a result of the service improvements, the churn rate in the last quarter had dropped to 1.5%, or 6% annualized. This was a 33 percent improvement over the previous year, and no additional price concessions were required to make those improvements happen.

The reduction in churn made the net repeatable revenue growth rate increase by another 3% to 46.9%, and this again added to the already significant improvements to the company valuation.

## The IPO – A Validation of Value

Later that year, ChangeCo conducted an IPO (Initial Public Offering) on the New York Stock Exchange. Their initial "going out" price was $202, which was 20 times higher than the price they were expecting to get just a couple of years earlier before Marta had joined the company.

Marta and her team made a huge impact on the value of the company as a result of their work.

In an interview with the *Wall Street Journal*, Marta was asked how she was able to achieve such massive increases in the growth rate of the company when others before her were unable to do it. Marta deflected the credit to the strength and dedication of her team. But in reality, we know how Marta was able to do it. First of all, she started with a **growth mindset**. She believed improvement was possible; she and her team just needed to find a way to get it done. She was open to ideas and experimentation. If something didn't work, she felt free to change it. She focused on where she thought the biggest opportunity might be. She felt that 18% margins were already fairly high, and that focusing on margins would be low impact, potentially risky, and largely unsustainable in terms of continuous price increases. So, she turned her attention to growth and conversion rates. She felt there might also be opportunity to reduce churn, but that would need to take second priority because there was less room for improvement there. Focusing on conversion rates was exactly the right thing to do because there was significant room for improvement. Marta knew the company could do better.

In the end, it wasn't because Marta was more charismatic. It wasn't because Marta worked harder or longer hours. It was because she worked "smarter" by forcing the focus to the opportunities with the greatest potential impact. And she was smarter because her expansive thinking and growth mindset allowed her to take in new ideas and not be constrained by the way things had always been done.

In the end, it wasn't that everything Marta tried ended up being wildly successful. Remember, her first attempt to improve growth and conversion rates actually put the company in a worse position. Her Operation Rescue didn't initially improve the churn rate. But she viewed these as valuable learning experiences that would help the whole company get smarter. And this ended up leading to overall results that were wildly successful.

*If you are interested in seeing some of the tools that Marta used to identify opportunities of the highest potential impact, you can see them in **Appendix B** at the back of the book.*

## Chapter Summary

The ChangeCo case parable is full of lessons that can benefit any company considering a change in their pricing strategy to achieve a larger company value.

- Try to focus first on the area of the largest potential impact. Marta focused first on growth and conversion rates because they seemed to have the most room for improvement. Conversely, profits were already high, above industry averages. She knew (from her tools) that improvements to the net revenue growth rate would have a massive impact on the value of the company.

- Experiment in a way that doesn't negatively change existing customer expectations. Marta did experiments in trial and onboarding incentives fairly liberally because she knew that they could be done on a very short-term basis without changing existing customer price expectations. As a result, she was able to learn and then go back to "normal" if she wanted to.

- Use every initiative and experiment as a learning opportunity. Operation Rescue wasn't very valuable as a pricing strategy, but it turned out to be a critical learning opportunity, which probably saved the company from a very bad fate. As a result, they were able to act on what they learned and turn the situation around before it became an out-of-control problem.

- Pricing strategies can be much deeper and more complex than simply moving prices up and down. The pricing strategies employed by ChangeCo were more about incentives to change customer behavior than they were about converging on an "optimal" price level. ChangeCo needed to find ways to dislodge customer buying inertia and overcome switching costs in order to increase their ability to capture new customers. Traditional elasticity models would never have worked in this situation. But it was clear that buyers had various sensitivities to price in the context of what behavior they were

- willing to change. In Operation Rescue, churned customers were offered a free month of service, and none of them accepted that offer, even though they were paying higher prices to another vendor. You cannot describe this phenomenon in terms of elasticity and maximum willingness to pay. It was more about willingness to switch or willingness to try, and free wasn't good enough to get it done.

By dissecting pricing strategies into focused objectives to capture, retain, and grow customer relationships, instead of using a blunt-force technique to try to "optimize" prices, pricing strategies become more manageable and achievable. In this case parable, Marta showed us that focusing on high-impact opportunities combined with hypothesis-driven experimentation can result in massive growth, which can exponentially affect the total sum of future profits—what really drives the value of a company.

---

**Next chapter preview:** *Now that we've discussed the attributes of customer loyalty and how customers typically move through the customer lifecycle, we are ready to make sure we have our bearings when it comes to elasticity. The next chapter will focus on what elasticity is and how it can be beneficial in helping us predict how customers will respond to changes in pricing strategies.*

# PART 3

# Building Focused Pricing Strategies

*Where focus goes, energy flows.*

—Tony Robbins

## CHAPTER 12

# The Concept of Elasticity vs. Growth

*We've done price elasticity studies, and the answer is always that we should raise prices. We don't do that, because we believe…that by keeping our prices very, very low, we earn trust with customers.*

—Jeff Bezos

The word "elasticity" gets thrown around a lot in pricing circles. But its meaning is not always clearly or correctly understood. There are many misconceptions about elasticity, even among people who have been in the industry for many years. This presents a problem. In order to construct growth-maximizing pricing strategies, it is critical to understand—without error or misconception—what elasticity is and how to apply its concepts.

Traditional elasticity-based price optimization models seek to predict the change in sales quantity for various potential price changes in order to calculate expected revenues and profits under each scenario. As you will soon see, these elasticity-based optimization models are simply not appropriate for repeat-purchase businesses, where most purchase decisions are made at the relationship level, and where customer loyalty and switching costs are such significant factors in the risk of customer churn.

Beyond the core concepts of elasticity, the more important and relevant questions for how pricing affects repeat-purchase customer relationships will include: How can price changes attract customers and incentivize them to learn about and try new products? How can price changes incentivize customers to change their long-term purchase behavior? How can price changes affect customers' perceptions of whether the price is fair or not? And what risks arise when prices start to get out of line with what is perceived as fair?

The question is not just whether a customer buys or not. No. The more important questions focus on how pricing strategies improve the way customers move through the customer lifecycle to become regular repeat buyers, and then what makes them continue. All of these questions build on the principles of long-term customer relationships that have been discussed up to this point.

The concept of elasticity has a role in how you should think about your pricing strategies, just not in the way it's usually talked about.

## What Is Elasticity?

When people in pricing use the term "elasticity," they are most likely referring to the conceptual relationship between pricing and sales volume. The notion that there is typically an inverse relationship between price and sales volume is perfectly fine. It is intuitive, and it seems consistent with real-world experiences. When prices get too high, fewer people buy. Nothing is wrong with thinking about elasticity in these terms.

But beyond that, things seem to break down.

Many people in pricing seem to believe, based on what they learned in their college or high school economics courses, that there is an inherent numerical relationship between price and demand—akin to a natural law (like gravity), such that one could discover this constant numerical relationship, and thereby engineer a precise number of sales, just by moving to the appropriate price. We will see shortly that this view of pricing and elasticity is problematic, and it typically leads to actions that do more harm than good to the long-term interests of the business.

The concept of elasticity is important to understand and master in order to properly interpret pricing and sales metrics. By the end of this chapter, you will have a solid understanding of elasticity, such that you will be able to apply its practical concepts to make high-value pricing decisions and appropriately infer the meaning of your observed results. You will have all the necessary tools to understand and leverage the concept of elasticity to your advantage in developing pricing strategies.

## The Real Meaning of Elasticity

In economics, the official term is Price Elasticity of Demand, and the formula to calculate it is:

$$\text{Elasticity} = \frac{\text{Percentage Change in Quantity Demanded}}{\text{Percentage Change in Price}}$$

What most people don't realize is that, based on the definition above, Elasticity is a backward-looking metric, not forward-looking. It looks back at two different points in time to compare two different prices, along with related quantity volumes. And contrary to the way most people use the term, there is no guarantee—or even an implication—that elasticity calculations at two different points in time would necessarily yield similar results, even for the exact same products sold to the exact same customer segments at the exact same price.

Elasticity is not a natural law. It is a metric used to succinctly describe a set of historical observations.

## Misuse of the Concept of Elasticity

Elasticity was originally meant as a way to report simultaneous movements of price and demand. When prices moved, and demand did not move very much, the demand was labeled **inelastic**. When demand seemed to be very responsive to small changes in price, it was labeled **elastic**. Even though the definition of elasticity does not specify that the changes in demand were necessarily caused by the changes in price, it was more or less presumed to be that way. One could theoretically change the price and wait to see what happened with respect to demand. Since the price change is typically presumed to have happened first, it would logically follow that it would be more likely that the price caused the demand than that the demand caused the price.

Unfortunately, as stated before, most people think of price–demand relationships as something more akin to a natural law, with a numerical constant that will automatically change sales volumes when prices are changed. But this isn't how it works. Changing a price doesn't automatically produce sales. Sales are produced when a customer's needs get big enough to cause a series of actions that result in something being sold. Demand curves vastly oversimplify the process of buyers and sellers coming together to make economically beneficial trades. Yet, because of the simplicity of the picture, it is tempting to try to forecast demand curves for the purpose of making "optimized" pricing decisions.

To aid in this practice, educators and consultants create illustrations of demand curves, revenue curves, and profit curves to help companies understand the theoretical "optimal" price for their products and services—the price that achieves "optimal" revenues and "optimal" profits. The example below shows how "optimal" prices are determined. The straight line represents the demand (or elasticity) curve, the larger arc represents the achievable revenue curve, and the smaller arc represents the achievable profit curve, based on the demand curve and associated cost estimates. $P_R$ would be the "optimal" price to maximize revenues, and $P_\pi$ would be the "optimal" price to maximize profits:

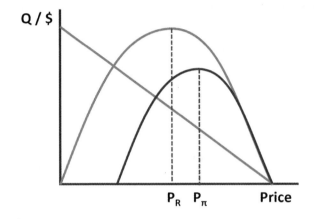

This is a nice, clean, and simple illustration of how elasticity-based pricing optimization systems work. They first forecast demand at various price points. Then they calculate the resultant revenue and profit for each potential price. And then they pick the price that has the highest revenue or highest profit, and that becomes the optimized price.

The problem is simply that these models to forecast elasticity often overlook important complexities and biases in the process. For most applications, these optimization models fall short and fail to achieve their desired results. This is not to say they're not helpful or that they shouldn't be pursued. I mean only to point out that if you don't take sufficient steps to mitigate the inherent complexities and biases, you're more likely to make bad, rather than good, pricing decisions, as a result of these types of models.

These attempts to model price–demand relationships often fail because they are based on:

- **The presumption that purchase decisions are driven only by price**. In reality, price is only one of literally hundreds of variables that affect customer purchase decisions, and most of the time, price is not the reason somebody decides to buy or not. The price–demand curve presumes that there is only a single variable that affects customer buying decisions—price. And it generally implies that there is a smooth, continuous relationship between price and demand. This has been proven false by numerous studies on what drives customers to make a purchase decision. The reality is that every customer has a "zone of indifference" where they don't care what the price is. Looking at the volume results from price changes in this area (the zone of indifference) won't tell you anything about price elasticity.

- **The failure to consider the mechanical steps in the buying and selling process required to onboard new customers**. Typical elasticity models ignore all the steps in the buying process, except for the actual purchase of the product. For example, elasticity models don't consider that customers need to educate themselves on a product or service, or that they may need to be sold to. They presume that all customers are in the market ready to buy, and the only variable they will use to make their decision is whether or not the price is low enough. In fact, elasticity models generally ignore whether or not the customer is already purchasing the product, and at what price. In real life, that would seem to be a fairly important factor in estimating whether or not a customer will buy at a certain price. If lowering the price is going to cause other new customers to buy the product, where are those customers going to come from? What selling needs to be done to get them to understand the value proposition and decide to buy from a completely new vendor?

- **The assumption perfect information.** Price elasticity models are based on the assumption that the customer has perfect information about not only the price of the product in question, but also all of the potential competing products. In reality, customers rarely have perfect information about prices. Many times, they don't even know where to look to find information on prices. B2B has a history of price opacity, where negotiations are done in secret, and new customers have very little information about what other customers are paying for similar products and services.

- **The lack of consideration for real-world market friction, buyer inertia, and switching costs**. In the world of B2B, repeat customers, and recurring purchases, price elasticity models tend to ignore market friction, such as buyer inertia and switching costs that tend to make switching vendors much

- more involved than just getting a better price. Often there are direct and indirect costs customers must bear to move from one supplier or product to another. At the very least, it is important to acknowledge the many potential sources of market friction that affect the complexity of actual buying decisions and customer behavior. These sources of friction go far beyond a single-price-variable model of demand.

The concept of price elasticity is real, but it's different than the way most people seem to understand it. It's very important, and it definitely should be considered in the creation of focused pricing strategies. The common biases and misunderstandings must be acknowledged and mitigated for pricing strategists to successfully manage pricing.

## Relevant Elasticity Questions

Now, with the understanding of the reasons why traditional elasticity-based optimization models tend to fail, it's appropriate to discuss where and how the concepts of elasticity can drive better decisions and better strategies. The **five sacred metrics of pricing success** deal with new customer revenue growth, existing customer revenue growth, reduction of churn, expansion of repeatable profits, and reduction of risk regarding future profits. This would indicate that the most important elasticity questions would be based on how to attract, retain, and grow customer relationships. For example:

- How does price affect a customer's willingness to learn about a product or service? Is there a price incentive that will cause a customer to watch a video or read a brochure?

- How does price affect a customer's willingness to try out a product or service? Is there a price incentive that will cause a customer to try something new?

- How does price affect a customer's willingness to purchase a second time? Is there a price incentive that would cause a customer to repeat a purchase decision or behavior? What about a third, fourth, or fifth time?

- How does price affect a customer's willingness to form a habit of buying a new product (instead of a competitor's product) all the time to fill their needs? Is it possible to create a price incentive that will prompt customers to develop a new purchase habit and start to establish buying inertia?

- Once a customer has formed a habit of purchasing one particular product or service line, what price incentive would cause them to try another product or service line?

- Once a customer has switched to another vendor, what price or price change would cause that customer to come back *before* developing entrenched buying habits with the new vendor?
- What price incentive would be required to get the customer to come back *after* becoming entrenched in their habits of purchasing from the new vendor?

These are the critical questions most relevant to relationship-level decision-makers who have needs for repeat purchases because they deal with how to attract, onboard, grow, and retain customer relationships. Almost none of these answers can be garnered from looking at price elasticity models for a single product. Rather than a simple hypothesized relationship between price and purchase volume, the focus must be on a specific price incentive to accomplish a specific progression in the customer lifecycle.

## "Fair" Price Elasticity Considerations

As discussed earlier, a sound pricing strategy seeks to get loyal customers paying fair prices. How does fair price relate to elasticity? How does a price or a price change impact a customer's belief that prices are fair? And what risks emerge when prices start to get out of line with fair?

These are particularly important questions because the long-term growth of the company depends on the ability to charge fair prices to the majority of the **regular repeat buyers**. If you miss on this question, you will likely lose customers faster than you mean to. And you will hurt your net growth rates.

Earlier, I discussed what a fair price means. To recap, it means:

- It is no better or worse than everyone else pays.
- It does not give the vendor unreasonably high profit margins.
- It doesn't change very often.
- It is consistent with advertised prices.
- It is not significantly out of line with competitive market prices.

In short, the fair price is the highest price that a customer doesn't mind paying because it is justifiable based on other price benchmarks. They are willing to pay the price because they believe it's fair.

So, what does fair price elasticity mean? It refers to how a change in price affects the customer's perception of how fair the price is. This is critically important to understand because the more a customer believes a price is unfair, the more likely that customer is to be dissatisfied and at risk of churn.

For the last several decades, study after study has shown that price is typically not the reason customers decide to stop buying from a company. The number one reason customers leave is because of a "service failure" or the company's failure to respond to a service failure effectively and respectfully. Most studies show that these service-failure-driven defections make up about 70% of customer decisions to switch vendors. And conversely, price related reasons account for less than 20% of customer defections.

That said, sometimes price increases end up being the straw that breaks the camel's back because they add to the existing level of dissatisfaction from previous service failures, and the increases give customers sufficient cause to move to another vendor. This is something that can and should be avoided.

As with regular elasticity, there is not a smooth and continuous relationship between price and a customer's sense of whether or not the price is fair. Here are some general observations/rules about factors that affect a customer's perception of fairness:

1.  **Price Decreases:** If the price is going down, most customers will tend to believe that the new price is fair, as long as other customers aren't getting even lower prices.

2.  **Stable Prices:** If the price is stable over a period of time (i.e., not changing), most customers will accept that it is a fair price, as long as the price seems to be in a competitive ballpark, and the customer doesn't see other customers getting lower prices.

3.  **Price Increases:** If the price is increased, customers may believe they are getting a fair price, if:

    a.   there is a justifiable rationale for the price increase (e.g., passing on a legitimate cost increase), and

    b.   the amount of increase is on par with the rationale, and not excessive.

As discussed in previous chapters, anytime a company increases prices, it is generally advantageous to communicate with the customers what is happening and why it is necessary or justified. **Price communication** is a very important part of shaping customers' perception of fairness.

Price increases are more likely to give customers the impression that they are not fair when they include one or more of the following elements:

*   **Lack of Rationale**: There is no justifiable or apparent reason why the price should go up (e.g., no change in market, etc.) or, worse, the company chooses to increase prices when market prices and costs are actually going down.

- **Excessive Increase**: The price increases by a larger magnitude than historical increases (e.g., prices have typically increased by 1%–2% per year, but this time they are increasing by 5%) or a larger magnitude than justified by market changes (e.g., market and costs go up by 5%, but prices go up by 10%).

- **Excessive Margins**: The customer has reason to believe that margins are unfairly high (e.g., company publicly reports margins of 70% while customers are struggling to break even).

- **Lack of Standardization**: There is clear evidence that different customers are getting different prices, and there is no clear, objective standardization regulating how different customers get better prices.

Before trying to mathematically model the relationship between price levels and customers' sense of price fairness, it would be beneficial to first ensure that any contemplated price increases pass muster with the guidelines listed above.

## Chapter Summary

Elasticity is an important concept, but it is often misunderstood. Sometimes it is used inappropriately to construct automated price optimization solutions, which often fail because they don't consider the inherent biases in the construction of the models. The important concepts of market friction, buyer inertia, and switching costs are often conspicuously missing in many of these attempted models, even though they have a massive impact on how customers make buying decisions.

The concept of elasticity is real and can be observed. But what is observed in history can seldom be turned around to engineer a target result just by changing the price. After all, a customer's decision to buy is a conglomeration of many different decisions, such as:

- a decision to pay attention
- a decision to learn
- a decision to try
- a decision to repeat
- a decision to substitute
- a decision to change behaviors to make buying easier

Good pricing strategists care about all of these decisions, and they are interested in how pricing, price strategies, or price incentives can lead customers to make positive decisions when the respective opportunities present themselves.

Studies consistently show that most customer defections are due to factors other than price. For that reason, churn models based solely on price should not be expected to yield much actionable insight.

Beyond initial incentives to buy a product for the first time, repeat-purchase customers generally like to settle into a repeated buying behavior based on the assumption of fair and stable prices. Unfortunately, price changes can potentially upset the stability of customer buying patterns. It is important to communicate to customers a reasonable rationale for raising prices in order to avoid the risk of losing the customer's trust.

---

*Next chapter preview: The next chapter explores the contrast between hypothesis-based objective-driven decisions and forecast-based cause-and-effect-driven decisions and their effect on pricing outcomes. The use of break-even thresholds in combination with the scientific-method-based approach to pricing strategies can enable both faster decisions and exponential learning.*

CHAPTER 13

# Objective-Driven Pricing Strategies

*Truth in science can be defined as the working hypothesis best suited to open the way to the next better one.*

—Konrad Lorenz

There are multiple approaches to determining the best pricing strategies in order to achieve your desired results. As far as this book is concerned, the primary objective of pricing is to maximize the sum total of all future profits.

Traditional price optimization techniques often involve forecasting likely outcomes of various potential pricing scenarios, and then using an algorithm to pick the one scenario that seems to have the highest probability of achieving the desired result. Somewhat ironically, this type of solution is often referred to as "science-based," even though it may not reflect the commonly understood elements of the **scientific method,** which the sciences have relied on for centuries to improve the collective understanding about how the world works. Instead, because forecasting-based methodologies use various mathematic techniques, and since the mathematics have somehow become confused with science, almost any methodology that uses advanced math seems to easily earn the label of a "science-based approach," whether deserved or not. Nevertheless, just because an approach uses math doesn't mean it leverages the scientific method.

We should not lose sight of the real value that comes from using the scientific method in our work—**learning and discovery**!

The **scientific method** is a process for using ingenuity and creativity to analyze the situation, formulate questions, develop hypotheses, conduct tests, observe results, draw conclusions, and repeat the process. This process is illustrated in picture below:

**The Scientific Method**

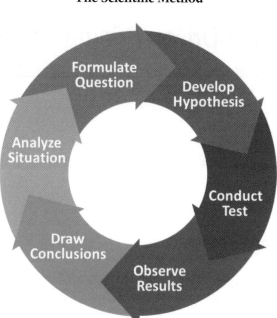

There is nothing wrong with using mathematical techniques to create a forecast. But this should not be confused with the scientific method, which opens doors to new discoveries and advancements in our collective understanding. For this reason, this whole chapter is devoted to **hypothesis-based, objective-driven** approaches for optimizing pricing strategies.

## Hypothesis vs. Forecast

The Oxford Dictionary defines hypothesis as the following:

**hypothesis** (noun): a supposition or proposed explanation made on the basis of limited evidence as a starting point for further investigation.

Contrast that with the definition of forecast:

**forecast** (noun): a statement about what will happen in the future, based on information that is available now.

Contrast these two words and their respective definitions. One of the words invites experimentation and learning. The other word seems, instead, to be a conclusive proclamation of a future reality. Oddly enough, the way people typically interact with these two words seems to match with the respective definitions. I'll explain what I mean.

## Forecast: A prediction of an Inevitable Reality?

Too often, the word "forecast" promotes the mentality that the future is already defined, and you can't change it. All you can do is forecast it. People sometimes drastically overweight the importance of a forecast, behaving as if it were an unavoidable fate. And when the forecast turns out to be wrong (as is frequently the case), people often blame the forecast for being wrong. And this allows people to separate themselves from the responsibility of the outcome. Because people often give too much weight to a forecast, they often tend to act helplessly instead of doing the things that would otherwise make them successful. And when they don't get the outcome they expected, they tend to blame the outcome on the forecast rather than their own action or inaction.

And yet, ironically, if you ask most people beforehand about the probability that the forecast will be accurate, almost everyone responds with confidence that the forecast will most assuredly be wrong. Nobody trusts the weatherman. But when it comes to action, they treat the forecast as though it will most certainly be correct. Otherwise, what would be the purpose of having a forecast? Although people frequently complain that the weatherman is wrong, as soon as they forecast rain, everybody grabs their umbrella.

Do you see the inconsistency here?

To me, this seems very close to insanity—acting as though the forecast were most certainly correct, while simultaneously believing that each individual forecast will almost always be wrong (even if the average of all the forecasts will be close to correct). Actions become disconnected from beliefs.

Is it any wonder that people don't take personal responsibility for their actions when the forecast is wrong?

## The Value of a Hypothesis

Conversely, people tend to discount the value of a hypothesis, as if it were some random guess pulled out of the air, with no connection to reality. But most would agree that a hypothesis is an invitation to experiment and test. It offers a chance to either validate or reject, and in that sense, it is much more valuable than a forecast...because a forecast is not up for discussion.

Given how often I hear people proclaim that the forecast will always be wrong, it seems ironic how much the word "forecast" seems to imply some inevitable reality that we can't change, despite our inability to correctly forecast it.

Depending on which word we use, we may be inviting a different mindset and a different string of potential outcomes. After all, a creative mind is required to analyze data, formulate questions, and develop hypotheses—all activities that utilize the growth mindset. And the hypothesis serves as the basis for experimentation and learning, inviting an open mind to examine the infinite possibilities.

A hypothesis is an educated best guess. Most of the time it's not disconnected from reality at all. And many times, it will outperform a forecast in terms of its predictive capabilities.

## Cause-and-Effect vs. Objective-Driven Approaches

Related to forecast vs. hypothesis, there are two opposing approaches to determining optimal pricing strategies. The first is the **cause-and-effect** approach, and the second is the **objective-driven** approach. The differences are fairly simple to describe. In the **cause-and-effect** approach, the focus is on the "causes," and in the **objective-driven** approach the focus is on the "objective."

To illustrate the difference in methodology, let's use a scenario of a company considering a price increase for the purpose of improving profitability.

### The Cause-and-Effect Approach

Typically, in the **cause-and-effect** approach, it is presumed that taking an action will cause some sort of resulting effect. The first step is to presume the cause. In the example of price increases for the purpose of improving profitability, the initial focus presumes that raising prices (the cause) will produce some sort of resulting effects. And so, the problem statement focuses on the cause more than the effect:

*How much should I raise prices to achieve the best business outcome?*

The question may seem to be focused and contained, but it is much more open-ended than it appears. In this case the causal actions would include various potential price increases. For example, the pricing team may look at various scenarios, such as increasing prices by 1%, 2%, 3%, 4%, etc. The next step is to attempt to forecast the effects or results of each price increase scenario: "What will happen if I raise prices by 1%?" The answer is typically provided by some sort of forecast or mathematical model. This is repeated for each potential cause scenario.

But every cause can have multiple effects. For example, raising price by 1% could result in multiple potential outcomes:

- Per-unit profits will increase.
- Existing customers might become upset.
- Some customers may decide to leave.
- It may become more difficult to capture new customers.
- Competitors may change their pricing strategies.
- Employees and salespeople could become confused.
- Billing errors could happen if systems are not all updated correctly.
- Etc., etc.

The action of raising prices could cause any number of resultant effects, probably too many for the company to forecast or even pay attention to, especially considering that these effects are multiplied by the number of causal scenarios. And so, the company must arbitrarily choose what to care about based on what they believe has the potential to be most impactful. Perhaps in this case, the company chooses to look only at resultant unit profits and potential decreases in sales because those two effects will likely have the most immediate and direct impacts on overall profitability.

The problem with this approach is that the company necessarily chooses to ignore some potential resultant effects for the sake of simplifying the problem. This approach might more appropriately be called **cause-and-some-of-the-effects** approach.

Sometimes this approach can be appropriate and even ideal—when there is only one potential causal action and the potential resultant effects are known to be contained or isolated. Conversely, this approach is less appropriate when there could be many potential causal actions to achieve the desired effect, or when the potential causal actions could have many different effects that touch many different parts of the company. In these cases, it might be more appropriate to consider using the **objective-driven approach**.

## The Objective-Driven Approach

The objective-driven approach is different in that it starts with the end objective, and then works backwards. One may say, "I want to increase prices, and I don't want to lose any customers. But my main priority is to not lose customers."

And so, the first step is to word the problem/objective statement such that it appropriately frames the priorities of the objective:

***How can I increase profits without losing any customers?***

While the cause-and-effect approach immediately presumed the causal action would be potential price increases, this problem statement does not restrict what the causal actions may be. Instead, the objective-driven approach might start making a list of all the potential ways the objective might be achieved by formulating several questions:

- What if I raised prices?
- What if I tried to increase profits by increasing the number of customers?
  - o What if I lowered prices to try to attract more customers?
  - o What if I hired more salespeople?
  - o What if I increased marketing investments?
  - o What if I tried to reduce customer churn by offering better service?
- What if I tried to increase profits by decreasing costs?
  - o What if I invested in people who could negotiate better costs?
  - o What if I committed to larger volumes with fewer vendors to get lower costs?
- What if I tried to increase profits by selling more to my existing customers?
  - o What if I found a way to resell somebody else's products?
  - o What if I developed new products to sell?
- Etc., etc.

Just as the cause-and-effect approach showed numerous potential effects, the objective-driven approach shows numerous potential causes. But there is a difference. The objective-driven approach is not constrained to focus on only one potential cause. The company could choose to take many simultaneous actions to try to achieve the objective.

But also, like the cause-and-effect approach, it's not realistic to evaluate everything, so you have to narrow down your choices by what seems most likely to be an effective strategy. At this point, gut feeling may be good enough.

The next step is to develop a **hypothesis**. Perhaps after reviewing all the potential causes, I form a belief that the quickest and easiest way to increase profits without losing any customers is to conduct a very small price increase. Perhaps, I believe I can justify a 1.5% price increase to keep up with inflation, but I would be worried to try anything higher than 1.5% for fear that customers would react negatively. And so, I form the following hypothesis:

**Hypothesis:** I can raise prices by 1.5%, attributed to keeping up with general inflation, with no material loss of customers and without materially increasing the risk of future churn.

And in the spirit of learning and experimentation, that hypothesis can be tested, and quickly verified or rejected based on the results. In the objective-driven approach, I am more likely to use' a hypothesis than a forecast due to the many different potential "causes" which may not have a ready-to-use forecast. In addition, the hypothesis-based approach provides more freedom to try something that may not have ever been tried, whereas forecasts are typically based on the analysis of only what has been done in the past, as recorded in the historical observations.

In the objective-driven approach, it is possible to develop a hypothesis, quickly test it, draw conclusions, and then revise the hypothesis and repeat the processes based on educated guesses about improving the results.

## Benefits of the Objective-Driven, Hypothesis-Based Approach

While the **cause-and-effect** (forecast-assisted) approach can be insightful and interesting, the **objective-driven** (hypothesis-based) approach is generally advantageous, especially for trying actions that have never been tried before. Key benefits of the **objective-driven, hypothesis-based approach** can be summarized as follows:

- **Focus**: It keeps primary focus on the desired objective, and it tries to ignore any potential option that will not help achieve it, thereby removing clutter from the thought process.

- **Engagement of Creative Thinking:** Because there is no pre-determined cause-and-effect forecasting model driving the process, decision-makers are free to explore multiple ways to accomplish the objective. Instead of just thinking, "How much will demand shrink if I increase prices by 3%?" creativity might be stimulated by the question, "In what ways might I increase profits without losing customers?" It doesn't necessarily have to be a price move, as shown above.

- **Provocation of Learning and Experimentation:** Because a hypothesis is a "best guess" at a potentially achievable outcome, it naturally invites efficient ways to experiment and observe results to quickly learn and adapt. Since forecasts are often seen as predictions of a future reality, when they fail it is often seen as either an easily-explainable short-term observation that is not

- really a failure or a failure of the whole system, not just another step in the learning process.

- **Freedom from Relying on Forecasts:** In the world of cause-and-effect decision-making, which depends on an accurate forecast to make decisions, companies often run into decisions that can't be made because there is not sufficient data to produce an accurate forecast. If your process has become dependent on a forecast, this lack of sufficient data will stall you. This is not the case in a world of objective-driven decision-making and hypothesized outcomes. You can test any hypothesis regardless of whether or not there exists sufficient data.

The point I am trying to make here is that hypothesis-based decision-making is generally superior, compared to forecast-dependent decision-making. This doesn't mean that a forecast is not helpful or interesting. Data analytics and forecast development can be insightful and educational. But the freedom of **hypothesis-based** decision-making simply cannot be achieved in forecast-dependent decision systems.

## The Fatal Flaw of Most Forecasting-Based Systems

Forecast-based decision systems typically suffer from a few problems, which can have disastrous results on their decision outputs. The most prevalent of these problems is the potential for wildly misguided answers because of data sparsity and/or data inaccuracy.

In the segmenting of forecasting entities, there is a constant trade-off between forecast fit and data sufficiency. In order to increase accuracy, it is preferable to segment by many dimensions and attributes. But that very act of segmentation causes increased data sparsity.

What data scientists typically find is that there will be a few segments which have sufficient data to produce very reliable forecasts, but data for the majority of the segments will be too sparse to produce reliable results. The default remedy for this problem is to roll up the data to higher level groupings. Unfortunately, this is not really a justifiable solution. Even though grouping these sparse, yet potentially unrelated, observations produces more available data, it does not solve the fundamental problem of data sparsity.

To illustrate this problem, let's say you want to forecast the weight of individuals based on their age. Your data contains plenty of observations of individuals between the ages of 15 and 65, but you have data sparsity in five of your predefined segments:

- only three observations in ages 0–2
- no observations in ages 3–5
- only one observation in ages 5–10
- only two observations in ages 10–15
- only two observations in ages 65 and older

You have determined that in order to produce a body-weight forecast, you need at least eight total observations. Since none of these groups have enough data to produce a forecast on their own, you roll them all up into one super segment that includes people of all the age groups. And every one of these eight individuals gets the same forecasted weight of 122 pounds. Yes, your system is producing a forecasted weight of 122 pounds for all three babies under three years old. Two full-grown, 66-year-old men receive the exact same forecast—122 lbs. This is an example of what happens when you roll-up data to the next level in the hierarchy to address data sparsity. This is an overly extreme example, but what if the decision system we are talking about is a drug-dispensing system based on age? Would you feel comfortable giving a 25-pound baby a drug dosage calculated for a 122-pound average human?

This is the fatal flaw found in many forecast-based decision systems—they perform well in the highly populated segments, but they break down when they have to handle data sparsity, which is a common feature in almost all segmentation schemas.

## The Cost of Being Wrong

Through much of my career, a great deal of attention was put on forecast accuracy as the measure of the quality of a price optimization system. I finally figured out that, most of the time, this was misguided. The attention was more about the hype of the seemingly magical powers of a forecasting model that could "predict" the future than it was about the actual **value** enabled by having a better forecast.

If a million-dollar forecasting system helps you save hundreds of dollars by avoiding bad decisions, it may be great, but it's not worth it.

If you only had one shot to get it right, and the cost of getting it wrong were unfathomably high, I would understand this concern over forecast accuracy. For example, if you were going to leverage billions of dollars of other people's money to bet on a stock, and you would either win big or lose big, I would understand the concern over forecast accuracy. But if I'm trying to decide whether I charge $8.99 or $9.00, and choosing wrong means I lose one cent on

100 transactions until I can correct it tomorrow, then it's probably not worth making a fuss over forecast accuracy.

## Most Pricing Actions Are Reversible

The reality is this: Most pricing decisions are not permanent, and for the most part, they are easily corrected. If I raise the price of a product by 2%, and customers don't like it, what's the worst that can happen? Relationship buyers probably won't leave, though they might complain. I may see a slow-down in new customer sales. But results probably won't be too disastrous, and I can always bring the price back down to the original level, if necessary, without too much consternation. And I've just had a learning moment. Of course, there are always some exceptions to this. But for the most part, pricing decisions are testable and correctable.

Now the important question: **How would I have behaved differently if I'd had an expensive forecasting system that told me a few customers would complain, and I might even lose a couple of price-sensitive customers?** If the answer is that I would have chosen not to conduct the actual experiment because the forecast indicated the results would not be good, then I have just proven the earlier point—that forecast-based systems lead to closed-minded avoidance of learning opportunities. I would have avoided the decision, made no incremental profits, and learned nothing more about my customers. Just because a forecaster tells you something bad might happen doesn't mean you shouldn't take risks and attempt to find new successful strategies to learn more about your customers.

## Designing Mitigation and Reversibility into Strategy Decisions

It is unfortunate that many companies have foregone good strategy, letting optimization solutions define the default pricing strategy for short-term profit maximization. Even companies who have not yet invested in pricing optimization systems have fallen victim to the default strategy of trying to maximize profits, just by listening to the sometimes compelling sales pitches of consultants and solution providers.

Good strategy is more than just the process of trying to "optimize" pricing decisions to maximize profits. Good strategy is the process of constantly moving the company to a better position to achieve better profitability in the future. That means every move should help the company learn more, expand options, and improve their position, enabling a better "next move" in the future.

This means pricing actions should be designed to test a hypothesis, learn about new opportunities, and move the company to a better position for a future move. Risk mitigation and reversibility should be designed into pricing actions. This is the essence of good strategy.

Just as it would be ludicrous to try to win a chess match in a single move, it makes no sense to think that there is some single optimized price that, once discovered, will lead to the optimal outcome.

Because of the inherent uncertainty involved in pricing, it is wise to design pricing actions that allow big learning opportunities, without locking into an irreversible future. This is typically accomplished by making pricing actions "temporary in nature" and minimizing changes in customer expectations around price and value. Making pricing actions "temporary in nature" means testing pricing reductions as "limited time offers" which "expire in 30 days." Advertising price incentives as temporary discounts or rebates to be paid later can distance the pricing incentive from the customer's expectation of price or value. Then, after multiple tests that have proven to be successful, companies can decide whether or not to make the experimental pricing actions more permanent, if they so desire, without weakening their strategic position.

Most price increases are easily reversible, unless customers who pay extremely high prices become upset to find out that they could have waited a few days and gotten much cheaper prices. An easy way to prevent this is either to keep price increases in small increments or to offer a limited-time price protection guarantee, which allows customers to benefit from any lower available price within a certain timeframe of their purchase.

If pricing actions are easily reversible, the cost of making a mistake becomes quite small, and more hypotheses can be tested. This is an important part of any good pricing strategy.

## Thinking in Terms of Break-Even Outcomes

Thinking in terms of break-even outcomes is an efficient way to make decisions in pricing (and probably most other aspects of our lives as well). The opposite of break-even outcomes is scenario modeling, which can be very taxing and still not lead to a beneficial result.

What does it mean to think in terms of break-even outcomes? The answer is actually quite simple. For any problem we face where a decision must be made, and where uncertainty exists regarding a range of possible outcomes, we naturally take a shortcut by finding the break-even threshold—the outcome that makes us at least as well off, if achieved, as we were before.

As a simple example, let's say I am considering buying the mineral rights to a piece of land that is thought to have over $20 million of oil to be harvested. It will cost $1 million to extract whatever oil is there, and the land mineral rights are priced at $1 million. So, the total investment would be $2 million. This is the cost. To determine the break-even outcome, I need to know the benefits and the units of benefit. For this example, let's say the benefits are extracted oil sales, and the units are $1 increments. What is the break-even outcome in terms of oil sales? Keeping it simple, I just divide the cost of $2 million by the $1 units of oil sales, and the break-even units equate to two million, shown in the table below:

| Break-Even Calculation | Incremental Cost (land+extraction) | Unitary Benefit (oil sales) | Break-Even Units (oil sales of $1) |
|---|---|---|---|
| ROI Break-Even | $2,000,000 | $1 | 2,000,000 |

Now all I need to do is figure out how likely it is that I'll achieve at least the break-even outcome, and I can make my decision. In the example above, if I believe I'll be able to easily get five million units of oil sales, I can feel very comfortable that I'll surpass the break-even value. And my decision to do the project is easy.

Alternatively, I could create a more complex decision structure by forecasting the probability of different potential extraction amounts in order to create a total, probability-weighted expected value of the investment, but that's not very efficient, and it usually doesn't improve the quality of the decision.

## Three Different Types of Break-Even

There are three different types of break-even calculations you can use. I recommend using all three simultaneously.

- **Profit break-even**: What has to happen to keep the actions and results profit neutral over a 12-month period?

- **ROI (Return on Investment) break-even**: What outcomes are required to achieve a positive ROI investment?

- **Company valuation-based break-even**: What outcomes are required to keep the company valuation neutral (requires a company value calculator)?

Break-even calculations are all about the incremental costs vs. the incremental benefits. Every pricing action has an incremental net cost. This can include foregone margins from existing or expected business when you lower a price or add a discount. It can also include the incremental costs to communicate the new pricing strategy to internal employees, resellers, and customers. It can include any additional administrative costs necessary to process any new pricing. You will need to decide what costs you will include in your break-even calculation.

Let's look at an example of a company that is considering expanding their trial incentive discount from 10% to 30%, an incremental 20% discount. For simplicity, let's include only the costs of foregone profits from our expected trial customers who would have otherwise purchased with a 10% discount. Let's say our current expectation is that, with a 10% discount, we are getting 100 new customers each month, and they typically purchase $500 (at list price) during the one-month trial period. After the 10% discount is applied, their spend is $450. Multiplied by 100 customers, that would total $45,000 in expected revenues each month from trial customers. An additional 20% discount would cost another $100 per customer, or $10,000 total. This is the cost.

Now, in order to calculate a break-even, we need to figure out what benefits will offset the additional $10,000 of incremental costs. If the average new trial customer typically ends up doing an average of $3,000 of business in the eleven months after the trial period at a profit margin of 15%, we should expect each incremental customer to produce $450 of additional profits. This is the unitary benefit. Now we can calculate the break-even quantity of incremental new customers by dividing the cost by the unitary benefit, as shown in the table below:

| Break-Even Calculation | Incremental Cost (foregone profits) | Unitary Benefit (profit per incremental customer) | Break-Even Incremental Units (new customers) |
|---|---|---|---|
| Profit Break-Even | $10,000 | $450 | 22.2 → 23 |

From this, it is clear that the profit break-even quantity is 22.2 new customers. If we round up to 23, we can see that if the new trial incentive produces a 23% increase in new customers, the new incentive will be "profit neutral" in the first 12 months. Anything above a 23% increase is a bonus from a 12-month profit perspective.

But that just covers the benefit needed to get to a profit-neutral position within the first 12 months. If new trial customers churn at a rate of 15% per year after the first year, it would be logical to expect the average incremental customer to produce $3,000 of profits over the customer lifetime (CLV = Annual Profit ÷ Churn Rate; $450 ÷ .15 = $3,000). If we instead use $3,000 as the unitary benefit, we get a much lower ROI break-even number, shown in the table below:

| Break-Even Calculation | Incremental Cost (foregone profits) | Unitary Benefit (profit per incremental customer) | Break-Even Incremental Units (new customers) |
|---|---|---|---|
| Profit Break-Even | $10,000 | $450 | 22.2 → 23 |
| ROI Break-Even | $10,000 | $3,000 | 3.3 → 4 |

When you look at the total return on investment, you really need only 3.3 incremental customers (four if you round up) to make a positive ROI. This means, if you can increase trial customer conversions by 4%, it is worth the additional 20% incentive from an investment perspective.

But what if you want to see what the additional growth rate does to the overall company value? Let's say that the current company value is based on current **annualized profits** of $3.6 million, and the company is growing at a **net growth rate** of 5% based on a **new-customer revenue growth rate** of 20% and a **customer revenue churn rate** of 15%. Using a **present-value discount rate** of 15%, the company valuation is currently $36 million. The value calculator shows that increasing the **net growth rate** from 5% to 6% would increase the value of the company by 11.1%, or approximately $3.996 million. Increasing the **net growth rate** from 5% to 6% would mean increasing the **new-customer revenue growth rate** by 5%, from 20% to 21%. Translating this to new trial customers per month would give a value of five (5% of 100). Since we are talking about annual numbers, we would need to multiply the monthly cost of $10,000 by 12 to get $120,000. Since an incremental 60 new customers per year would result in an increase of $3.996 million in company valuation, each incremental customer would be worth $1/60^{th}$ of that, or $66,600 of incremental company value per incremental customer. The resultant valuation break-even would be as shown in the table below:

| Break-Even Calculation | Incremental Cost (foregone profits) | Unitary Benefit (profit per incremental customer) | Break-Even Incremental Units (new customers) |
|---|---|---|---|
| Profit Break-Even | $10,000 | $450 | 22.2 → 23/mo |
| ROI Break-Even | $10,000 | $3,000 | 3.3 → 4 /mo |
| | Annualized Cost | Incremental company Valuation (per new incremental customer) | Break-Even Incremental Units (new customers) |
| Valuation-Based Break-Even | $120,000 | $66,600 | 1.8 → 2 /yr<br><br>Less than 1 per month |

What this shows is that, if you are looking at the impact to the valuation of the company, you would need only two new customers per month to justify the value impact to the company of spending an additional $120,000 of profits.

Now that you have calculated three different types of break-even values, you can easily see the range of potentially justifiable outcomes.

The break-even outcome is helpful in that it provides a quick benchmark for considering the likelihood of success with a particular strategy. If, looking at the break-even outcome, you feel very confident that you will easily exceed that benchmark, you should take that as a green light to proceed with your strategy. If not, you may want to pause and potentially consider a different strategy.

## The Addition of the Hypothesized Outcome to the Break-Even Values

The hypothesized outcome is a best guess of what you believe will happen as a result of a strategy or action. In the example above, perhaps you believe that tripling the incentive as you have will double the number of conversions. This would mean that you believe the 20% conversion rate would rise to a 40% conversion rate. So, the hypothesized outcome is a 40% conversion rate. And you can compare the hypothesized outcome to the various break-even rates by adding a column to the break-even table, as shown below:

| Break-Even Calculation | Incremental Cost (foregone profits) | Unitary Benefit (per incremental customer) | Break-Even Units (new customers) | Hypothesized Incremental Units |
|---|---|---|---|---|
| Profit Break-Even | $10,000 | $450 | 22.2 → 23/mo | 100/mo |
| ROI Break-Even | $10,000 | $3,000 | 3.3 → 4 /mo | 100/mo |
| | Annualized Cost | Incremental Valuation (per new customer) | Break-Even Units (new customers) | Hypothesized Incremental Units |
| Valuation-Based Break-Even | $120,000 | $66,600 | 1.8 → 2 /yr<br><br>Less than 1 per month | 1200/yr |

This example shows how the hypothesized outcome can be massively larger than the break-even outcomes. Even using the profit break-even number as a comparison, the hypothesized outcome is more than four times more. This indicates that this investment is a very easy decision. Most pricing decisions are like this in that they don't require a great deal of precision in the hypothesized outcome, especially when the ballpark estimates are so lopsidedly in favor of taking the action.

Why is the hypothesized outcome important? Because it gives an initial expectation and a beneficial checkpoint in the learning process. Forcing yourself to put a best guess out there gives you the opportunity to test your gut instincts. Record your hypothesis, and then see if the results are statistically in the range of your hypothesis, so you can accept or reject it. If you accept the hypothesis after the results come in, then your gut feel was good. If you reject it, you have a learning opportunity.

By hypothesizing and experimenting, you are continuously learning and developing your creative problem-solving skills. It's important to think in terms of hypothesized outcomes and break-even outcomes because it employs both sides of your brain to achieve your high-priority objectives. The break-even calculation comes from your logical, mathematical side, and the hypothesized outcome comes from your creative and intuitive side.

And as you think about the objectives you wish to accomplish, your mind will grow more expansive in terms of imagining possible solutions to reach your desired objective.

## Chapter Summary

Effective pricing strategies include a series of sequential steps to identify opportunities, hypothesize results, take controlled actions, observe results, draw conclusions, improve your position, and revise your strategy. In this chapter, we covered some important lessons on why objective-driven, hypothesis-based approaches to pricing strategies are so advantageous in comparison with traditional cause-and-effect, forecast-dependent pricing decisions, including the following:

- Forecasting systems encourage pricing decision-makers to place responsibility and blame on the forecast rather than their own actions, even though most people agree that forecasts will almost always be wrong.

- Using a hypothesis-based approach encourages creativity and the consideration of solutions that have never been tried, leading to accelerated learning and improvements.

- Objective-driven problem solving is more expansive than the cause-and-effect approach because it is not limited to focusing on only one presumed set of causal actions. Objective-driven approaches allow for creative and compound

- solutions that can easily be transformed into a single hypothesis that can be tested and revised if needed.

- Even though much attention has been devoted to forecasting systems over the last few decades, most of these pricing systems continue to suffer from data sparsity in many of the forecast entities. For this reason, the value of forecasting systems tends to be vastly overrated for pricing decision-making.

- In reality, most pricing decisions can be reversible, especially if mitigation and reversibility are designed into the pricing action.

- Advancements in pricing strategy are achieved when pricing actions are designed to produce both the hypothesized strategic benefit and the potential to learn from the results of the pricing action.

- Thinking in terms of break-even outcomes allows for rapid evaluation of potential pricing actions with a built-in outcome hypothesis (which can always be used in the absence of another outcome hypothesis).

While there are clearly times that forecasting and automated decisions can improve processes and outcomes, most of the larger-impact pricing-strategy-driven outcomes are achieved by using creative thinking to take advantage of high-impact opportunities, using the scientific method to formulate questions, develop hypotheses, conduct experiments, measure results, and draw conclusions. Automated decision systems should be reserved for after the large strategic questions have largely been settled, and the organization is looking to fine tune.

---

*Next chapter preview: In order to achieve the largest potential impact to the value of the business, it's important to understand that certain actions will have a bigger impact than others. The 80/20 principle is a concept that will improve your perspective and allow you to focus your efforts on those opportunities that will have relatively larger impacts on the overall business.*

## CHAPTER 14

# Applying the 80/20 Principle

*Believe it or not, it's not only possible to accomplish more by doing less, it's mandatory.*

—Tim Ferris

*The 80/20 principle is so prevalent in so many aspects of business and life that Richard Koch, one of my all-time favorite nonfiction authors, wrote a whole book about it—***The 80/20 Principle***. Learning about the 80/20 principle and truly understanding it will give you a tremendous advantage over others who fail to prioritize, and instead insist that "everything" is high priority. In both pricing and life, the 80/20 principle can enable shortcuts to success by finding smarter ways to increase productivity and double down on higher-yield investments.*

Efficiency and effectiveness are almost universally portrayed as the hallmarks of productivity and results. Over the last few decades, "Work smarter, not harder" has been at the forefront of the more progressive literature on achieving more output in a culture-friendly manner. The implication is that higher productivity and its commensurate rewards await those who are willing to find ways to work smarter, cut out wasted efforts, and replace them with higher-value activities.

The Tim Ferris quote above embodies a new style of progressive thought on productivity that it is catching the attention of people across the full spectrum of life's pursuits: business, athletics, games, investments, technology, etc. Anywhere productivity matters, people are finding ways to be ultra-successful in the aspects of their lives they deem most important. They are achieving new levels of success by adopting insights from *The 80/20 Principle*.

# What Is the 80/20 Principle?

The **80/20 principle** (which is sometimes called the **Pareto principle**) basically states that, in systems of variable output, typically 80% of the output is produced by 20% of the inputs, and the remaining 20% of the output is produced by the remaining 80% of the inputs. Explained another way, when you rank observations by a particular metric in descending order, you will often observe that the first 20% of the observations account for 80% of the total metric. The long tail, which includes the other 80% of the observations, conversely accounts for only 20% of the total metric.

Most people in the business world are somewhat familiar with the reference to the 80/20 principle, usually in the context of their own business. It's not uncommon to see references such as:

• 20% of customers make up 80% of revenues or profits

• 20% of the products generate 80% of the revenue

• 20% of the salespeople generate 80% of the sales

• 20% of the stores make up 80% of the profits

I am sure you are familiar with your own favorite 80/20 observation. These types of observations are most common anytime you have a system with variable output.

And even though it is called the 80/20 principle, it applies to any sort of disparate productivity, whether it's 80/20, 90/10, 70/30 or anything in-between. If a relatively smaller proportion of inputs are responsible for a relatively larger proportion of outputs, it's all applicable under the 80/20 principle.

# Why the 80/20 Principle Exists

The 80/20 rule is actually quite easy to explain. It boils down to variability in outputs, combined with the tendency of more successful outcomes to be given the opportunity to repeat, along with the compounding nature of investments.

### An Illustration from Baseball

Let's look at a baseball analogy. With a hypothesis that 20% of the players hit 80% of the home runs, we can dig into Major League Baseball data from 2019, the last full year of play, prior to the publishing of this book. It turns out that, in 2019, a record-setting 6,776 home runs were hit. If you take 30 teams and multiply by their 40-man rosters you get 1,200 total MLB players, 20% of which would total 240 players. Adding up all the home runs hit by the top 240 players adds up to 5,466 home runs (Source: mlb.com Statcast). And what would you guess you would get if you divided 5,466 by 6,776? That's right. Exactly 80.7%. It doesn't always happen that way. But it did in 2019. Twenty percent of the players accounted for 80% of the home runs.

Why does this happen? Is it just variability in player abilities?

Let's look at a comparison of the two groups in the table below:

| Metric | Top 20%<br>240 players | Bottom 80%<br>960 players |
|---|---|---|
| Average Home Runs per Season | 22.8<br>home runs per player | 1.4<br>home runs per player |

The data shows that the top 20% of players are 15 times (1500%) better than the bottom 80% of players in total home run output for the season. But does that mean they are 1500% better players in general? The answer is no.

When you look at batting average, a key measure of hitting proficiency, the bottom 50 players average .193, and the top 50 players average .277. Yes, the top players are better, but they're not 1500% better. They are 43% better (according to batting average), but they produced 1500% more home runs. Why? Because they were given many more opportunities. The top 50 players in this list had 545 at bats on average—meaning they were given, on average, 545 opportunities to hit a home run. However, the bottom 50 players who have any recorded stats were given only 7.6 opportunities, on average. The top 50 players got 71 times more opportunities than the bottom 50 players. Baseball managers were smart enough to know that their better hitters had a higher probability of hitting a home run, so they gave better hitters more opportunities.

This is why the 80/20 principle exists—because things that are even moderately more successful tend to get more focus, more opportunity, and more ability to experience compound growth. To bring this back to the business statistics discussed earlier:

- Perhaps 20% of the customers account for 80% of the revenues because everyone tends to focus on the customers with higher revenue potential.

- Perhaps 20% of the sales reps produce 80% of the sales because they are given the best leads and opportunities.

- Perhaps 20% of the products generate 80% of the sales because salespeople tend to sell the most popular products.

The main message of the 80/20 principle? Do more of what yields more and do less of what yields less.

# Critics: That's It? Just Do More of What Yields More?

Critics could look at the main message of the 80/20 principle and scratch their heads in mild disgust: "That's it? Just do more good stuff and less bad stuff? Where's the magic? Where's the a-ha discovery?"

It could be argued that not only is this lesson obvious, but also somewhat patronizing. It implies that there is an unlimited supply of high-yield opportunities, and people are missing them because they simply prefer to spend time on lower-value opportunities, or worse, they're too ignorant to know the difference.

Critics of the 80/20 principle might appropriately observe that it exists only because of the natural variability in output from similar inputs. Therefore, they see it as more of an observation to be observed than a strategy to be implemented.

In the baseball example above, how smart do you have to be to know that you should give your better players more opportunities? It is entirely possible that critics may dismiss the **80/20 principle** as a nice buzzword that has little relevance in how business decisions are actually made. And while I agree that the 80/20 principle is not universally applicable to all situations, I think it would be a mistake to dismiss it all together.

# The Real Power of the 80/20 Principle

If you look a level deeper, I believe you can find some incredibly valuable insight lurking beneath the surface-level dismissals of what may seem overly obvious and largely irrelevant.

And this is the insight: Not universally, and not in every situation, but frequently enough to be incredibly powerful...you can find valuable shortcuts that can massively improve outputs by doing things in a different (smarter) way, and it's often worth the time and effort, in an extremely lopsided way, to pause lower-yield efforts in order to find these smarter paths to success.

### An Illustrative Story: The Room with a Million Logs – Part 1

To illustrate the point, let's say you enter a large room with one million logs, each 18 inches in length, that need to be split into four pieces lengthwise. There is a single bed in the corner. One ax and a sharpener lie on the floor. There is nothing else in the room. You are told that you may not leave the room until all the logs are split. You will receive a brief meal every four hours, and the lights will be turned off for eight hours each night for you to sleep. As soon as you finish splitting the logs, you will be given $1 million.

From your previous experience, you know that you have the ability to manually use the ax to split the logs at a rate of approximately one log per minute (because you are obviously in incredible physical shape). You do some quick calculations in your head, and you realize that, using your normal process, it will take one million minutes of regular work to accomplish the task. So, if you can work 14 hours per day, you can finish the task in approximately 40 months or 3.3 years. The $1 million payoff at the end will represent approximately $300K per year. And so, you get to work to finish the task using your traditional method of splitting logs with an ax at a pace of one log per minute. And, just as expected, you finish the task in exactly 3.3 years and get your million dollars.

## Part 2 – Now with Forced Innovation

Now let's replay the same story, but this time you are given one more piece of information: The person who was there in the exact same situation before you split all the logs and got out in 90 days.

Now, that changes things.

After hearing this, you decide that if someone else can do it, you can do it too. So, you decide to restructure your work so you can discover the innovations necessary to do it faster. You determine that you will spend only two hours per day splitting logs, and at least 12 hours per day dreaming up better approaches to splitting the logs.

I won't tell you how you did it, but I will tell you the ending. You were able to split all the logs and reach your million-dollar payday in 60 days, even faster than the person before you.

Now, let's examine your productivity. On average, each split log was worth $1. Because you could split 60 logs in one hour, your productivity was $60 per hour. And we know that you spent two hours per day for 60 days manually splitting logs. In total, you generated $7,200 of productivity by manually splitting logs for 120 hours in a 60-day period.

Overall, you generated $1 million of productivity over that 60-day period. If you subtract the $7,200 of productivity created from manually splitting logs, you have $992,800 of productivity, which came from the remaining 720 hours, for an average hourly productivity of $1,379 per hour. If you compare that to the productivity of manually splitting logs, the $1,379 is roughly 2200% bigger than the $60 per hour productivity.

That means you forced yourself to be more productive by getting smarter. And, on average, whatever thinking work you did to improve your productivity was well worth it. This illustrates the power of the growth mindset and the recognition of potentially endless possibilities for positive change.

## The Deeper Meaning of the 80/20 Principle

The 80/20 principle is all about finding shortcuts to productivity by "getting smarter," for lack of a better way to describe it. There are better solutions to be discovered, but they will never be discovered if we spend all of our time on lower-yield efforts.

As this story was told, the difference in productivity between Part 1 and Part 2 was massive. But what if, instead of shaving off three-plus years, you were only able to shave six months off the total time by spending most of your time trying to think of more efficient ways to accomplish the task? Wouldn't it still have been an improvement worth the switch? Of course it would.

In situations like what was described in this story, the increased productivity from thinking of smarter solutions doesn't typically come uniformly, but rather in short spurts of time when the more productive discoveries are made. Perhaps a single one-hour time period frames the discovery of something so powerful that it halves the effort needed to accomplish the task—in the story scenario, that would have been a $500,000 hour.

Imagine if that single flash of brilliance happened in hour 500. Imagine how you felt in hour 499, having invested over 70 days with no major breakthroughs, perhaps second-guessing whether the thinking time would have been better spent just chopping logs. And what if you had changed your mind and decided to go back to just chopping logs right before the hour that gave you your breakthrough revelation.

There are no guarantees. But the universal history of progress shows that smarter solutions are there to be found in almost everything. Impactful ideas come because time is consciously reallocated from a known lower-yielding effort to the effort to find smarter solutions.

# How to Use the 80/20 Principle to Your Advantage

The 80/20 principle has deeper meaning and benefits than simply identifying disparities in outputs and doubling down on more productive input investments. There is a benefit to engaging in the 80/20 mentality—a pervasive consciousness that there is room for improvement and that you can attain massive improvements in productivity through innovative thinking and literally getting smarter about the process. The 80/20 mentality is an extension of the growth mindset, which approaches problems with an openness to change and experimentation. When you expect a universe of infinite possibilities, new solutions will come to you.

Using the full power of the 80/20 principle means following four driving principles:

1. **Create time and space for thinking.**
    a. Allocate high-value thinking time.
2. **Adopt the 80/20 mentality.**
    a. Everything is an opportunity to improve.
    b. Question everything.
    c. Make everything a learning experiment.
3. **Take actions to enable 80/20 benefits.**
    a. Simplify.
    b. Reallocate time.
    c. Reallocate investments.
4. **Analyze and measure.**
    a. Analyze to find opportunities.
    b. Measure the benefits of every action and change in strategy.

We will cover each of these in detail below.

## 1. Create Time and Space for Thinking

The first step to start taking advantage of the 80/20 principle and its related opportunities is to create time and space to think. This is extremely important. As we saw in the log-splitting scenario, thinking time can be the highest yielding investment. The first step is to proactively schedule time just for thinking. To make this possible, you may need to clear some lower-yield activities off your plate. After that, you can use your newly allotted thinking time to find ways to get more thinking time.

I recommend everyone set aside at least 30 minutes per day for thinking time. This time can be used to solve an urgent or important problem. Or it can be used to find high-impact opportunities for improvement and to ask key questions to drive new and valuable ideas.

There is an old saying that "necessity is the mother of invention." Thinking time allows you to review high impact necessities and proactively drive inventive solutions and improvement ideas. Don't let a false sense of urgency drive you to make the wrong decisions. Take time to pause and think. Focus on your ultimate objectives and think about what might be preventing your desired level of success.

## 2. Adopt the 80/20 Mentality

The second step to unleashing the benefits of the 80/20 principle is to adopt the 80/20 mentality. This includes three important aspects:

**1. Everything is an improvement opportunity**: The first aspect of the 80/20 mentality is to see everything—your pricing strategies, your customer base—as an improvement opportunity, just waiting to be made better. When you see everything as an improvement opportunity, two great things happen. First, you see improving it as a worthy challenge, and you stimulate your mind. Second, you realize there is room for improvement. Conversely, when you look at the world as a collection of mostly solved problems, you typically don't feel any urgency to make improvements. This part of the mentality is very important.

**2. Question everything:** The second important aspect of the 80/20 mentality is to constantly formulate questions, looking for new possibilities. This includes questions like: What if I could double the customer acquisition rate? What would make more customers want to buy from me? In what ways might we improve customer revenues? Remember, the scientific method is about formulating open-ended questions and developing new ideas that can be tested. Generating questions shortens the distance between your current situation and new and improved strategies and results. It's the difference between an active mind and a passive mind.

**3. Make everything a learning experiment**: One way to learn is to observe what's happening. A more proactive way is to consciously formulate testable experiments. Get in the habit of thinking in the pattern of the **scientific method**: Analyze the situation; formulate questions; develop a hypothesis; conduct a test; observe results; draw conclusions; and repeat.

Anytime you make a pricing change, you can add a hypothesis before the fact, and then draw a conclusion after the fact, using the scientific method to test your ideas and draw important conclusions. This creates a structure for documenting key learnings. In addition, it pushes your mind to consider how reasonable a hypothesis is before taking action. Sometimes forcing a hypothesis is enough to realize something is not a good idea. Remember that leveraging the 80/20 rule is all about getting smarter about which investments have the highest return. That means it's critical to learn at every opportunity. Just like Marta's discovery of quality issues, it may be that the value in some pricing actions is derived more from the learning than from the actual monetary value of a specific action.

Adopting the 80/20 mentality helps you to easily recognize improvement opportunities and learn new things, leading to important innovations that can sometimes drive significantly better results.

## 3. Take Actions to Enable 80/20 Benefits

The third step to using the 80/20 principle to drive significant improvements is to take key actions that enable more productive outputs, specifically three key actions:

**1. Simplify**: The 80/20 principle might suggest that 80% of your complexity is unnecessary. The first key act is to remove unnecessary complexity. Complexity tends to slow things down. It takes more time to understand. It takes more time to communicate. It causes more effort on the part of your customers and co-workers. Wading through complexity is rarely a high-yield activity. When in doubt, simplify.

**2. Reallocate Time Investments:** Look at how you and your team are spending time. Categorize activities as very-high-yield, high-yield, medium-yield, low-yield, or very-low-yield. Then take decisive action to eliminate, offload, outsource, or delegate your low-yield and very-low-yield activities. If you've categorized everything as high-yield or higher, then re-index and recategorize. If everything is high priority, then nothing is. Focus on what matters most, while spending less time on what matters less. This is a good opportunity to exercise good time management, so you don't let the urgent distract you and your team from what's most important.

As in the example of the home run hitters, finding higher value activities to spend your time on is the way you give your activities and efforts more opportunities for success. It's the equivalent of a baseball manager putting the best hitter in all nine batting spots in the line-up. Of course, in baseball it's illegal to do this. But it's not necessarily illegal in your life. You can stack the deck in your favor by spending more of your time and effort on the highest value opportunities. Prioritizing your activities is the way to find out how.

**3. Reallocate Other Investment Inputs:** This is the common and obvious task of finding out what decision inputs are yielding more output than others, and then doubling down on your high-yield investments. In pricing, 80/20 opportunities are plentiful. But they don't all have the same returns. Some pricing strategies and actions will generate very large results, and some pricing strategies and actions will generate relatively small results. Pick a topic, and rank investments by performance. These are high-likelihood opportunities for improvement. If 20% of your sales reps are producing 80% of the profits, look for ways to increase investment in those sales reps. If 20% of your products are producing 80% of your revenues, look for ways to increase sales of those products. This action can apply to anything. These are the actions you discover in your thinking time.

## 4. Analyze and Measure

The last step for leveraging the 80/20 principle to drive abnormally high returns on your time, efforts, and strategies is to constantly analyze and measure key data to reveal potential opportunity areas and to gauge the success of efforts underway.

Analyzing is part of thinking, learning, and getting smarter about the business. In order to find potential opportunities, look for disparities or irregularities in the data. Wide variations often indicate the presence of 80/20 opportunities. Here are some examples of things to look for:

- Which products account for a disproportionate amount of revenues? Or profits? Or customers?

- Do you have an 80/20 situation where 20% of the customers generate 80% of the revenues? Or profits? If so, what products or services are they buying? How does their purchase frequency differ from that of other customers?

- Are certain regions or salespeople outperforming the others? If so, what do the more successful ones have in common? Is there a profile that seems to be more successful? Are they selling the same or different products?

Measuring the results of pricing actions can also point to opportunities. It's important to understand not only which pricing actions were most successful, but also why. The "why" is important to understand so you can know if the result is repeatable. Without this knowledge, it can be dangerous to repeat actions that inexplicably turned out to have a successful result. You can learn this in the stock market by buying stocks that have just had record performance— "past performance is not an indicator of future results." You have to understand the "why" in order to know if the performance is likely to repeat.

By going into the data and looking for irregularities or the existence of specific 80/20 relationships, your thinking will expand, and you will start to see opportunities that you perhaps didn't see in the past.

# Bonus Ideas for 80/20 Benefits

Here are some bonus lessons, regarding the 80/20 rule in pricing.

**Learn to say no in a positive and liberating way:** Saying yes to higher-priority activities means saying no to lower-priority activities. Saying no is a requirement. You must learn to say it. People don't like saying no because they don't like disappointing others or coming across as unwilling to help. This doesn't change the reality that you have to say no sometimes in order to succeed. The way to make it easier is to learn how to say no in a positive way. You can do this by focusing on the benefits to the person you are talking to. Here's a template I sometimes use: "I don't think we can afford to put *[the higher priority results]* at risk by letting focus become diluted. I worry that *[fill in the blank with the thing you're saying no to]* will get in the way of accomplishing what we both care about the most—*[name the higher-priority activity that will take the place of what you're offloading]*. So I'm offloading this activity to *[insert what will happen to the activity you won't be doing]*."

Let's say you realize you need to say no to the "TPS reports" in order to focus on analyzing data to find high-impact growth opportunities, which will lead to higher-value impact to the company growth rate. *"I don't think we can afford to put our company growth at risk by letting focus become diluted. I worry that spending time on the TPS reports will get in the way of accomplishing what we both care about the most—analyzing data to find high-impact growth opportunities. So, I'm offloading the TPS reports to the reporting administrator in India."*

Feel free to create your own template for saying no. But just make sure you have a good way to say no.

**Block at least 30 minutes each day to just think and reflect**: It will help you ensure that all the rest of your time is spent on the highest-value use. Thinking makes you smarter. Asking yourself questions makes you smarter. Make sure giving yourself daily time to think is a high-priority activity. In your thinking time, ask yourself questions: In what ways could I make my time investments more valuable? What do I care most about accomplishing in my life? What things could I do to improve my chance of accomplishing those things? What decisions could I improve for higher impact? What activities produce relatively low benefits? In what ways could I help other people and generate good will? In what ways could I gain new ideas to innovate a better path for accomplishing the most important goals? Write down questions like these and pull them back up in your thinking sessions.

The 80/20 Principle is an extremely valuable tool if you use it to your advantage. It works by helping you find higher quality investments for your time, energy, and focus. When you find those higher quality investments, you can achieve extraordinary results by giving your efforts more opportunities to succeed. Thinking creatively and asking provocative questions will allow you to discover opportunities that come with a high probability of success. The more you succeed from smarter investments of time, energy, focus and resources, the more you can experience the compounding effects that bring about extraordinary results. Apply this principle to your life, and let it guide you to make exponentially better pricing decisions.

## Chapter Summary

The 80/20 principle is often simply a way to marvel at disparity and variability in output. For many who see examples of the 80/20 principle, for example that 20% of the products make up 80% of the profits, or something equally insightful, the surface-level insight can lead to helpful ideas, such as reallocating sales and marketing dollars, or increasing R&D investments. But the deeper-level benefits come only to those who get beneath the surface of the 80/20 principle, along with why it exists and what actions can be taken to leverage its influence in almost any aspect of pricing or life in general. As a precursor to the chapters on specific pricing strategies, this chapter should drive a different way of thinking about how to approach pricing opportunities and how to make strategic decisions, including the following key lessons:

- The 80/20 principle exists anywhere there either is—or could be—disparity of output, indicating variable productivity.

- The obvious, no-brainer action is to prioritize investments based on their relative productivity; invest more in the inputs that result in greater-productivity outputs and less in the inputs that result in lesser outputs.

- The deeper-level lesson is to invest the time and focus to understand why the potential disparities exist in order to discover innovations beyond the obvious—to think of new and better approaches to achieve the same or more output.

- Doing more by doing less has two different meanings. First, do less of what produces relatively lower output. Second, spend more time imagining how to produce more output with relatively less effort.

- A few key practices together enable the types of game-changing innovations intended to be discoverable in the context of the 80/20 principle:

  - Allocate time for high-value thinking.

  - Adopt the 80/20 mentality: Opportunities are everywhere. Question everything. Make every major action a learning experiment.

- Take actions to enable 80/20 benefits: Simplify. Reallocate time to high-yield activities. Reallocate other investments toward higher-yielding opportunities.

- Consistently analyze and measure results to find opportunities and determine the effectiveness of strategies and actions.

- Saying yes to high-value activities means saying no to lower-value pursuits. Learn how to eliminate, offload, delegate, or outsource lower-value tasks in order to make room for efforts that will lead to much larger results—even if it's just thinking time. And learn how to say "no" in a positive way that maintains the growth mindset.

- Block a minimum of 30 minutes each day for a thinking session. Use this time to determine the most important questions to find the largest opportunities. And, like using one of your three wishes (in the genie story) to wish for more wishes, use your thinking time to figure out how to get more thinking time. Thinking is often the highest value activity you can spend your time on.

Using the 80/20 principle is an important prerequisite to improving the impact of investments in time, effort, attention, and any other scarce asset. Keep this in mind as you reflect on opportunities to use focused pricing strategies to make sizeable impacts to the value of your business.

---

*Next chapter preview:* With an eye on the highest impact opportunities and strategies, we are ready to start reviewing segment-focused pricing strategies, starting with strategies to increase the acquisition of loyal customer relationships.

## CHAPTER 15

# Focused Pricing Strategies to Increase Customer Acquisition

*New customers are the best source of new business.*

—Frank Bettger

I've now come to the important part of the book about the elements to construct focused pricing strategies to accomplish the specific objectives of acquiring, growing, and strengthening customer relationships. After all, growing the value of the company means growing the value of present and future customer relationships. One-size-fits-all pricing strategies won't be effective at driving ideal outcomes for all potential business situations. Pricing strategies to expand margins are fundamentally different than pricing strategies to attract new customers.

This chapter will cover key aspects of pricing strategies specifically tailored to increase customer acquisition. Customer acquisition is a core responsibility of many different functional groups in the organization. However, Pricing, combined with cross-functional participation, should be the primary owner of price-driven growth strategies. These strategies commonly include price incentives to motivate customers to learn about, try, and purchase products in repeat fashion.

Pricing strategies alone are not sufficient to drive maximum potential growth. In order to be successful, pricing strategies must be integrated with sales, marketing, and product strategies. Together, these coordinated growth efforts can produce the desired improvement across the core metrics of growth.

The 80/20 principle should always be in play to determine the areas of greatest potential impact. Hypothesis-based decision-making and break-even thresholds should be used to determine the dimensions and magnitude of each individual pricing strategy. This foundation will enable you, though continuous learning and experimentation, to ultimately arrive at the most effective pricing strategies.

## Why Is Customer Acquisition So Important?

For most companies, customer acquisition will be the most important lever for growing the value of the company. The fact that you have made it this far into the book indicates that you consider your company to be a growth company, and customer acquisition is the primary basis for repeatable, sustainable, and compounding profit growth. There is only so much you can sell to an existing customer, and there is only so much you can raise a price. Without new customer acquisition, your growth eventually hits a wall.

If a company can build a proven customer acquisition model that is both successful and sustainable, that company's potential growth is constrained only by its desired level of investment and its physical ability to scale operations.

And even when success has been achieved, companies can still improve upon their existing customer acquisition strategies in order to become more efficient at growing the business. Each new successful model becomes a foundation for further improvements and growth. This is why the 80/20 mentality is so important.

Ironically, despite the fact that most companies believe growth is important, very few companies have dedicated pricing strategies focused on customer acquisition, most likely because they are too busy trying to protect and expand margins. This is usually a mistake. Failing to focus pricing strategies on customer acquisition reduces the effectiveness of other non-price-related efforts to capture new customers. This not only results in partially wasted sales and marketing investments, but it also limits company growth.

For most companies, a small increase in the growth rate of new customer revenues translates to an exceptionally large increase in company value. Therefore, failing to create pricing strategies for improved customer acquisition is, in essence, the same as choosing to limit the value of the company. Very few investments can yield higher returns than investments in customer growth.

It is very possible to drive higher levels of new customer acquisition for long-term revenue growth through the use of tailored pricing strategies. Typically, the cost of that growth comes from short-term price incentives that can negatively affect short-term profitability. If your ultimate goal is to grow the present value of all future profits, you should NOT be unduly concerned with the relatively small short-term profit decreases required to unlock much larger sources of future profits.

If your company cares about growth, you should have pricing strategies specifically tailored to attract and onboard new customers. And those pricing strategies should be getting better over time.

## Tailored Incentives to Accomplish Specific Growth Objectives

As discussed earlier, many of your target customers may be heavily entrenched customers of your competition. In order to move these customers, you will likely need sufficiently large incentives to offset the switching costs these customers would bear by switching to you as their new provider.

This chapter will cover three specific types of incentives to help you achieve improved new-customer-acquisition rates:

- **learning incentives**: incentives to **learn** about your products and services
- **trial incentives**: incentives to **try out** your products and services
- **onboarding incentives**: incentives to **purchase** your products and services on an ongoing basis in order to form a new habit of buying from you

As will soon be shown, there are different ways to structure these incentives, depending on the specific situation in your markets, and what will have the most impact on your prospective customers' behavior. These customer acquisition incentives typically include one or more of the following incentive forms:

- a **discount off the price** of a product or service realized at the time of purchase—this would also potentially include free products or services
- a **credit** with some monetary value, which can be used to purchase goods and services within some pre-defined boundaries or time periods
- a post-purchase **rebate** of money spent on a particular product or service
- a **money-back guarantee**, where a customer can recover some or all of the money spent with you if they are not completely satisfied with the purchased products or services (in some cases, the amount of the guarantee can be more than 100% of the purchase price)

Customer acquisition incentives attempt to either remove obstacles or compensate a customer for acting outside of their normal process in exchange for considering, learning about, trying, and/or purchasing products or services from you. These incentives can include both monetary and/or non-monetary features.

Sometimes, especially when the value of the incentive becomes larger than the value of the purchase, the incentive works more like an "ethical" **bribe** than a discount or a guarantee. Of course, when this happens, the hope is that the customer will like the experience enough to repeat it later without the bribe.

## Customer Journey and Key Behavioral Incentives

**Customer journey** models can be helpful for outlining the steps a customer must take to become a regular repeat customer. These are very similar to customer lifecycle models, but they are more focused on the customer's point of view than the company's.

There are many different **customer journey models**. Some have three steps. Some have 25 steps. I prefer the model below because it illustrates a few different behaviors a price promotion could incentivize.

In addition, it maps nicely onto the standard universal customer lifecycle model I introduced in Chapter 10.

### Universal Customer Journey Model with Key Incentives

1. **Awareness** → *Learning Incentives*
2. **Learning** → *Trial Incentives*
3. **Trial** → *Onboarding Incentives*
4. **Onboarding**
5. **Regular Repeat Purchases (retention)**
6. **Advocacy (promoting to other customers)**

Let's assume awareness is a marketing function, and marketing will deliver on it. There are many ways to incentivize someone to learn about your product once you have their awareness. But first you need to make your potential customers aware of your incentive in order to move them to learning, trial, onboarding, etc. Most of the time, it's easier to incentivize a customer to learn about a product than it is to get them to outright buy the product. Learning about the benefits of the product can increase customers' openness to trying the product.

## The Dimensions of a Pricing Incentive

Pricing strategies for customer acquisition are largely comprised of pricing incentives to motivate customers to act or behave in a certain way. All incentives are defined by seven key dimensions:

1. **Magnitude**: the size of the incentive, typically in monetary terms

2. **Required Action**: what the customer has to do to receive the incentive

3. **Rationale**: the reason for the incentive—what outcome is desired

4. **Timing**: when the incentive is given and received by the customer

5. **Form**: defines whether the incentive is in the form of money, credits, free goods, services, warranty, refund, etc.

6. **Complexity**: how difficult the incentive is to understand or communicate

7. **Qualification**: refers to the limits of the incentive, which can be size, product scope, time limits, customer eligibility, etc.

Every incentive should have these dimensions defined before launching to customers. Any one of these dimensions can be defined to make the incentive more or less successful. For example, higher-magnitude incentives are more likely to be impactful than lower-magnitude incentives. Incentives with easier required actions are more likely to be successful than incentives with more difficult required actions. Incentives that are more immediate are more impactful than incentives designed to be received several months later. Each of these dimensions will serve as a lever you can use to shape the potency of the incentive.

These dimensions also affect the cost of an incentive. Prior to launching any incentive, the potential costs should be well understood in order to model incentive productivity.

As different strategies and structures are outlined on the following pages, you should think about how each of these dimensions could be varied to improve the effectiveness of the incentive and make it more impactful for your business.

# Learning Incentives

Although not typically at the top of the list for most pricing teams, it is both possible and sometimes advisable to incentivize customers to learn about your product through a price incentive. A simple example of this might be:

*Watch this YouTube video to learn how to get a free month's supply of coffee. The coupon code and instructions for redemption are found at the end of the video.*

The price incentive is the free month's supply of coffee. The intended behavior is for the customer to watch the YouTube video, which should help them learn about the virtues of the product. Thus, by making a free offer to them, the company is incentivizing a customer to teach themselves why they want to buy their product.

This is something that is measurable.

- You can measure how many customers watch the YouTube video.

- You can measure how many of those customers follow the directions at the end of the video to get their free month's supply of coffee.

- You can measure how many begin purchasing from you after watching the video and getting the free sample.

This is the type of incentive where Marketing and Pricing should be collaborating. Marketing generates more awareness. Pricing improves conversion rates, which could be defined as the percentage of video watchers who follow up for a free month's supply of coffee. This is just one example to illustrate the mechanics. But the offer could really be anything. It could be a 20%– off coupon code. It could be a buy-one-get-one-free offer. All of these offers are in the realm of Pricing.

If the customer is already familiar with the product or service offering, along with all the relevant benefits, learning incentives may not provide much value. On the other hand, if the customer doesn't already have a desire to use the product, or understand why they should want to use the product, a learning incentive could be a very effective way to change this.

## Trial Incentives

Trial incentives are incentives for customers to experience the product without having to bear the full economic burden of a regular purchase. To determine the potential effectiveness of trial incentives in your business, consider the following questions:

- Do customers generally show a much greater willingness to purchase the product after they have tried it?

- Do your target customers often point to uncertainty about your product as a reason for not buying?

- Does it seem like the percentage of leads that convert to the trial stage is lower than it should be?

If the answer to one or more of these questions is yes, trial incentives should definitely be under consideration as a key part of your strategy.

Measurements of the effectiveness of trial incentives should include both the number of leads that convert to trial and the number of leads that convert all the way to regular repeat customer. As we saw in the case parable with Marta and ChangeCo, it's possible to increase the trial conversion rate in such a way that the overall conversion rates actually get worse. For this reason, it's important to look at conversion rates as a whole, rather than just looking at one of the individual conversion rates that ultimately contributes to the whole.

There are five common structures for trial incentives:

1. **Discounts**
2. **Free Product Samples**
3. **Post-Purchase Rebates**
4. **Free Spending Credits** (with monetary value)
5. **Money-Back Guarantees** (which could be up to 100% or more)

All five of these structures have their own pros and cons, which shape their relative effectiveness, depending on the situation. After reviewing each structure, you should have a good idea which structure would be best in your business.

## 1. Discounts

Discounts are essentially reductions to the price of the product or service. They can come in the form of either a percentage or fixed dollar amount off the regular price of the product. Trial incentives are also typically limited to a specific quantity, dollar amount, or timeframe. Below are a few examples:

- **25% off first purchase**
- **$50 off first $100 spent**
- **30% off first $200 of purchases this month**
- **20% off all purchases that occur within 30 days of first purchase**
- **50% off first 20 units**

Discount trial incentives are usually administered as time-of-purchase coupon codes or discounts. They can be offered for trials of specific products or categories, or they can be offered across all products as a way to try out the general commerce experience.

A simple percent-off discount is typically a good structure when the customer already believes they will get benefit out of the product, and the price reduction tips the scales enough to induce the trial. However, if the customer is uncertain about whether or not they will get benefit from the product, or the customer must also overcome very entrenched buying habits or very strong product preferences, a simple percent-off discount may not be enough.

Consider the examples of toothpaste vs. paper towels. Most people are particular about their toothpaste, but less particular about paper towels. A simple percent-off discount, such as 40% off, will probably not be sufficient to get you to try a new toothpaste. However, if you were offered a free tube of toothpaste plus a $50 gift card in exchange for trying it out and providing a review, then you might think about it. Conversely a 40%-off discount might be more than enough to get you to try a new brand of paper towels. Why? Because there is little doubt that you'll be getting some benefit out of the paper towels, even if they don't end up being your favorite. But if you don't like the toothpaste, you will likely get no value out of it.

Discount trial incentives can also be ideal for customers who are predisposed to try something new. This could include customers who are looking for some new way of satisfying a preexisting need because their old solution isn't working. It could also include customers who have a new need, but don't yet have a solution. For these types of customers, a relatively small trial discount could push them to try your product first.

One of the benefits of a percentage-off discount structure is that it allows the company to offer percentages that align with the typical margin of the product. This can help companies avoid going into negative margin. A 25%-off incentive would be safe on a 28%-margin product, but not with a 10%-margin product.

Discount incentives are low-risk ways to incentivize trials for customers who are already receptive and just need a small push.

## 2. Free Product Samples

Free product samples are a great option when the customer doesn't know if they'll like the product or not, and they're not willing to take any monetary risk to find out (often because they are already happy with whatever they are currently buying). The free product trial is designed to take all of the economic risk out of the equation, so the customer can try the product if they are at least curious to try an alternative with no financial risk. One of the downsides of a free product trial is that the customer is not obligated to try the product, even if they receive it for free. Since they didn't pay for it, there's no urgency for them to experience it, and there's no cost to them if the product goes to waste. For this reason, free product trials should be used in situations when it is highly likely the customer will try the product on their own, as long as they have free access to it.

If customers are unlikely to try the product on their own, free product trials should be avoided, unless there is an acceptable mitigation to minimize wasted product.

There are a few different ways to mitigate the situation to change the odds that the customer will take advantage of the free trial:

1. Make the customer have to exert some effort to request the free product before making it available to them.
2. Give the product away in the form of a 100% rebate, contingent on a written product review.
3. Give the customer only a partial supply of the free sample until they try it and request the remaining portions. For example, a company could offer a free one-month supply, but it's offered in four weekly units. The customer must request each additional week's supply after they finish the prior week's. This is good, also, because the company learns about who likes the product enough to request more.

As in the toothpaste example above, it's possible that a customer will require something more than free samples to actually try the product. In these cases, free product trials can be packaged with other credits or rebates, but they should come with some sort of requirement for the customer to prove they are actually trying the product and not just throwing it away. This can come in the form of a customer product review or even a second purchase of the product at regular prices. It's probably worth some 80/20 thinking time to figure the best way for the customer to demonstrate proof of trial without an awkward invasion of their privacy.

Free product samples can be effective ways to get customers to try your product when a simple product discount isn't enough to make them buy it, but the product is something they're likely to try on their own once the financial cost is removed.

## 3. Post-Purchase Rebates or Credits

Post-purchase rebates can also be effective trial incentives. However, they generally require more effort on the part of the customer because they must file, track, and wait for the rebate or credit to be fully executed.

That said, if the incentive is large enough to compensate the customer for the inconvenience, a rebate structure could be an effective way to get them to set up an account, along with payment information, thereby removing friction that might otherwise get in the way of repeat purchases.

There's no rule that says the rebate can't be larger than the customer's actual spend. It is possible to offer a $150 rebate on the purchase of a $99 power tool if that's what it takes to incentivize the customer to try it out. Part of the rebate offsets the purchase price, and part of the rebate offsets the inconvenience of setting up their user account and entering their credit card information in order to remove friction on future purchases.

The difference between a rebate and a credit is simply that the rebate is a payment back to the customer, and the credit is like money, but it can only be used for future purchases from that vendor. One of the obvious benefits of offering the incentive in the form of a vendor credit is that it ensures the customer will buy more from you. This can result in additional buying inertia and reduced friction for future purchases.

Rebate incentives can be based on either a percentage off the regular price or a specific dollar amount. Percentages make it easier to control margins, and specific dollar amounts make it easier to contain the maximum cost of the rebate.

Rebate incentives can be an excellent way to "bribe" your customers into a first purchase that requires a little extra effort due to setting up accounts and payment information that will remove friction for future purchases. It is also a good structure for getting the customer to show interest (through their efforts) in the product that you'd like them to try, without worrying that they won't actually try the product or buying experience.

## 4. Free Spending Credits (with Monetary Value)

Another way to incentivize customers to try a new product or purchase relationship is to offer free monetary credits that can be used to make purchases from you. That's right. Free money. This can be a good incentive structure to get a customer to try out the experience of doing business with a company independent of any particular product. And if the buying experience is excellent, the incentive can be an effective way to acquire new customers. The incentive structure could be as simple as a dollar amount and a time dimension, such as:

*$200 to spend on any product in the next 30 days—no obligation.*

In addition to providing the customer an incentive to try out a business relationship, it can also help companies understand the product preferences of their customers, based on what the customer chooses to buy.

The beauty of giving away "free money" is that you can often get the customer to jump through a few hoops to receive it. For example, the credit could be made contingent on the customer setting up a new account, along with payment information. Or, depending on the size of the credit, you might even ask the customer to fill out a new customer survey. Whatever it is, you should make sure you ask for something that will help you sell to the customer with less friction in the future.

There are many different ways to structure free credits. One of the great aspects of gift incentives is that they can be structured in creative ways, and the customer will almost always see it as a positive gift. One creative structure could be a declining multi-month incentive, designed to reinforce recurring purchase behavior across multiple months. The following would be an example of this:

*Sign up and receive a total of $350 in shopping credits in your first three months. Receive $200 in month one, $100 in month two, and $50 in month three. No obligation.*

A multi-month incentive is typically used during the onboarding phase, but it can also be structured to incentivize both the initial trial and future purchases with slightly smaller incentives in the onboarding phase.

As with all trial incentives, the intent is that once the customer tries the product or buying experience, they will be so satisfied that they will want to repeat the purchase even if the incentive is not being offered. For this reason, it is important to ensure that the post-incentive value proposition is strong enough to attract the customer into the relationship after the incentives have run out. This is especially important with large gifts of money, as they can be expensive and have almost no teeth. For this reason, "free-money" incentives should be targeted only to high-probability prospects who are likely to convert.

Monetary credits are great for getting target customers to try out a whole customer relationship, although they can also be used to incentivize product-specific trials. Because they can be so expensive, they should be reserved for situations when there is a high likelihood of conversion after the customer samples the experience.

## 5. Money-Back Guarantee (up to 100% or More)

Most people are familiar with the well-known 100%-money-back guarantee, where a customer can return what's left of the product for a full refund if they are not completely satisfied. This structure can work great as a trial incentive because it removes nearly all the financial risk for the customer, and it costs the company nothing, as long as the customer is satisfied with the product. So, if you have a great product, this can be a very economical way to incentivize trial.

The beauty of the money-back guarantee vs. the other trial incentive structures, is that the customer pays whatever price you charge for the products or services only because they intend to benefit from them, not because they are being bribed. When a customer buys with a money-back guarantee, it tells you something. The customer buys only because they have an intention of doing business with you in the future, provided they are satisfied. With free goods or free credits, a customer might take the incentive even if they have no intention of doing business with you further.

And lately, the money-back guarantee has evolved to something that can be even more powerful and just as economical. Over the last couple of decades, the 200% money-back guarantee has come onto the scene as an even more compelling incentive to try new products or services. This means that if the customer is not completely satisfied, the company is willing to refund the customer's purchase price, plus another 100% of the purchase price. Here's an example to illustrate:

*Buy our new battery pack for $200 and try it out for 60 days. If at any time in the first 60 days you are not completely satisfied, return the battery pack and we will send you a check for $400 for your trouble. No questions asked.*

This is very compelling because, not only does it remove the entire financial risk, but it also conveys the company's high degree of confidence that the customer will be satisfied—otherwise why would the company be willing to put so much money at risk? And it doesn't have to be limited to 200%. Companies have also used this structure for 300% money-back guarantees, depending on the size of the potential inconvenience in relation to the cost of the item.

Of course, there is a possibility that customers could game a greater-than-100%-money-back guarantee just to get free money, but this can be mitigated in a few different ways. One way is by making the excess amount roughly the equivalent to the size of the inconvenience—the time and effort it would take to place the order, receive the goods, show proof of trial, and go through the administrative hassle of requesting the refund. Another way to mitigate this problem is to offer it by special invitation only to prospects that would be unlikely to behave in such a way. Along the same lines, it could be a general invitation to customers that meet specific qualification criteria.

Companies that have successfully used 200%-money-back guarantees as a trial incentive have almost universally reported that customers did not abuse the incentive very often. The impact of the few who claimed the refund was relatively small compared to the number of new customers onboarded through the incentive. Overall, the benefits largely outweighed the costs.

Some companies that offer monthly subscription services offer an ongoing 200%-money-back guarantee, but only for the last 30 days of service. This is good because it conveys to the customer that the company will always be concerned with delivering high-quality service, while at the same time limiting the company's exposure to just two months of service revenue. This same structure could be imitated by non-subscription businesses as well.

As one might expect, most CFOs are reluctant to approve this type of incentive structure because it presents the possibility of a large, open-ended risk that they can't control. But companies that have experience employing this type of promotion typically say that it is a remarkably effective trial incentive, and very few customers ask for the refund. Furthermore, you can keep the liability from getting out of control by restricting it to a limited amount and expiring the refund offer after a specific timeframe, such as 60 days or six months, or whatever is reasonable.

The money-back guarantee can be a very effective incentive structure for situations when the customer is looking for a solution, and you are confident that customers will be highly satisfied by your product or service. And for an even more compelling incentive, companies can offer a 200%-money-back guarantee, as long as the risks for abuse have been positively mitigated. Of all the structures, the money-back guarantee can be both the most economical and the lowest risk when properly mitigated.

## Summing up Trial Incentives

There are many different ways to incentivize trial. Which type of incentive will be most effective for you and your company will depend on how your target customers currently think about your product. If they are likely to desire the product without objection, then a small trial incentive or a money-back guarantee might be good enough to get them to try it. On the other hand, if your product or service is not already desired by your customers, then you may need a little more incentive to get them to move. And you may need to first incentivize them to learn about the benefits of your product or service before you can jump to incentivizing trial. Refer back to this section when you start designing incentives for your company.

# Onboarding Incentives

Onboarding incentives are those intended to make it easy for customers to buy from you during the onboarding period—the period of time it takes for customers to develop regular-repeat-buying inertia. The goal is that, by the end of the onboarding period, customers not only want to buy from you, but have already created habits and behaviors around this practice.

Unfortunately, onboarding incentives are often ignored or overlooked. Companies may successfully get customers to try their products and even get excellent ratings from those customers, but then wonder why the customers don't continue to buy the product, even after they expressed a preference for it. The reason is simply that the customers haven't yet developed the habits or momentum of making regular purchases from you yet. After the trial, the customer needs just enough incentive to continue their trial behavior for a little longer, until almost all friction is removed from the buying process. The good news is that if you find a way to incentivize your customer to try the product, you can almost always find a way to incentivize repeat purchases.

Onboarding incentives are different than other types of incentives. Because you are trying to get the customer to form a habit of buying from you in a certain way, it's important to design an incentive that reinforces the behavior and experience of regular buying, so the behavior will continue after the incentive has expired. For this reason, **post-purchase rebates or credits** are generally preferred because they are somewhat disconnected from the actual purchase experience. Here's an example:

*Buy our product for three straight months and get a rebate credit in the amount of 30% of the product price—must make a purchase of our product each month for three consecutive months to qualify for the rebate.*

Another popular approach to onboarding incentives is a declining rebate, where the larger discounts are offered up front when the relationship is young, and then, over time, as more buying inertia is being created, the discount slowly gets smaller, until it ultimately fades into the background. The following is such an example:

*Three months of savings! Get a 30% rebate on all purchases in the first 30 days. A 20% rebate on all purchases in the second 30 days (days 31–60). And 10% rebate on all purchases in the third 30 days (days 61–90).*

Although this structure introduces more complexity, it can be effective as long as it is understood by the customer. If you have a sales force, the complexity can be mitigated by having salespeople explain how the incentive works to ensure that your customers understand it.

Another approach is to structure the incentive so the customer gets the rebate after a feedback session with customer service. During this session, the customer can report on how well they like the product or service. This gives your company one more touchpoint during which the customer's temperature can be taken to gauge the likelihood of future purchases after the incentive has expired. The following is an example of such an incentive:

*Get a 25% rebate on all purchases occurring in the first 90 days by participating in a service-quality survey at the end of the 90 days.*

If, for whatever reason, the customer is not happy with some aspect of the product or service, the company has a chance to try to fix it. If necessary, the company can offer an extension of the incentive for an additional 30 or 60 days to allow time to get the problem fixed.

Pricing strategy isn't just about numbers. Pricing always wants to capture and analyze information, especially about the strength of customer relationships. These relationships are the primary asset Pricing seeks to maximize because they are the source of future profits. Since Pricing thrives on information, pricing strategies are more valuable if they provide ways to gather important information about the customer.

In summary, onboarding incentives are an important part of an overall customer acquisition strategy, and they should not be ignored. Like all incentives, they should be the product of hypothesis and experimentation until the most effective approach can be found. They should allow the customer to experience the regular long-term buying process as much as possible, so the desired habits can be formed. This means post-purchase rebates are usually the best onboarding incentive structures. Lastly, incentives with built-in mechanisms for customer feedback can be highly beneficial in gauging when onboarding incentives are no longer necessary.

## Important Considerations for Customer Acquisition Incentives

A number of important considerations apply to nearly all incentives designed to improve the rate of new customer acquisition. The following topics should be part of your thinking as you design, evaluate, and employ the incentives I've just reviewed.

## Don't Let Incentives Set Wrong Customer Expectations of Fair Price

As discussed early in this book, a customer's fair price expectations are set based on what prices they think are generally achievable in the marketplace. Poorly defined incentives can erroneously set customer expectations that the lower incentive price is the regular fair price. This generally happens for one of two reasons:

1. Providers don't clearly communicate that the incentive price is different than the regular "fair" price, or that the purpose of the incentive is to make it easier for the customer to try the product or service before purchasing at regular price.

2. Providers allow the incentive to last too long, thereby causing the customer to believe that the incentive price is the same as the regular fair price.

If your customer is allowed to believe that your incentive price is the same as the regular fair price, then you may have a difficult time trying to charge them the regular price later without upsetting them.

In order to prevent the situation where customers confuse the incentive price for the regular fair price, it's advisable to follow a few key guidelines:

1. Label the incentive as a **trial** incentive (or something appropriately similar), so the customer understands that the purpose is to get them to try the product, and it is not meant to be a long-term price inducement.

2. Make it clear that the incentive is available for a limited time or limited use, such as "valid only for first 30 days of purchases" or "valid only for first $500 purchased," so the customer has a clear expectation that the promotional price will expire.

3. Give the customer visibility into what the regular price will be after the incentive.

4. Limit the duration of the incentive to only what is needed to achieve the stated effect. Generally, 30–90 days should be sufficient.

5. If you ever run into a situation where you believe a long-duration incentive is required, it will likely be better to charge the customer the regular price, and then give the incentive in the form of a rebate or free equipment, or some other lump sum approach, so the customer will be accustomed to paying the regular, fair price after the incentive has expired.

### Avoid Making Existing Customers Angry with Discounts They Can't Have

It's important to always consider how your new customer incentives might affect the attitudes of existing customers. If existing customers see you handing out lower prices to new customers, you should expect that they will feel entitled to the same lower prices, especially if they are long-time, loyal customers. If you refuse to make the lower pricing available to them, they may become angry and question their relationship with your company. Here are a few tips to minimize and avoid this awkward situation:

1. Never offer new customers long-term pricing that is not offered to existing customers. Typically, if existing customers see a very short-term or a limited–scope promotion, they are less likely to be affected by it than if they see something that is longer in duration or scope. For example, an incentive like *Get 50% off your first $500 spent on our new website* will be much less concerning to an existing customer than an incentive that leaves it very open ended, like *New customers get 30% off all items!* It helps to make the incentive feel smaller by boxing it into a limited timeframe or dollar amount. A good test is whether or not an existing customer would be tempted to have another employee try to create a separate account just to get the savings from the new-customer incentive. If so, you probably need to go back to the drawing board. This is not a behavior you want to promote.

2. Always state the objective of the incentive in order to make it clear to existing customers that the incentive is not applicable to them. For example: *Register your business account on our online store and get a $300 credit toward your first purchases.* Clearly, the objective is to get the customer to register their account online. Existing customers who have already registered their account online would logically not qualify for this incentive.

3. Try to structure and describe the incentive such that it seems reasonable; so that it seems like a fair exchange for the prospective customer's burden; and so it doesn't sound discriminatory to existing customers. For example, a $5,000 reward for registering a new account would seem excessive and discriminatory in comparison with a $300 reward.

## Justifying the Cost of Growth

Before concluding this chapter, I must bring up an important struggle that often occurs when pricing people try to justify pricing incentive strategies to improve the acquisition of new customers. Usually, someone in the finance department questions the expected return on investment or profitability of the proposed pricing incentives. WARNING: These may not be the right comparison metrics.

If the benefit of acquiring a customer is a lifetime of revenues and profits, why would the **customer acquisition costs (CAC)** be compared to only one single year of revenues or profits? Think back to the discussion on break-even values.

In order to make good decisions and justify investment decisions, the ideal way to evaluate the investment is to use a company value calculator in conjunction with the **five sacred metrics of pricing success**.

Let's look at an example of a $100 million company that is generating $24 million of profits and is growing by 9% annually. It is estimated that it will require a pricing incentive investment of $2.5 million to improve the growth rate from 9% to 10% annually, producing another $1 million of revenues and $240,000 of profits. How do you decide whether or not to make the investment?

If you use traditional accounting metrics, you see that it will cost you $2.5 million to increase profits by $240K annually. Most CFOs will veto that. It will take over 10 years of profits just to pay back the investment to acquire the customer.

## Company-Value-Based Break-Even Benchmarks

Using a company value calculator and the company's current valuation of $400 million, the implied discount rate is 15%. The company value calculator shows that increasing the net growth rate from 9% to 10% increases the theoretical value of the company by 20% to $480 million, assuming no change in the recurring profits of $24 million. That extra $1 million of growth produces $80 million in incremental value. But the cost of the incentive will eat into the current recurring profits. Each incremental dollar of lost profits reduces the company value by approximately $20. This is shown by again using the company value calculator. With the increased growth rate, the company can lose $4 million in annualized profits to get back to its original theoretical value. The company-valuation-based break-even is shown in the table below, using a benefit-based break-even calculation (instead of a cost-based break-even calculation).

| Break-Even Calculation | Incremental Benefit (company valuation increase from increasing new revenues by $1M) | Unitary Cost (value decrease per $1 of lost profits) | Break-Even Units (profit decrease) |
|---|---|---|---|
| Valuation-Based Break-Even | $80,000,000 | $20 | $4,000,000 |

In other words, the company is better off increasing the recurring growth rate from 9% to 10%, as long as the incremental cost is less than $4 million. The break-even profit decrease or cost is $4 million in annualized profits. Since it has been estimated that the cost will be only $2.5 million, well below the break-even threshold of $4 million, the company valuation should increase by making this investment.

Sure enough, recurring profits drop from $24 million to $21.5 million, and the new theoretical value of the company grows from $400 million to $430 million. The investment of $2.5 million in growth incentives produces only $1 million of incremental revenue, and only $240K of profits, but the real value comes because of the $30 million increase in the theoretical value of the company. The opportunity cost of not making the $2.5 million investment is $30 million of company value.

## A Simpler Shortcut Approach

Although less precise, there are several industry **rules of thumb** for how to value recurring-purchase customers and how to determine whether the customer acquisition cost is justifiable. The most common is a benchmark that divides the **customer lifetime value (LTV)** by the **customer acquisition cost (CAC)**. This is called the **LTV/CAC ratio**. (Keep in mind that this LTV calculation is based on the future value of all future profits from each customer. This is not the CLV calculation which attempts to calculate the present value of all future profits.)

A simple way to calculate customer lifetime (future) value (LTV) is to divide annual profits by the expected churn rate.

In the example above, let's say there is a 4% expected annual churn rate. The LTV of the additional $1 million of revenues and $240K of profits would be calculated as follows:

**Customer LTV = $240K / .04 = $6 million**

This basically tells you that you can expect this investment to produce $6 million in profits over the lifetime of the customer(s). Calculating the LTV/CAC ratio is just simple division:

**LTV/CAC ratio = $6 million / $2.5 million = 2.4**

This means you can expect to earn back 2.4 times your original customer acquisition investment in future profits. Any value over 1 indicates that this would be a positive investment. But the important question is how it compares to other potential investments. An industry rule-of-thumb benchmark is that the LTV/CAC ratio should be 3:1 or better. However, if your company's goal is to grow, and you can only get to an LTV/CAC ratio of 2:1, there's nothing to stop you from continuing to invest. Growth is a strategic priority, even if it costs a little more than industry averages. Most companies will be better off making the investment to grow. As a rule of thumb, I would use a ratio of 1.5:1 as a good lower limit. Anything above 1.5:1 should be easily justifiable.

In the example above, I've greatly oversimplified customer acquisition costs to include only the cost of the incentive, but typically CAC includes any expense used to acquire new customers, such as advertising, sales, etc. In this case. I assumed that the only incremental expense was the $2.5 million cost of the incentive, which could be plausible because I was evaluating the difference between a 9% growth rate and a 10% growth rate.

## Other Considerations

While the investment decision should be primarily based on how the investment is likely to affect the value of the company, it will also necessarily include the company's current cash situation and access to capital, along with a realistic appraisal of the company's ability to execute the respective pricing and sales strategies. And, lastly, it should be based on the company's ability to scale to handle the incremental sales without letting the customer experience deteriorate. It is not always easy to decide.

While one could argue about the potential difference between the theoretical value of the company and the actual market value, that difference should not be so big that it makes or breaks this type of investment decision. Theoretical company value and actual market value often move together, even if there is a slight lag in timing.

The reality is this: Most companies massively underinvest in their own growth, and as a result, they make themselves vulnerable to competitors that decide to make growth a priority. If you want your company to be a Star—a market share leader in a high-growth market—company growth should be the primary focus of nearly all investments.

The five sacred metrics of pricing success and the company valuation calculator will give you the tools you need to make the case to justify the necessary investments for growth. In order to succeed, you will likely need to make the case that the opportunity cost of not making the investment is just too big. One might say, from a company valuation perspective, that it's irresponsible for a company that intends to lead the growth in your industry to forego any investments that have a positive break-even value.

# Chapter Summary

In summary, new customer acquisition must be among the most important objectives of growth-focused companies. But the pricing strategies to achieve new customer growth are more complex than just providing a lower price. Most new-customer-acquisition-based pricing strategies are defined in the form of incentives. It is important that these incentives be seen as an integral part of a standard pricing schema that is fair, rational, and transparent. All incentives are defined and constrained by seven dimensions: **magnitude, required action, rationale, timing, form, complexity,** and **qualification**.

Focused pricing strategies to increase new customer acquisition include three main categories: (1) learning incentives, (2) trial incentives, and (3) onboarding incentives.

- **Learning incentives** are useful for helping your customers learn about the benefits of your products and services and hopefully increase their desire to try or to purchase them. An example of a learning incentive might be a credit or discount that becomes available after watching an online video explaining the benefits of buying from your company.

- **Trial incentives** are useful for getting prospective customers to sample the experience of buying from you and using your products. They can come in the form of discounts, rebates, spending credits, or money-back guarantees of 100% or more. Their main purpose is to reduce the prospective customers' risk and/or the inconvenience associated with trying a product they don't know whether they will like or not.

- **Onboarding incentives** are meant to make it easy for a customer to develop recurring purchase habits with you and to make it difficult for them to switch to another provider that comes along in the future. The important aspect of onboarding incentives is to separate the incentive from the regular purchase experience in order to condition the customer to the regular buying experience they will receive when the incentive period is complete.

It is critically important to ensure that your targeted pricing incentives are seen for what they are—short-term incentives for customers to try and onboard—in order to prevent accidentally setting the wrong customer expectation for long-term, regular prices. The incentives should last no longer than necessary (rarely longer than 90 days) to accomplish their intended objective.

It is also important to make sure that NEW-customer acquisition incentives don't negatively impact the attitudes of existing customers. This may take a little extra work, but it's worth the effort to maintain good customer relationships.

When considering the cost, benefits, and ROI of acquisition incentives, it's important to look at the real opportunity cost, which is the amount of increase in the value of the company that would be foregone by not investing sufficiently in new customer acquisition incentives. Accounting and Finance departments are famous for crushing investments that would otherwise make the company a Star.

As stated at the beginning of the chapter, focused pricing strategies to increase the acquisition of new customers may be the most important strategies in terms of their potential impact on overall company growth and therefore the overall valuation of the company. Impact can be determined by using the tools enabled by the five sacred metrics of pricing success, which will be described in *Appendix E*.

-----

*Next chapter preview: In the next chapter, we will cover focused pricing strategies to increase revenue from existing customers, which is measured by the second sacred metric of pricing success.*

## CHAPTER 16

# Focused Pricing Strategies to Increase Existing Customer Revenues

*It is generally agreed that it costs 5 to 10 times more to bring on a new customer versus keeping and developing an existing one.*

—Julian Patel

For most companies who sell to repeat buyers, existing customers often represent the easiest source of incremental revenue growth, even though they are often overlooked. Theoretically, it should be easier to sell incremental products and services to existing customers because so much data already exists on what they buy, what prices they pay, and how long they've been developing purchase habits with your company. Depending on how fast your customer numbers are growing and how your customers are moving through the customer lifecycle, expanding revenues from existing customers can potentially be a very sustainable vehicle for repeatable revenue growth. This chapter is about selling more to your existing customers, independent of price-based margin changes. Growing revenues and profits by raising prices will be covered in Chapter 18.

# Revenue Growth Opportunities from Existing Customers

Increased sales to existing customers typically fall into one of two categories: (1) the organic growth of existing customer needs, and (2) selling existing customers products they're not currently buying from you. Both are important to understand and recognize.

## Organic Growth of Existing Customer Needs

The second **sacred metric of pricing success** is **existing customer revenue expansion rate (ECRER)**, and organic customer growth can definitely be a sustainable source of growth from existing customers.

In the B2B world, most customers are trying to grow their own businesses. If you are selling to customers with growing needs, you may have a sustainable source of revenue growth without doing much of anything. Just continue to serve your customers and keep them happy, and your business will grow. Depending on the industry, organic customer revenue growth can easily be as high as 2%–5% per year, and in some cases, 10% or more. The beauty of this source of customer growth is that it usually requires no additional price incentives. For this group, the most important price-related practice is keeping customer relationships strong through fair and transparent pricing. This includes avoiding any new-customer incentives that could make existing customers question the fairness of your overall pricing practices.

Even though this source of growth is typically not driven by pricing incentives, it's important for Pricing to measure, track, and understand how organic customer growth affects the overall revenue growth from existing customers. By keeping this growth separate from incentive-driven sales of additional products, you will better understand the impact and effectiveness of all of your pricing strategies and incentives.

## Selling Additional Products to Existing Customers

The big opportunity with respect to existing customers is to use pricing incentives to get them to buy additional products and services that they are not currently buying from you. But the opportunity is not equal for all companies. It exists only where customers need the other products and services you sell but aren't buying them, at least partly due to price. If the reason they are not buying those products from you is not something that can be affected by pricing incentives, then pursuing additional product sales may be a waste of time.

This is one area where research and understanding are critical. Transaction data analytics can tell you what customers are and are not buying from you, but they don't always tell you why. You could waste a lot of time, effort, and expense on pricing incentives if you don't understand why certain customers aren't buying some of the other products you sell.

Perhaps they don't need those products. Maybe they need the products, but they don't know you sell them, and it's more of a sales and marketing problem. Maybe they have a company policy that requires them to buy from multiple vendors. Maybe they are buying from another vendor because of a product feature they need, but which your company doesn't offer. And finally, maybe they are buying from other vendors simply because they can get a better price.

It's important to do research, where possible, to understand what factors are at play, so you can appropriately target any potential incentives. Research can also help you estimate the size of the potential revenue growth opportunity. That being said, there is a lot that can be learned from experimental pricing incentive strategies. Measuring how existing customers respond to specific pricing incentives can help you understand the extent to which an opportunity exists. But before putting too much effort into incentives, I recommend conducting a few customer interviews to better understand the situation.

If you find that there are opportunities to increase revenues from existing customers, then some of the pricing incentive strategies described in this chapter should be quite helpful.

## Pricing Strategies to Sell More to Existing Customers

In order to accomplish the objective of selling more to existing customers, pricing strategies must incentivize customers to act in a slightly different way. In this case, you want customers to buy additional products that they are not currently buying from you. Presumably, they're already buying those products from another vendor. Maybe the price–value equation with the other vendor is more attractive. Maybe it's just a result of buying inertia created over a long period of time. In either case, the new pricing incentives must be compelling enough to disrupt their existing behavior and get them to see a better overall value proposition by purchasing those products from you.

Even though existing customers may have already developed significant buyer inertia with your company, they may also have equally strong buyer inertia with the vendor who is currently providing them with additional products. Getting them to buy products they are currently buying from another vendor may require a larger incentive that looks more like a trial incentive than a typical volume-discount incentive. In order to win the maximum amount of additional business from your existing customers, you will likely need a combination of some of the **trial and onboarding incentives** discussed in the last chapter and the **purchase-volume incentives** I will discuss in this chapter.

There are five different types of incentives you can use, either individually or in combination with another incentive, to try to increase sales to existing customers:

1. Overall-purchase-volume incentives

2. Product-specific purchase-volume incentives

3. Portfolio-breadth incentives

4. Purchase-volume growth incentives

5. First-spend incentives (on specific products or categories)

Before getting into the specific details of each, I should restate that whatever you do, **you do not want exception pricing** (pricing out of the ordinary for an individual customer). It is imperative that customer relationships are treated with extreme care. This means always adhering to a **standard pricing and discount schema** that customers can trust, as I covered in earlier chapters. This will ensure that customers feel like they're being treated fairly as they continuously evaluate their existing relationship with your company.

As described in the last chapter, there are seven dimensions to all incentives: **magnitude, required action, rationale, timing, form, complexity,** and **qualification.** Each of the following incentives can be altered along any of these dimensions to fit your particular situation. As I review each of the five different types of revenue expansion incentives, think about how they might be modified along any of these dimensions in order to make them ideal for your business situation. Refer back to the incentive dimension section in the last chapter if necessary.

## 1. Overall-Purchase-Volume Incentives

When they are well designed and easy to understand, **overall-purchase-volume incentives** can be effective for incentivizing customers to spend more money with you. The most common and effective approach is a simple set of volume tiers, along with a simple discount or rebate percentage. Unless your point-of-sale systems are capable of calculating the discount on the spot, these incentives are usually administered via rebates, typically at the end of a defined period that could be monthly, quarterly, or annual. Rebates are also preferable if it's important to distance the incentive from the product price in a trial or onboarding period when customer buying habits are being formed. However, this distancing is not as important during regular ongoing purchases after onboarding.

A simple, overall-purchase-volume tiered incentive can look like the following:

### Earned Discount Volume Tiers

| If you spend... * | ... you get ... |
|---|---|
| Over $5,000 per month | 5% rebate on all purchases |
| Over $10,000 per month | 7% rebate on all purchases |
| Over $20,000 per month | 8% rebate on all purchases |

*\* calculated based on the average monthly purchases over the last three full months*

**Marginal vs. Overall Discount Rates:** There are two different ways that tiered incentives are calculated: (1) as **marginal discounts** on purchases in each respective tier, or (2) as **overall discounts** on all purchases, once the respective tier is reached. To illustrate the difference, using the table above, let's say a customer purchased an average of $13,000 per month over the last three months.

In the marginal tiered discount approach, that customer would receive a 0% rebate on the first $5,000 of purchases, a 5% rebate on the second $5,000 of purchases, and a 7% rebate on the $3,000 over $10,000. The total rebate would be $250 + $210 = $460.

But in the simpler, overall discount approach, the customer would be paid a 7% rebate on all purchases, which would be equal to $910.

If you are trying to get the customer to buy more from you, the simple overall discount approach is typically more effective because buying more not only contributes to a lower price on the extra purchases, but it can also lead to a higher discount across all purchases.

Imagine, using the rebate schedule above, that a customer is purchasing $9,000 per month and getting the 5% discount ($450). If that customer purchases just $1,000 more, not only do they get the 7% rebate on the last $1,000, but now they get the 7% rebate on all $10,000 (a rebate of $700). Increasing their purchases by just 11% increases their overall rebate by 55%. They essentially get 25% off the last $1000 of purchases because they get an additional $250 rebate for making $1,000 of additional purchases.

This can be immensely powerful, as long as your customers understand the compound impact of moving to higher rebate tiers. That's one of the reasons it's so important to keep incentive structures simple. You never want to be in a situation where your customer is frustrated because they misunderstood the rebate incentive, and they got less than they were expecting. It's not good for keeping relationships positive.

A simple, tiered, overall-purchase-volume-based incentive can be useful not just for getting customers to expand their purchases across more products, but also for keeping price structures competitive relative to other vendors that might offer discretionary volume discounts. Due to its simplicity, it is probably the most common form of purchase-volume incentive.

## 2. Product-Specific Purchase Volume Incentives

The benefit of a product-specific incentive is that it keeps the focus on a single product or product category you are trying to grow. This could be a good solution if the majority of your existing customer expansion opportunities are related to the same product or product category, as is often the case after an acquisition or after the introduction of a new product line. Or perhaps you just want to focus on a specific category of products due to an aggressive competitor in that category, but you don't want to needlessly lower prices across other categories.

One of the downsides of product-specific incentives is that administration of the incentives can become more complex. This can create a problem if you decide to simultaneously maintain multiple incentives for various products or categories.

The simplest way to structure a product-specific purchase-volume incentive is either a single percentage-off discount or a tiered purchase-volume discount structure like the example above, limited to a single product or category. And the simplest versions of this would have only one tier, such as this:

*Take an additional 20% off all break room supplies, after your first $1,000 of break room purchases this year.*

This type of incentive can work as an overlay on top of a regular tiered purchase-volume discount schema, and it can be implemented for a limited period of time, while the overall purchase incentive is potentially more permanent in nature.

The other obvious benefit of a product-specific incentive is that it can be scaled based on the cost and margin of the particular product. For example, if you sell software, training, and consulting services, but you only care about growing software, then restricting it to software will help you avoid having to pay out expensive rebates to customers who just spend a lot on consulting services. Restricting the incentive to certain products can also help you ensure that you don't enter negative margin territory with your rebates. For example, if your services are low-margin, but your software is high-margin, this is a way to ensure the rebate goes only against high-margin products.

## 3. Portfolio-Breadth Incentives

Another type of incentive is a discount or rebate based on the number of product categories your customers purchase from. This is a good way to incentivize your customers to buy more of what you sell.

This type of incentive system rewards customers as they purchase from more categories. As an example, let's say your company has five major product categories: (1) Paper, (2) Office Supplies, (3) Technology Products, (4) Furniture, and (5) Janitorial Supplies. The table below shows an example of how you could create an incentive system to get customers to purchase from additional categories:

### Category-Breadth Purchase Incentive

*Every 90 days, we will give you a rebate based on how many of our five product categories you buy from. To receive credit for a category, at least 5% of your total purchases must come from that category.*

| If you spend at least 5% of your total purchases on ... | ... you get ... |
|---|---|
| Each of two different categories | 2% rebate on all purchases |
| Each of three different categories | 3% rebate on all purchases |
| Each of four different categories | 4% rebate on all purchases |
| Each of all five different categories | 5% rebate on all purchases |

This is potentially a good incentive structure to encourage a homogeneous customer base who have similar needs to buy products from across all your product categories. It's generally not as effective if most customers are heterogenous (different from each other) and don't need to buy from the same categories.

This type of incentive can also be used as an overlay on top of an overall-purchase-volume incentive. In the example above, in addition to a regular purchase-volume incentive of 8%, customers could get up to another 5% off purchases by purchasing from more product categories. This would mean up to 13% off in total.

The potential problem you need to be aware of is the added complexity of overlaid incentive programs and whether or not your customers will clearly understand how they work and how they get benefits. Stacking incentives should be kept to a minimum. Thinking in the 80/20 mindset can help you decide which ones will have the most impact.

## 4. Growth-Based Pricing Incentives

**Growth-based pricing incentives** provide an excellent way to incentivize growth without paying discounts or rebates to all high-volume purchasers. Like the raw spend volume tiers above, growth-based incentives can be administered based on monthly, quarterly, or annual growth. An example of **growth-in-spend discounts** is shown in the table below:

### Growth-in-Spend Discount Volume Tiers

*The following discount schedule specifies the rebate on all purchases that occur in the last full month, based on a comparison of that month's purchases to the average monthly purchases for the previous 12 months.*

| If you spend... | ... you get ... |
|---|---|
| 10% more than your average monthly purchases for the last 12 months | 5% rebate on all purchases for that month |
| 20% more than your average monthly purchases for the last 12 months | 7% rebate on all purchases for that month |
| 30% more than your average monthly purchases for the last 12 months | 10% rebate on all purchases for that month |

And then, each month, you can send a reinforcement email that lets the customer know how much they need to spend to get various rebates, like the example below:

*Dear Customer:*

*Your average monthly purchase amount for the last 12 months ending August 31, 2020 was $2,914. You can earn extra rebates next month if you spend $3,206 or more as follows:*

| If you spend... | ... you get a ... |
|---|---|
| Over $3,206 next month | 5% rebate |
| Over $3,497 next month | 7% rebate |
| Over $3,789 next month | 10% rebate |

Making the new target visible at the beginning of the month can reinforce the impact of the incentive because the customer can see exactly what they need to spend to get each level of discount or rebate.

First, a caution. Relatively speaking, this is a fairly complex rebate program. It will be more difficult to communicate this type of program to customers such that they understand it fully. It should be used only for sophisticated customers who will take the time to understand it. If you have a sales force that can help explain it and make sure the customer understands it, all the better. Incentive programs work only if customers understand how they work.

That said, this can otherwise be an incredibly effective incentive program. The beauty of the structure is that it incentivizes larger growth sooner, and then, after the customer hits their growth target, you do not have to continue to pay the larger incentive.

This can be a very effective program for incentivizing trial and onboarding for new customers without really discriminating against existing customers. This is because, for the first 12 months, each progressive month's purchases are likely to be higher than the 12-month average for new customers. Existing customers can receive the same discounts, as long as they are growing their business at the same rate.

This is an incentive that can be used in combination with overall-purchase-volume incentives to form an effective long-term incentive system for all customers. Combining a growth-based incentive with an overall-purchase-volume incentive helps prevent a situation where growth incentives go away and leave your prices significantly higher than your competitors' prices.

As with all incentives, you should continuously monitor incentive effectiveness and customer net pricing needs (vs. the market competitiveness of your pricing) to ensure that customers are getting fair and competitive prices at all levels.

## 5. First-Spend Product-Based Incentives

Another way to incentivize customers to buy different products or categories is a first-spend discount incentive. This is like a product-specific trial and onboarding incentive. It can be used to get existing customers to try—and get accustomed to purchasing—specific products or categories. An example of this is shown in the table below:

## New Product Purchase Incentive

*For each new product you buy that you've never purchased before, you will receive the following rebates:*

| For... | ... you get a ... |
|---|---|
| The first $1,000 spent on a new product | 25% rebate |
| The second $1,000 spent on that product | 15% rebate |
| The third $1,000 spent on that product | 5% rebate |

You can apply this discount/rebate structure to specific products or to all products. However, if you choose to apply this to all products, you need to make sure you are very clear about how it applies. Is it for the first time buying a specific product? Or is it for the first time buying any product in the category? The answer to those questions can make a very large difference in what customers expect and how much you end up paying out.

The above shows the incentive broken out by dollar spend, but you could also administer it based on number of units. For example, instead of saying *the first $1,000 spend*, it could say *the first 10 units of product purchased*.

This incentive structure can be an effective way to increase sales volume in a targeted product category that customers are currently buying from a competitor. As an example, let's say an exercise equipment company is doing great, but they are having a hard time getting customers to purchase workout video programs. This type of first-spend incentive could potentially be a good way to get existing customers to try purchasing the workout video programs at a discount.

Depending on how the incentive is defined, this structure can be relatively complex and difficult to explain. Complexity is an important dimension to consider when evaluating new incentives.

# Ten Guidelines for Successful Incentives

As you put together your incentive structures to try to increase revenues from existing customers, it's helpful to follow ten key guidelines.

1.  **Simple and straightforward:** Make sure your incentives are easy to communicate and easy to understand. Avoid complexity, especially unnecessary complexity.

2.  **Connect incentives to controllable behavior:** Customers need to be able to see a connection between the reward and behavior they can control.

1. Customers need to see how they can easily win. They don't want to feel like they are set up to fail by being offered an incentive they can never earn. This is VERY important. Poorly set up incentive programs can be demotivating and even make customers angry.

2. **Make new or experimental incentive programs limited-time opportunities,** so you can retract and/or alter them if they're not yielding desired results.

3. **Focus on just one or two incentives at a time:** Too many incentives are difficult to keep track of and can actually hurt customer motivation.

4. **Test different incentive values:** Start with an initial hypothesis and see how it works. If it's not working the way you expected, try something else. Always be learning.

5. **Communicate frequently and reinforce communication:** Incentives work only if they are present and understood in the minds of your customer decision-makers. This means you need to communicate frequently with your customers, and reinforce your communication with reminders on invoices, rebate statements, and any other logical communication with your customers.

6. **Measure and simplify:** If your incentives are not producing desired results, get rid of them. In the world of pricing, incentives, and customer attention, less is more. Fewer incentives will be more powerful than many incentives.

7. **Make sure everything seems fair and transparent:** You never want a customer to feel slighted because they didn't know about a rebate opportunity. Make all rebate programs visible, so all customers can see them. The number one priority for existing customers is to keep them happy.

8. **Keep track of overlapping incentives.** Don't let overlapping incentives kill your profitability or confuse your customers. Keep overlapping incentives to a minimum.

9. **Avoid frequent incentive changes and contradictory incentives:** Give your customers a sense of stability and security. Avoid changing incentives every week or every month. Give them time to play out. Give your customers time to process them and take the necessary time to act. It doesn't all happen overnight. You don't want to give your customers incentive fatigue, or worse, pricing fatigue. And definitely avoid contradictory incentives.

# Chapter Summary

Selling more to existing customers can be a sustainable way to grow revenues at a repeatable rate, thereby growing the value of your company.

There are two main drivers of revenue growth from existing customers: (1) the organic growth of existing customer needs, and (2) selling existing customers products they're not currently buying from you.

As far as pricing is concerned, there is really only one growth scenario that seems to be primarily driven by price—cross-selling additional products that the customer is not currently purchasing from you.

Pricing incentives can be used to capture additional sales from existing customers, but they must be compelling enough to disrupt the existing buyer inertia your customers have developed with your competitors. Sometimes the trial and onboarding incentives discussed in the previous chapter are more appropriate than the purchase-volume incentives covered in this chapter. Sometimes both types of incentives can effectively be used together to dislodge inertia and grow the volume of purchases from your company.

There are five different types of pricing incentives that can be used to incentivize existing customers to purchase more from your company:

1. Overall-purchase-volume incentives

2. Product-specific purchase-volume incentives

3. Portfolio-breadth incentives

4. Purchase-volume growth incentives

5. First-spend incentives (on specific product or category)

Each of these incentive structures have their own respective pros and cons, which make them more or less appropriate for different situations. Some of them can be overlaid on top of other incentives to create a comprehensive, long-term, pricing incentive system that can effectively deliver your desired outcomes.

You must use your knowledge of these incentives, combined with the specific situation of your business, to hypothesize and experiment to determine the best combination of incentives to drive maximum growth for your business.

Effective incentive programs for existing customers should follow ten key guidelines:

1.  Keep incentives simple and straightforward.

2.  Ensure incentives are connected to controllable behavior.

3.  Default to short-term, limited-time opportunities.

4.  Focus on just one or two incentives at a time.

5.  Test different incentive values to find what works best.

6.  Communicate frequently and reinforce communication.

7.  Measure and simplify by removing ineffective incentives.

8.  Make sure everything seems fair and transparent.

9.  Don't let overlapping incentives hurt profitability or confuse customers.

10. Avoid frequent changes to incentives and the presence of contradictory incentives.

The key to maintaining and growing existing customer relationships is to consistently deliver good service combined with fair prices and effective long-term, volume-based discount structures that never undermine customer satisfaction. In all cases, the strength of the customer relationship should be the highest priority, even higher than gaining additional revenues. This means never breaching the implied commitment to offer fair and standardized prices and discounts to all customers who objectively qualify.

---

*Next chapter preview: In the next chapter, we will cover focused pricing strategies to reduce customer churn.*

## CHAPTER 17

# Focused Pricing Strategies to Reduce Customer Churn

*The key is to set realistic customer expectations, and then not to just meet them, but to exceed them— preferably in unexpected and helpful ways.*

—Richard Branson

I have repeated, chapter after chapter, that a large portion of company value hinges on the strength of long-term customer relationships that drive all present and future profits. Of course, there are many potential ways to either strengthen or damage customer relationships. There is no single shortcut. There is no silver bullet. High value customer relationships require a culture of care and a total company commitment to meeting customer expectations—or, ideally, exceeding them.

High levels of customer churn can cripple net growth rates. The big question is: What pricing strategies can you implement to reduce customer churn? This chapter will answer that question.

But first it's important to understand what causes customer churn, what types of churn are preventable, and what types are not. Let's start with some examples of unpreventable churn. The number one cause of churn in daycare is the growth and maturity of children. That is not preventable. The number one cause of churn in apartment rentals is the tenant moving to a different location. That is mostly not preventable. The number one cause of customer churn in nursing homes is the death of the tenant. There is no pricing strategy that can prevent some types of customer churn.

Before attempting to prevent or reduce churn, it is advisable to first understand what is causing churn in your own business and what proportion of churn is theoretically preventable.

## Preventable Churn

Preventable churn is when a customer leaves for a reason that could have theoretically been prevented by the company. Over the last three decades, an immense amount of research has been done to better understand why preventable churn happens, and how it can be prevented.

Due to the way we were all taught elasticity in high school and college, as discussed in Chapter 12, most people in pricing tend to over-inflate the importance of price in attributing reasons for customer churn. However, as discussed in earlier chapters, only about 20% of churn is typically attributable to price. While this is a large enough percentage to merit consideration, it is important to first understand what is causing the other 80% of preventable churn. Is there a bigger problem that needs to be addressed instead?

Approximately two-thirds of all preventable churn can be directly attributed to service failures and/or poor handling of service failures. And included in this are ill-timed price increases close to the timing of service failures. So, at the very least, pricing people should have awareness of service failures, so they can avoid increasing prices at the wrong time.

## After the Fact May Be Too Late

Unfortunately, in the context of repeat purchases, where buyer inertia and switching costs are big impediments to change, when a customer finally decides to leave, it is usually too late to change their mind. If the incumbent vendor doesn't see this coming until after the customer has moved, the customer has already incurred the majority of the switching costs. The ship has sailed. Whatever was keeping the customer in the relationship before, despite the service failures or poor customer experience, is now gone.

In my career, I have interviewed numerous customers in high inertia buying environments who finally became sufficiently dissatisfied with their previous vendor that they decided to switch. In every case, they said that, at that point in time (after the decision to switch), there was nothing the previous vendor could do to win them back. And, furthermore, they said that the only thing that would cause them to consider returning to the previous vendor would be if their new vendor screwed up as badly as the old one did.

The best time to mitigate customer churn is before it happens.

This is why it's so valuable to have an early warning system to alert companies to situations that could result in churn before the customer crosses the threshold of "too late."

But how can pricing strategies assist in creating an early warning system?

## Rescue Pricing

Unfortunately, once a loyal customer becomes so dissatisfied that they decide to switch, it is usually too late to save them under almost any circumstances. That doesn't necessarily mean companies shouldn't try. It just means expectations should be set appropriately.

Attempting to lure a churned customer back with some sort of price incentive is called **rescue pricing**, and it rarely works once a loyal customer has made a switch. However, there is one type of scenario where rescue pricing has a chance to work: when the customer leaves due to frustration and anger, but without a better place to go. These customers might be receptive to a rescue effort. But pricing alone will typically not be sufficient. They will need apologies and sufficient convincing that the service failures they experienced will not be repeated. This requires participation of functions beyond the Pricing department. If you are interested in learning more about churned customer rescue attempts, you can read ***Appendix C***: *Rescuing Angry Customers Who Have Nowhere Good to Go.*

**Rescue pricing** should not be confused with **price chasing**. Rescue pricing applies only to churn due to service failures or actions that made the customer angry. It is not intended to be a response to low-price competition.

## Price Chasing

**Price chasing** is the attempt to win back a customer who has stopped purchasing because a competitor offered them a better price. This could theoretically apply to either loyal or disloyal customers (remember those **opportunistic customers** and **unprofitable bottom feeders**?).

When customers leave because a competitor offered a lower price, the natural reaction of most customer-focused people is to consider matching or undercutting the competitor's price to try to win the customer back. But the practice of **price chasing** seldom leads to a better outcome.

First of all, disloyal customers who leave due to price should not be a surprise to anyone. The defining characteristic of disloyal customers is that they buy from whoever offers the lowest price. For many reasons that have already been discussed, it's not a good idea to chase disloyal customers with a lower price—primarily because it can undermine the value of fair and transparent pricing. If you think about it, low-margin bottom feeders carry almost no weight in the valuation of a company because they represent almost no profit, and they can never be counted on for future profits. Companies that chase price-sensitive, disloyal customers are wasting effort on low-yield activities—the opposite of the 80/20 principle.

With respect to loyal customers, price-based churn should be a very rare occurrence. For a multitude of reasons already discussed, loyal customers don't typically leave due to price, so, if and when this ever happens, it's imperative that you take a PAUSE and make sure you really understand the situation. If you recall the earlier chapter on the attributes of customer loyalty, you'll remember that loyalty is mostly a misnomer. Loyalty is really all about cost avoidance. Considering the deeply entrenched buying habits and the associated switching costs that apply to loyal customers, it would seem that the price savings would have to be unreasonably significant for the customer to leave. Remember, we are not talking about service failures here. We are talking about loyal customers leaving due to a lower price. Because of the large switching costs involved with moving to a new vendor, most satisfied customers will first give the incumbent vendor a chance to match the competitor's price (unless, of course, you've done a flawless job of letting customers know that price is not up for discussion under any circumstance).

Either way, you now have a situation where a competitor is using a deep discount to successfully steal one of your loyal customers. This now creates a strategy-level problem that must be addressed. Something must be done, but what needs to be done is not **price chasing**. It needs to be bigger than that. A loyal customer leaving due to price may indicate an important vulnerability in your customer strategy that requires urgent attention. If you ignore it, other customers may soon follow, and the churn problem could snowball into something much larger.

Pause, investigate, analyze, and act.

What is the real problem? Is your overall price too high? Is something changing in your market that reduces switching costs? Are customers less satisfied than your company has been led to believe? Is there an important customer need that your current offering is not meeting? Or is this possibly a sales messaging issue that is allowing a competing vendor to craft a believable attack on your competitive value proposition?

Whatever the case, it's important to understand the situation as fully as possible, and then make any necessary changes to your overall strategy to prevent future customer defections. Once the principal issues have been addressed, you will be better equipped to go after churned customers.

## Pricing Strategies to Prevent Customer Churn

The best way to use pricing to reduce churn is to prevent churn from happening in the first place. In addition to fair and transparent pricing, which is the most important strategic imperative for churn prevention, there are four incentive-based pricing strategies that can also potentially help the churn prevention effort:

1. Customer satisfaction survey incentives
2. Commitment discounts
3. Earned discounts or rewards
4. Deferred-reward loyalty incentive systems

These pricing strategies, each detailed below, can be used by themselves or in combination with other incentive strategies. There's nothing wrong with having both a **customer survey discount** incentive AND an **earned discount program** overlaid on top of each other. Just remember how important it is to keep things as simple and understandable as possible to keep things clear in the minds of your customers.

### 1. Customer Satisfaction Survey Incentives

In order to prevent churn in a high-inertia environment, it's helpful to know about any customer dissatisfaction issues *before* the customer goes through the effort to change to another vendor. This information can be obtained through regular customer satisfaction surveys.

The best solution is to implement a proactive customer support organization that is constantly communicating with customers to find out if they've had any service failures or negative experiences that would cause them to seek out another potential vendor. While this type of customer communication is typically a function that sits outside of Pricing, Pricing can help by creating incentive programs that motivate customers to regularly participate in customer satisfaction surveys. By investing in this type of incentive, you are really investing in an early warning system that can expose potential churn before it happens.

The easiest way to approach this type of incentive is to offer a specific discount or rebate in exchange for participating in a regular customer satisfaction survey.

When you do this effectively, you will typically find three categories of customers:

1.  Customers who say they are mostly happy

2.  Customers who say they are mostly not happy

3.  Customers who do not take the time to fill out the survey

Somewhat ironically, the highest risk customers are often found among those customers who do not take the time to fill out the survey. They are the ones who are not engaged. And they are the ones you need to do something about. That's where the budding churn possibilities are lurking. Of course, there are always non-responses due to reasons other than customer dissatisfaction. But, since the potential cost is too big to ignore, all negative and non-responses need to be escalated to the attention of managers to ensure that follow-up contact is made with each customer. Unfortunately, this is the only way to find out which customers are really at risk in order to mitigate potential churn events before they occur.

Certainly, you should also address the customers who say they are not happy. When issues are addressed early, relatively small (non-pricing) changes for the better can make a significant impact on keeping unhappy customers away from the edge of the "cliff."

The value of customer satisfaction information cannot be overstated. Pricing incentives that increase the amount of available customer information can be well worth the cost.

## 2. Commitment Discounts

**Commitment discounts** grant customers access to a specific discount in exchange for verbally committing to regularly purchasing a certain dollar amount or exhibiting some specific loyalty behavior. One such behavior might be a "first-call" supply relationship, where the customer promises to first shop from your company and buy from you as long as the product they seek is available at a competitive price.

Commitment discounts don't typically require the customer to do anything other than verbally commit in order to get the discount. And there's rarely any enforcement. After all, what are you going to do if a "committed" customer stops buying from you? Raise the price? Will that make the customer buy more?

This type of discount is really nothing more than a price reduction packaged up with some loyalty vocabulary to make both parties feel like the discount is somewhat deserved.

Oddly enough, this is the most common type of loyalty discount. The reason is because it is easy to manage. Once the customer agrees to be "loyal," the company can enter the discount into the point-of-sale system, and that's that. Or, if the point-of-sale system can't handle the discounts when orders are placed, the discounts can easily be administered as a rebate after the fact.

The obvious downside of this type of incentive is that it doesn't really have any teeth. What's to keep the customer from suddenly becoming disloyal if some other vendor comes around with a lower price? Maybe some switching costs if they are present—which is why buyer inertia and switching costs are so powerful. But the loyalty discount doesn't really do anything at that point because it becomes useless once a lower price is offered by a competitor.

If that's the case, why offer it at all?

Good question. Although commitment discounts typically don't have any teeth or enforcement mechanism, they can be a valid part of a successful churn prevention strategy. For starters, there is a proven psychological effect that customers experience when they receive a special loyalty discount—it can make the customer feel like they're part of an elite or select group. And, while sometimes that may not be so powerful, it can contribute to developing customer loyalty early in the relationship until more entrenched **buyer inertia** and **switching costs** can develop. Once buyer inertia is established, price becomes a lesser factor in the purchase decision. At that point, the commitment discount has successfully served its purpose, and now it's just helping to keep prices competitive.

## 3. Earned Discounts or Rewards

**Earned discounts or rewards** give the customer something to work toward. If the reward is significant enough, it can definitely influence behavior. Just ask the airlines.

There are many different flavors of earned discounts or rewards. The basic structure creates an incentive that the customer can receive after they've achieved some sort of behavioral milestone. A simple example might be a punch card where, if you get five haircuts, the sixth one is free. Another example might be a monthly discount that changes based on how much a customer spends in the previous month. Of course, in airline frequent flyer programs, customers get access to additional rewards as they fly more miles or spend more money. In essence the customer is earning the rewards through their loyalty.

Earned discount or reward programs can be very effective, but only if the customer really cares about the reward AND it doesn't take too much effort on their part to earn it.

Earned discounts are just one notch above commitment discounts. They have teeth, in that the customer doesn't get the discount or reward without earning it. But the influential power of the reward varies depending on how close the customer is to the next milestone and whether or not they see it as achievable or worth the effort.

In the punch card example, the customer's incentive to buy more is highest when they have achieved four of the five required haircuts. At that point, they buy one more haircut, and they get one free. But once the fifth haircut is achieved, the customer's incentive level may be low again. Similarly, in airline frequent flyer miles, if it's close to the end of the year and a customer needs only 1500 more miles to get to the next status level, they have a much higher incentive to act than if they are 20,000 miles from the next level.

Once the reward has been received, there may be a period of vulnerability during which a competing vendor with a similar reward structure could attempt to steal the customer's business. That phase can last until the customer starts the process of earning the next reward. Again, the hope is that, by this point, the customer has developed enough buyer inertia to stay, even when the rewards have been cashed out.

It's important to design earned reward systems that have continuous relevance and that balance the size and significance of the reward with achievability and positive feedback to keep the customer engaged.

CAUTION: In B2B, individuals often make purchase decisions on behalf of their company. Airlines and other companies have found ways to reward individuals for how they spend the company's money. While this can create incredibly effective incentive dynamics, it can also create a strong temptation for the individuals to behave in their own personal self-interest instead of the company's best interest. If the incentive program is not specifically designed to prevent individuals from behaving unethically, the whole system could backfire due to individual misuse of the incentive program for personal gain at the expense of the company. Many companies have actually banned their employees from benefitting from frequent flyer programs when the company is paying for travel. This is to protect the company from paying high prices unnecessarily. Because of the potential for a conflict of interest between individuals and their employers, it's important to ensure that earned rewards loyalty programs are not prone to abuse by self-interested employees.

Incentives should primarily benefit the company rather than the individual. Otherwise B2B incentive programs could backfire and actually become deterrents. This is not to say that individual buyers cannot not also benefit, just that the rewards should be ethically balanced between individuals and companies—where individuals benefit from helping the company benefit. One way to do this is to tie individual rewards to the rewards the company receives. Imagine a frequent-flyer program that awarded individuals frequent-flyer miles as a percentage of reward points earned by the company.

Earned reward incentive programs can be powerful, but they must be well designed. If not, they could actually work against customer loyalty. There are many considerations that must be understood and fine-tuned for earned reward systems to be successful.

## 4. Deferred Reward Loyalty Incentive Systems

**Deferred discounts or rewards** are simply programs where the customer gets a reward of significant value, but the reward is deferred by some specific amount of time. The magic is in the deferral period. The customer must first make the purchases to earn the reward, and then they must continue doing business for the waiting period until the rewards become **vested** and can be received. And since the customer has to do business with the company during the waiting period, they are building the value of the next reward, and this accrual continues as long as the customer continues the buying behavior.

A good example of this type of incentive is a deferred rebate where a customer is offered a 10% rebate for purchases, paid every six months, but paid out after a six-month vesting period which starts at the end of each earning period. The customer receives the rebate after the waiting/vesting period provided they are still purchasing close to the same amount or more while they are waiting for their reward to **vest**. Here's an example:

*A customer buys in months 1–6. At the end of month 6, the amount of the rebate is calculated for the first six months, but the customer is not eligible for the rebate until after month 12, provided their purchases for months 7–12 stay within 20% of the original six months' purchase amount. After month 12, a new reward amount is calculated based on purchases for months 7–12. As long as the amount purchased for months 7–12 is at least 80% of the amount purchased in months 1–6, the customer gets the full rebate for months 1–6. Six months later the process repeats for the rebate for months 7–12.*

This is similar to stock option incentives with deferred vesting. Deferring the reward and ensuring that the customer knows there is always something of significant value down the line may make customers more willing to trade off a short-term inconvenience, like a service failure or even a higher price, for a significant reward later. This is why deferred incentives can be so effective.

There are few potential downsides of deferred incentives:

1. The time deferral element adds complexity, which could make the incentive difficult to communicate or understand.

2. Deferred rewards are not as valuable to customers as immediate rewards. Customers may not have the patience to wait for long-term rewards, especially if competitors are offering immediate rewards. The value of a future reward must be significantly larger than a present reward to keep the customer motivated.

But once the customer gets past the first deferral period and starts receiving incentives, a deferred incentive program can become a powerful driver of customer behavior.

Sometimes companies will prime the program with a first-time gift reward that will be granted at the end of the first earning period, regardless of purchases, so the customer doesn't have to wait two periods before receiving any reward. This adds a little more expense and complexity, but it can help make the incentive more powerful and immediate.

A word of caution on deferred incentives (and really any incentive program that effectively controls or influences customer behavior): Don't rely on an effective loyalty incentive program to make up for bad service or poor pricing. Sometimes incentive programs can become so powerful that they actually mask a deteriorating customer experience and value proposition. If companies become complacent, they can unwittingly become overconfident about the value they are providing to their customers and fail to recognize or remedy a declining customer experience or pricing misalignment. All the while, customers may feel like they are trapped in a bad vendor relationship, wading through poor service or poor prices just because the reward at the end is too big to ignore. This eventually ends with the customer actively looking for a way out. When it finally gets bad enough for customers to leave, it can be nearly impossible to get them back. Once the incentive is gone, there is no longer a reason to continue the relationship.

To prevent this type of situation, companies need to have a good way to gather information on customer satisfaction levels. Strong incentives should provide customers with incremental benefit on top of an already great customer value proposition.

## General Guidelines for Loyalty Incentives

Loyalty incentives can be an effective way to reinforce positive customer relationships and interactions. Sometimes, they are not needed. Remember, some churn is unavoidable. Some churn is theoretically preventable, but only a small fraction of avoidable churn is due to price. Most of it is attributable to service failures. Companies would often do better to focus on minimizing and appropriately addressing service failures, rather than implementing loyalty incentives.

That said, a well-designed loyalty incentive can almost always help to provide another layer of protection against customer churn. And loyalty incentives will generally perform better if they adhere to the following eight guidelines:

1. The magnitude of the incentive needs to be significant enough to affect the customer's behavior.

2. The incentive will work better if the customer has to do something to earn it. This makes it feel personal and deserved.

3. It should be simple enough to be understood and present in the minds of customers as they make purchase decisions.

4. Customers should always be able to easily see how they're doing on meeting the incentive criteria and what the impact of the incentive is likely to be. This will reinforce the mental awareness of the incentive when customers are making purchase decisions.

5. Deferred incentives tend to outperform immediate incentives because they create a situation where there is always significant benefit down the road, as long as the customer keeps buying.

6. Incentives should never create a situation where an employee is influenced to behave unethically.

7. The loyalty incentive should never replace good service and compelling value. It should be an addition to good service and compelling value.

8. Loyalty incentives should always be measured and monitored to evaluate their effectiveness on a cost–benefit basis. Simple is better, and less is more. When in doubt, cut it out.

Loyalty incentives can be an effective way to reduce churn when they are well designed and well communicated to the customer base. But they should never be the whole answer. Most importantly, loyalty incentives should be integrated into the overall pricing strategy for the whole business.

## Chapter Summary

Customer churn happens in all repeat-purchase businesses. Some is preventable, and some is not. Companies should do research to understand why customers leave and what portion of their churn is preventable, so action can be taken if desired.

Studies show that, on average, only about 20% of preventable churn is due to price. The other 80% is due to other factors, such as service failures, that cause dissatisfaction in the relationship. This is important to understand because a large portion of service failures are preventable. While pricing is typically not responsible for operational service failures, an ill-timed price increase can sometimes push high-risk customers over the edge. For this reason, it is critical that Pricing has the pulse of the current levels of customer satisfaction and the company's history with service failures.

Once otherwise loyal customers have decided to switch, it's usually too late to try to mitigate. At that point they've decided that it is more costly to continue buying from you than to bear all the switching costs and change to another vendor. **Rescue pricing** almost never works. The one exception is when customers have no better place to go. Even then, rescuing the customer requires more than just a good price. Price is almost never the reason customers leave when they have no other place to go. Rescuing an angry customer will typically require personal attention, combined with a genuine effort to mitigate the service failures that are causing the customer's dissatisfaction.

When customers leave due to lower prices offered by the competition, **price chasing**—offering a lower price to try to win back the customer—is almost never a fruitful effort. Disloyal customers will always chase lower prices, and their business will have little impact on long-term company valuation.

On the other hand, when an otherwise loyal customer decides to stop buying from you due to a lower competitive price offer, that generally means something big is going on because loyal customers seldom leave due to price. Whatever it is, it must be understood and addressed to ensure that you don't have a strategic vulnerability with your other loyal customers.

Simply put, an ounce of prevention is worth a pound of cure. There are four different types of pricing strategies that can help prevent customer churn:

1. **Survey participation discounts:** Pricing incentives for customers to participate in regular customer satisfaction surveys can serve as an early warning system for simmering problems that could later turn into churn.

2. **Commitment discounts** give customers financial incentives to commit to giving the company a certain amount of their purchases. While they can make the customer feel like they are receiving special treatment, they typically don't have enough teeth to keep customers from moving to a lower-priced vendor. But they can be a part of a total solution.

3. **Earned discounts or rewards** require customers to do a certain amount of business before they get the reward. Even though these programs are more compelling than commitment discounts, their potency can vary as customers get closer to or further away from the next reward.

4. **Deferred reward loyalty programs** are systems of reward that have incentives that customers earn but are deferred in their vesting for some predetermined time period. This helps to keep the customer loyal and simultaneously earning their next reward while they wait for the previous reward to vest. While these are inherently more complex and difficult to explain and understand, they can be among the most powerful incentives when well designed and successfully implemented.

While loyalty discounts and rewards programs can be effective in preventing customer churn, it's important that they are built on top of the foundation of solid customer experiences. Too often these programs turn into bribery to make up for an otherwise poor customer experience, and companies end up paying more than necessary to keep customers coming back. Worst of all, this can cause customers to feel angst about the relationship—having to put up with a poor experience in order to receive the rewards that have built up.

In the end, there are many ways to reduce churn through pricing. But the most important way is to ensure that your pricing is fair, transparent, rational, and easy to understand. This will build trust and make it easy for your company to be the default choice for your customers' future purchases.

---

*Next chapter preview: In the next chapter, we will cover focused pricing strategies to increase margins.*

## CHAPTER 18

# Focused Pricing Strategies to Expand Margins

*Look for companies with high profit margins.*

—Warren Buffet

I've spent most of the book downplaying margin expansion strategies in relation to net growth strategies because, most of the time, growth strategies will have a much greater impact on increasing the value of the company because they are more sustainable than margin expansion strategies. For too long, growth pricing strategies have largely been ignored while margin expansion strategies have received the majority of the attention.

Nevertheless, there will occasionally be situations when margin expansion strategies need to be implemented. Sometimes margins are simply too low, and they need to be elevated. In those times, margin increases will have more leverage on the value of the company than just adding another increment of growth. It's important to understand when it is appropriate to focus on margin expansion vs. when it is more of a fool's errand that is likely to add risk and devalue future profits.

## When Is Margin Expansion Appropriate?

The simple answer is: when margins are close to zero or when the overall company profit percentage is close to zero. If your profit percentage is very low, then a 1% increase in price can make a much more disproportionate impact to company value. There will be times when growth has been the focus long enough that a company is achieving outstanding growth rates, but the margins haven't been touched. Eventually there will come a time of harvesting where a company needs to raise profits to help monetize the value of the impressive growth they have achieved.

For margin expansion, companies should use caution to avoid hampering growth rates or increasing customer churn. To do this, it is critical to understand the lifecycle stage each customer is in because price increases are more likely to be accepted by customers who have already developed entrenched buyer inertia.

Since margin is simply price minus cost, there are effectively only two ways to expand margins: either increase net prices or reduce costs. And there are multiple ways to increase net prices, but most boil down to either increasing list prices or reducing discounts. And so, in this chapter I will cover three categories of margin expansion:

- **Reducing Costs**
- **Removing Discounts**
- **Raising Prices**

Each of these can individually contribute to expansion of margins. However, margin expansion strategies are different from growth strategies in that they are generally implemented as one-time corrections, not sustainable or repeatable sources of profit growth. Furthermore, margin expansion can add significant risk to existing growth and churn-prevention efforts if it pushes beyond what is considered fair and competitive in the marketplace.

## Reducing Costs

Although Pricing is not typically responsible for costs or cost reduction, it is important for Pricing to be aware of how costs can affect margins and how costs can be reduced to improve margins. After all, "**annualized profits**" is the fourth of the **five sacred metrics of pricing success**. Since Pricing is typically responsible for all the metrics of pricing success, cost reduction should be an important area of knowledge where Pricing can contribute to strategies and discussions. Too often, Pricing is left out of the discussions on cost, while they are measured on margin improvement. Both of these practices should be challenged. Pricing should be responsible for improving the overall value of the company, and costs are an important part of the equation that must be managed responsibly.

There are two separate cost categories: (1) **direct product costs**, which includes anything that translates to a per-unit cost and is factored into the gross margin calculation, and (2) **indirect costs and overhead**, which includes all other business costs, including the CEO's salary.

## Indirect Costs

With respect to indirect costs, it is definitely a good practice to look for opportunities to "trim the fat" by eliminating costs that don't directly add justifiable benefit to the business. But most of the time, these will be relatively small amounts that won't make a big impact on overall profits. It's simply good housekeeping to make sure you review these "overhead" costs from time to time to ensure that you're not letting good money go to waste.

## Direct Costs

Direct costs include any costs that can be traced to a specific product or service being sold, and these are the costs that are most relevant to future profit growth. For this reason, these are the costs that are of most interest to Pricing.

Most of the companies I've worked with have found numerous opportunities to reduce direct costs, including the cost of raw materials, finished products, or anything in-between. Companies can find opportunities to either buy better or reduce costs through greater efficiency. Here are some possible suggestions to reduce costs:

- **Negotiate lower prices with existing vendors:** Many companies originally negotiate costs from their suppliers when they are purchasing lower volumes. Over time, as companies grow, they also develop more negotiating leverage, and they can go back to suppliers and ask for—or demand—lower costs based on increased volumes or future loyalty. Trust me, as you grow, your suppliers can less afford to lose you as a customer, and it is often possible to negotiate lower rates from time to time. (Lucky for you, most companies don't have good price discipline or price integrity, so they will likely be willing to make an exception rather than lose you as a customer.)

- **Conduct a Request for Proposal (RFP)** from several companies and let them know that you plan to go with the supplier that offers the best overall value and economics. Often, just the presence of competing suppliers will be enough to make your existing suppliers lower their prices.

- **Dual source your supply:** Many companies find that forcing themselves to use two different suppliers, each supplying a portion of their needs, allows them to keep prices in check. Dual sourcing also provides a built-in

- comparison benchmark, not just for pricing, but also for the purchase and service experience with another supplier. This is also a useful way to try out another supplier before making the decision to switch to another vendor should the need arise in the future.

- **Ask for alternative payment terms:** Sometimes just asking the question opens up a dialogue that leads to some sort of reduction in cost. One of my customers once asked one of his suppliers for extended payment terms. The supplier said they could offer 45-day payment terms, but that would mean removing the 2% cash discount the customer was otherwise eligible for. The only problem was that the customer wasn't receiving the cash discount at the time. After a little back-and-forth with the supplier, they ended up moving to 10-day payment terms and getting the 2% cash discount applied. And since they hadn't been receiving the cash discount in the past, the supplier offered to give them an additional 2% on all purchases for the next year. So just by having the discussion, my client ended up getting a 4% cost reduction for the entire year.

There are many ways to get lower costs from your suppliers. Analytics can be used to identify areas of potential cost reduction. This is the opportunity to use any of the tricks your customers might use on you to get lower prices, but typically without any of the downside. Getting lower costs is a way to increase margins without putting your customer relationships or growth rates at risk.

# Removing Discounts

There are two ways to effectively increase the prices for customers who are currently receiving a "discount." You can either increase the list price or reduce the discount. In this case, I am using the word "discount" to mean any agreed reduction to list prices, whether it be an on-invoice discount or some sort of rebate or credit after the fact.

## When Discounts Should Be Removed

While there are clear situations when discounts should be removed (discussed below), you should never remove a discount when it would be a breach of ethics or when it would cause a profitable customer to stop doing business with you. **Growth** and **ethics** should both be at the forefront of your mind anytime you are contemplating whether or not to take something away from your customers. With this in mind, here are three situations where discounts should probably be removed:

1. **Customers are unprofitable**: If the customer is costing you money, you are fully justified in removing a discount, provided you are not breaching any contracts or promises. Of course, you will probably want to do it with good communication that helps the customer feel better about the situation in the hopes of keeping a customer who may one day be profitable.

2. **The discount is based on criteria the customer doesn't meet:** Often a customer will receive a discount based on some sort of criterion, like a volume commitment, purchase frequency, product mix, or overall loyalty, but, over time, the customer has stopped meeting that criterion. This is a perfectly justifiable reason to remove a discount.

3. **The reason for the discount has expired:** Perhaps you offered a short-term discount to move excess inventory, but, over time, that justification doesn't apply anymore because you no longer have excess inventory. If the discount is still being used, it should probably be removed.

This is not an exhaustive list, but this serves to show examples of when removal of discounts could be appropriate.

## How to Communicate Justifiable Removal of Discounts to Customers

In order to reduce potential negative effects of removing discounts, it's important to avoid either directly or indirectly communicating unjustified negative news to the customer about what effectively amounts to a price increase. This is a specific category of **price communication** that must be done effectively in order to avoid a negative experience that can reduce a customer's willingness to continue buying from your company. To accomplish this, the following guidelines should be employed:

- Focus on the company's commitment to offer fair and transparent pricing. This is a noble cause that ultimately works to benefit the customer.

- Remind the customer of how they benefit from fair and transparent pricing practices—primarily that they will never have to worry about overpaying.

- Explain how the change in discount is in line with the company's fair pricing commitment and, specifically, why it is justified.

- Talk about why the new price situation is still a good value for the customer.

While good price communication is sometimes a hassle, it can make a big difference in keeping customers in a good place and minimizing disruption to their existing buying inertia. An example of a pricing communication using the above principles might look something like the following:

*Dear Customer,*

*As you know, we are committed to offering all of our customers fair and transparent pricing in order to improve your overall customer experience and our ability to offer you and other customers a consistent value proposition.*

*Four months ago, we offered you a 20% discount as an incentive for you to try our products and services for 90 days, in order to get a get firsthand experience with our products and services. This temporary discount will expire this month.*

*We hope you have enjoyed the experience so far, and we'd like to hear any suggestions you might have for us. Beyond our commitment to offer fair and competitive prices, our goal is to make your buying experience the best in the industry. This includes the ease of ordering, the constant updates on the status of your orders, and the generous return policy that makes it so easy to place orders without risk.*

*We appreciate the opportunity to serve you, and we hope you will share suggestions about any areas we might improve.*

*Sincerely,*

*Jeff Robinson*

*VP Customer Support*

When you base your pricing practices on the concept of fair and transparent pricing to all customers, it becomes much easier to justify the removal of unjustified discounts.

## Raising Prices

Sometimes, companies simply must raise prices to get profit margins in the right range. The most critical element of raising prices is to successfully communicate to the customer why the price change is justified, fair, and necessary. This requires effective **price communication**.

Effective price communication depends on the type and magnitude of the price increase. There are three main "flavors" of price increases, each with unique communication challenges:

1. **A general "across the board" price increase**: This is where a company undertakes a general price increase, raising the prices of most or all products and services, typically in response to **rising costs** or **a new business year**. This type of mass price increase should almost always be accompanied by some sort of communication to give context to the price increase. Customers should be informed, so they don't imagine for themselves what is happening and inadvertently reach the conclusion that the increase is not justifiable. As a general rule, if the customers are not expecting a price increase, then there should be some communication around the rationale and justification for why the company is raising prices. This can be as simple as: *"Due to recent cost increases from our suppliers, you may notice a small increase in the prices of some of the products you buy from us."* It doesn't have to be elaborate.

2. **A select price increase**: This is where a company raises the prices of specific products, typically in response to either a cost increase or a reassessment of the market value of a product that might be selling too fast. When companies decide to raise the prices of just a few select products, it is not generally necessary to send out a broad communication to all customers because only a portion of the customers will likely be affected. However, it may be a good idea to inform customers selectively, either on the website where they select products to order, on the invoice itself as a separate note, or in an email to customers who have recently purchased the products in question. And it is not always necessary to identify which specific products are increasing in price and by how much. Just as with the general price increase, the communication can be simple and straightforward.

3. **A mix of price increases with a few price decreases**: This is where a company seeks to better align margins or prices with movements in the market by using a mix of price increases and price decreases. Although there are plausible scenarios where this strategy makes sense, as a default this should be avoided. Companies seldom get the same credit for lowering prices as the penalty they get for raising them. Furthermore, there is no guarantee that the customers who buy the products whose prices are being raised will also buy the products whose prices are being lowered, so some customers may see it only as a price increase. And some companies make the mistake of communicating that the net effect of the price changes is negligible, when some customers see only large price increases. In general, price increases and price decreases should be evaluated separately and independently. However, in rare situations where most customers buy a full portfolio of products, it can be advantageous to mix price increases with price decreases. It allows you to communicate that, even though some product prices had significant

1. increases, there were also some price decreases, making the overall net price change closer to zero.

## Justifiable Rationale for Raising Prices

Although most companies would like to have higher margins, repeat customers can be skeptical when learning about a price increase to the products they buy. They will be more accepting of price increases when they seem justified. "Unjustified" price increases may be received as a breach of trust that can put vendor relationships at risk.

Based on my observations and research over the last 20 years, there are four main potentially justifiable reasons for raising prices. The first two are typically more accepted by customers. The second two are typically not very well accepted by customers. Ultimately, the success of any price increase depends on your ability to effectively communicate the justifiable rationale to your customers. Successful price increases will most likely be communicated with one of these reasons, listed in descending order of acceptability:

1. **Passing on a cost increase**: The most acceptable rationale for raising prices is to pass on a cost increase. Most customers don't expect vendors to unreasonably absorb cost increases from their vendors. Most customers also accept that vendors should be able to make a fair profit. And more than any other reason, most customers will eventually accept this as a justifiable reason for raising prices.

2. **Generally keeping up with inflation**: Many companies take a mild price increase at the end of the year under the general rationale that inflation is broadly increasing the cost of living, and therefore price increases are acceptable to keep pace with overall price levels. This typically works only once per year, unless you happen to be in an economy whose currency is experiencing rampant devaluation, in which case it can be justified more frequently. This is also an opportunity that many companies neglect, costing them potential additional margin. At the very least, this opportunity and rationale should be considered.

3. **The product has been previously underpriced leading to scarcity of supply in the market and an adjustment is needed**: Most customers do not like this rationale, and they are more likely to resist and challenge it. Customers do not like to hear that their prices are being raised because of limited supply. But if it is true that there is scarcity in the market, some people think it almost doesn't matter how you communicate the price increase because you will have plenty of customers who will buy at higher prices. Just keep in mind that customers have a memory, and you may be able to protect

1. future relationships by connecting with your customers in a meaningful way. Sometimes scarcity can also mean rising costs, and you can blame price increases on that instead. CAUTION: NEVER USE SCARCITY AS A JUSTIFICATION FOR PRICE GOUGING. PRICE GOUGING IS NEVER OKAY.

2. **The value of the product has increased:** Sometimes companies increase prices due to the addition of incremental features and benefits. This is another one that customers don't typically like very much. Customers don't like paying more for a product just because new features were added. There are some cases when the product improvements are so transformative that they put the product in a different tier of competition. In this case, it's almost always better to release a new premium version of the product, in addition to the existing product, and charge more for it. However, there are times when this is not practical or feasible, and the incremental value costs you more and really does provide additional value to the customer. In these cases, it may be better to use the **cost-increase** rationale rather than the **new-product-features** rationale.

## How Much Is Too Much?

When considering a price increase, you must answer the key questions:

- By how much should I raise prices?
- How much is too much?

The ideal outcome would be the maximum price increase but with no customer dissatisfaction, no resultant churn, and no material additional risk to any customer relationships.

Although it will depend on the specific situation and industry, there are some general rules of thumb based on the impact to customers who regularly purchase the product in question, outlined in the table below:

## Price Increase Range vs. Risk Table

| Price Increase Range | Noticeability and Impact | Risk Level |
|---|---|---|
| 0–1% | Negligible impact. Customers won't take much notice. | Very Low |
| 1–2% | Small, but potentially noticeable. Most customers won't object. | Low |
| 2–5% | Questionable. Will raise eyebrows. Will need to be justified by acceptable rationale. Might want to look at competitive prices again. | Medium-Low |
| 5–7% | Significant. Likely to send customer looking at alternatives. | Medium-High |
| 7–10% | Warning: probably too high for the customer to accept without seeing corroborating evidence in the market that all prices are going up. Customer may conclude that you are attempting a profit grab. Either way, the relationship should be re-evaluated | High |
| 10–15%+ | Red Alert: If this is not happening across the whole market, the customer has reason to look for another vendor. | Very High |

I strongly recommended that you create a table like this for your own industry and customers based on your own company experience. It can be extremely helpful for planning price changes when necessary.

But, in almost any case, price increases less than 2% are not likely to have much effect on the buying behavior of repeat customers who have developed a reasonable amount of buying inertia.

## Are Price Increases Repeatable?

Keep in mind that every time you raise a price, you add risk to the customer relationship, especially if the particular product is already priced relatively high compared to alternatives in the market. And so, if you've already raised prices in recent history, another price increase may be significantly riskier, even if the customers seemed accepting of the previous increase. Just because they accepted it last time doesn't mean they will accept the price increase this time. As I have said repeatedly, raising prices is not a sustainable source of profit growth. Most price increases should be seen as one-time corrective actions.

## Low-Risk Price Increases

If you have determined that you should attempt a price increase, but you want to avoid changing prices for high-risk products or customers, you can attempt a **low-risk price increase**, meaning that customers are more likely to accept the price increase without objection. Assuming all customers are paying the same price for a given product, the easiest way to do this is to find the products that are lower-risk and attempt to raise their prices by a low-risk amount, as classified by the table above. Lower-risk products are products that meet many of the following criteria, in descending order of importance:

- products that are currently low price or low margin relative to the rest of the market

- products that are seldom purchased

- products that are not easily substitutable or "commodity" in nature (highly substitutable products or commodities are not good candidates for low-risk price increases unless they are currently underpriced relative to the market)

- products that haven't had a price increase for a long time (ideally a year or longer)

- products that are NOT high-visibility or image products (an image product is a product where customers already have an expectation of what the price should be, and from which customers form opinions of how the company prices ALL their products)

There are several tools that can help you identify good product candidates for low-risk price increases, depending on what data you have available.

If you have a scenario where you have different customers paying different prices for products, you could also target price increases only to the customers who are paying significantly below-average prices for the products they buy. A popular term for this is **segmented price targeting**. But as I've stated repeatedly in this book, customer-specific pricing typically goes against the principles of fair and transparent pricing, and you'll probably get better results moving to a standardized pricing structure where prices are not negotiable, presuming you have a repeat-purchase type of business where customer relationships are important.

## Estimating the Outcomes of Price Increases

Because of the risk associated with raising prices, if it were possible, it would be extremely helpful to have a way to estimate the extent to which price increases will affect customer purchase behavior—how many unit sales will be lost or how many customers will decide to leave.

Unfortunately, due to the complexity of customer relationships, it is exceedingly difficult to produce an accurate forecast of what customers will do as a result of a price increase, especially considering that rationale and messaging are such an important factor in the success of a price increase.

The ideal outcome of any price increase is that no customers leave, and no customer relationships are damaged. But this is not always the case. Sometimes price increases happen at inopportune times or are simply too much for customers to bear, and they decide to stop purchasing from you. And because of the unpredictability of the many factors that affect customer attrition, it is nearly impossible to forecast, even if you have historical observations of previous customers who have churned in response to price increases.

While I do not recommend trying to model the elasticity of a price increase or putting much confidence in such a model to make pricing decisions, I have included a short commentary in *Appendix D* at the end of the book. Some companies have found ways to control variables in such a way that they can accurately forecast attrition due to price increases, and it would be unfair to exclude this possibility altogether. But successful elasticity-based attrition forecast models are a rarity and are best reserved for later phases, after all the lower-hanging fruit has been harvested.

Furthermore, if you are conducting regular customer satisfaction surveys, you may be able to measure a change in customer attitudes before and after a major price increase to understand how churn risk is increasing as a result of the price change before the churn actually happens.

In summary, rather than try to forecast the customer churn caused by price increases, it will likely be more productive to plan and execute price increases with the objective of not injuring any customer relationships or losing any customers, as this is more preferred than any trade-off between customers and profits. Even in the attempt to expand margins, preserving and growing customer relationships should be among the top priorities.

# Chapter Summary

While margin expansion is rarely a repeatable source of profit growth, there are times when it should be a high-priority strategy. Usually, it should be approached as a one-time, corrective action rather than an ongoing effort. However, sometimes regular price increases are necessary in order to maintain existing margins, especially in markets that experience constantly increasing costs.

Margin expansion typically becomes important when margins have become unacceptably small or when growth strategies have stopped yielding sufficient results. Margin expansion strategies can include cost reduction or net price increases. And net price increases can be achieved by either raising list prices or removing discounts that are no longer valid. Either way, companies should be careful not to do anything that would risk damaging customer relationships. Giving undeserved discounts to one customer can damage relationships with other customers, as it erodes the perceived fairness of pricing practices.

Discounts should be removed when customers have become unprofitable or when the discounts are no longer deserved or valid. Effective communication can reduce the relationship risk when discounts are removed or when prices are increased. As a general rule, good communication should accompany any price increase that is not expected to occur without a notification to the customer.

Price increases can be accomplished as general overall price increases or as select price increases in response to cost or market changes. Most customers will accept moderate price increases in response to increased cost or as an annual adjustment to account for general inflation. However, customers generally don't like price increases due to supply shortages or added product features they didn't ask for.

The probability of successful price increases also depends on the magnitude of price increase. For customers with entrenched buyer inertia, most of the time, price increases of 2% or less are usually accepted without adding much risk to customer relationships, especially when customers understand the price increases are happening in response to cost increases or general inflation. Price increases of 5% or more are generally noticeable and higher risk. They should be avoided unless absolutely required due to cost or market price increases.

Keep in mind that every time you raise a price, you add risk to the customer relationship, and if you have already raised prices in recent history, another price increase may be significantly riskier, as you're now starting from a riskier starting point.

Price increases can also be less objectionable by focusing them on lower-risk products (non-image products whose margins may be relatively high and that have not had their prices increased in the last year or more).

Finally, since every pricing action should be a learning opportunity, the outcomes in terms of customer risk and churn should be hypothesized and measured, both before and after any price increase. And since the objective is to increase prices without creating additional risk or churn, the ideal approach will use "zero" impact as the hypothesis, and then plan and execute the price increase in a low-risk way, which should support the likelihood of proving the hypothesis true.

---

***Next chapter preview:*** *In the next chapter, we will cover focused pricing strategies to reduce risk.*

## CHAPTER 19

# Pricing Strategies to Reduce Risk

*Risk comes from not knowing what you are doing.*

—Warren Buffet

This quote by Warren Buffet is refreshingly straightforward: "Risk comes from not knowing what you're doing." It would logically follow that risk reduction can be achieved by increasing knowledge and understanding about the business. When you have more knowledge and information, you can predict outcomes sooner, with more time to take mitigating actions if necessary.

The last of the **five sacred pricing metrics** is the **present-value discount rate**, which is used to value future expected profits. When there is more risk to the expected future profits, the present-value discount rate is higher, and those future profits are worth less. But as companies become more predictable in their ability to deliver consistent growth rates, investors will begin to value those future profits more, leading to lower discount rates.

This is not something that can be done overnight. It takes time to demonstrate consistency in growth and profitability—typically several years. But reducing risk should not be ignored. A company with a 10% net growth rate is 50% more valuable with a 13% present-value discount rate than an identical company with a 15% discount rate. The same stream of future revenues and profits is much more valuable when there is greater certainty (less risk) of achieving that projected stream.

Actual discount rates are based on market comparisons, so the link between specific risk metrics and discount rates can be somewhat murky and usually delayed. But over time, there is definitely a link between risk reduction and company valuation, so investments to reduce risk can certainly be worthwhile.

Before jumping into how pricing can help reduce risk, I should point out the main ways pricing strategies can increase risks:

1. Higher growth rates inherently increase risks.
2. Higher churn rates inherently increase risks.
3. Higher margins and higher prices inherently increase risks.

Growth is important, so lower growth rates to achieve lower risk is not an acceptable trade-off. But it might make sense to try to find ways to make growth rates more predictable, without constraining them in any way.

It's clear that reducing churn is generally desirable, and in doing so, overall risks to future revenues and profits are also reduced. So, any pricing strategy that reduces churn should also be good for reducing risk.

Raising prices and margins can have beneficial short-term results, but they can also add risk to customer relationships and increase future churn. Therefore, attempts to increase margins through price increases should happen only when additional risks can be sufficiently contained, and when it is certain that the new prices will not cause damage to existing customer relationships.

In accordance with Warren Buffet's quote above, one way to reduce risk is to increase knowledge and information. Therefore, any pricing strategy that results in the acquisition of new knowledge should be helpful to a company's efforts to minimize risk.

This chapter will cover thoughts and ideas about how pricing strategies can help reduce risk by increasing the information available to make decisions, mitigate problems early, and increase predictability of results. Although most of these topics have been covered in earlier chapters, reviewing them in the context of risk reduction will increase the breadth of their usefulness in formulating overall pricing strategies.

As a general rule, there are three main ways pricing can reduce risk to present and future profits:

1. It can make growth rates more predictable.
2. It can reduce churn.
3. It can reduce variability of existing revenues and profits.

Let's talk about each of these in a little more detail.

# Making Growth Rates More Predictable

Unfortunately, higher growth rates inherently come with higher risk and potential for variability, primarily because there's more to lose if you stumble and miss your target. So, in the quest for higher growth rates, achieving reduced variability and risk is likely to be more difficult than it would have been for lower growth rates (as lower growth rates are usually easier to achieve). Of course, it would be ludicrous to recommend intentionally reducing growth rates just for the purpose of reducing risk because growth is the primary objective of this book. But it's important to understand that higher growth rates also bring higher challenges with respect to risk. For this reason, higher growth makes it more important to find ways to mitigate the higher risk that comes with it.

One of the most effective ways to reduce risk and variability associated with higher growth is to have an early warning system that allows for early mitigation to any potential problems that may get in the way of achieving your target growth rates.

For most companies, new customer revenue growth is really a conglomeration of many different marketing-funnel metrics and conversion rates that typically start way before leads become trial customers. Therefore, mitigating potential shortfalls starts with visibility to the entire range of marketing-funnel metrics, starting with marketing investments to generate new leads. Pricing should have the ability to monitor all of these marketing-funnel metrics and conversion rates in order to suggest mitigating actions to Marketing or to make changes to pricing strategies further up the funnel if necessary. In almost all cases, Marketing and Pricing should be collaborating and sharing information about mitigation efforts.

# Reducing Variability in Customer Churn

Most companies want to keep churn rates close to zero. Minimizing churn also tends to reduce variability in churn, as long as the churn-prevention efforts are sustainable. The natural way to reduce unwanted churn is to increase the strength of customer relationships. This is typically achieved by adhering to fair and transparent pricing and providing a good customer experience, which includes minimizing service failures. Pricing can help by ensuring fair pricing practices and by ensuring proper timing of pricing actions based on continuous visibility of customer satisfaction and unwanted service failures.

In addition, Pricing can add a layer of protection with well-designed loyalty incentive programs, ideally with deferred rewards that keep customer incentives more consistent over time. While loyalty programs seldom make up for a poor customer experience or value proposition, they can provide an added level of protection for unanticipated gaps in good service. Combined with efforts to ensure an overall good customer buying experience, loyalty incentive strategies can help reduce variability and risk related to customer churn.

# Reducing Variability of Existing Customer Revenues

If you are experiencing unacceptable levels of variability and risk associated with existing customer revenues, there are some pricing strategy mechanisms that have been proven to be effective in reducing this variability.

## Subscription Pricing

Many companies have found that they can reduce variability of customer purchases through the use of subscription pricing programs. This can potentially work for any business that has repeat purchases, including both products and services, to satisfy recurring customer needs. By moving to a subscription arrangement, companies can save on sales, marketing, and order management costs, which can allow them to afford additional standardized pricing incentives to lure customers to the subscription arrangement.

## Long-Term Contracts

Sometimes, long-term contracts can align customers' and vendors' expectations for a consistent long-term relationship, which ultimately can reduce variability and risk. It is important that these contractual relationships don't undermine fair and transparent pricing based on standardized discounts and incentives. It's not worth all the negative effects that accompany the pricing tug-o-war and negotiated pricing. Long-term contracts can and must coexist with strong price integrity, using standardized pricing.

## Vendor-Managed Inventory

Some recurring purchase businesses have customers whose needs are large enough to justify vendor-managed inventory, where the company monitors when the customer needs to order more products to replenish depleted stocks, and then automatically places the order to get the customer back to their desired stock levels. This is more complex than it seems on the surface, but it can also be a way to reduce variability and improve long-term customer relationships. And while the service itself is typically handled by Sales and Customer Service, the prices and pricing strategies should obviously be determined by the Pricing department.

### Targeting Customers Who Are More Likely to Be Loyal

In addition to low margins, disloyal customers typically add variability and risk to overall sales and profits. Pricing can help to keep disloyal customers out of the picture by avoiding any pricing incentives or pricing strategies that might attract the low-price-loving crowd. This is another reason why it's not a good idea to chase low price competition to try to win back disloyal customers. They just add future risks.

In addition, Pricing should work with Marketing to actively identify and target the types of potential customers who end up turning into loyal repeat-purchase customers. This can also help reduce risk and increase predictability. Essentially, you are reducing risk by working with customers who are less likely to be risky.

## Pricing Strategies to Increase Available Information

Increasing available information is a way to universally reduce risk by enabling early warnings and mitigation actions. This applies to both acquiring new information and accessing existing information in different ways, including new ways to analyze existing data to provide new insights.

Chapter 17 covered pricing incentives to reward customers in exchange for participation in regular customer satisfaction surveys. This can absolutely provide information that can reduce risk by improving the quality of decisions and mitigating churn. Anytime you include a customer touchpoint opportunity in a pricing strategy, you provide an opportunity to capture more knowledge and information, which can help reduce risks.

## Chapter Summary

All else equal, lower risk and variability are preferred because they usually translate to higher company valuations for the same amount of future expected revenues and profits. Risk is captured in the **present-value discount rate** (PVDR), the last of the five sacred metrics of pricing success. It's been demonstrated that a minor reduction in the discount rate can translate to an exceptionally large increase in company value. For this reason, risk and variability should not be ignored.

However, for growth-focused companies, reducing risk should not take priority over increasing growth rates if faster growth is possible. Reducing risk should almost always be a secondary priority. Yet there are some strategies that, by increasing predictability of results, can simultaneously aid in both accelerating growth and reducing risk.

There are three main ways to use pricing to reduce risk:

1. **Make growth rates more predictable**: Capturing early information on marketing-funnel and conversion rates allows for potential mitigating actions to achieve results that are more in line with targets, thereby reducing variability and maintaining desired growth.

2. **Reduce churn**: Improve customer relationships by fair and transparent pricing combined with good service and a good customer experience. Pricing strategies to incentivize customer loyalty can serve as another layer of protection to prevent customer churn and reduce variability in results.

3. **Reduce variability of existing revenues and profits:** Companies may also consider other risk-reducing commerce mechanisms like subscription pricing, long-term contracts, or even vendor managed inventory to reduce customer purchase variability. But in no case should companies let these mechanisms destroy their pricing integrity by devolving into customer-specific pricing. Any benefits achieved that way will not be worth the long-term damage to your customer relationships.

Lastly, risk reduction can also be achieved by avoiding disloyal customer types like **low-margin bottom feeders** or **opportunistic buyers**. To accomplish this, avoid any pricing strategies or incentives that would attract disloyal customers, and focus your incentives on dislodging the loyal customers of your competitors instead.

Pricing strategies focused on incentivizing customer participation in customer satisfaction surveys can help reduce churn and variability of profit results.

In summary, there are many ways to reduce risk, which can ultimately increase the valuation of future expected profits—the basis for total company valuation. While risk reduction should almost never take priority over growth, thoughtful strategy design can sometimes incorporate elements of both and allow companies to benefit from both higher growth and increased certainty of future profits.

---

*Next chapter preview:* In the next chapter, we will cover the complete, step-by-step process to create focused pricing strategies to produce the biggest potential impact on overall company value.

# PART 4

# Putting It All Together

*Without execution, 'vision' is just another word for hallucination.*

—Mark V. Hurd

# The Complete Step-by-Step Process

*If you can't describe what you're doing as a process, you don't know what you're doing.*

—W. Edwards Deming

We've come to the highly anticipated chapter of the book where all the philosophies, tools, and frameworks can finally come together in a cohesive, step-by-step process that you can follow to start making significant improvements to the value of your company.

In the next few pages, I will lay out an easy-to-follow, step-by-step process that you can use as a starting point. And I expect that over time you will adapt it to the specifics of your business as you apply your 80/20 thinking to discover new ways of making it work for you.

First, I'll briefly outline each of the eight steps, and then I'll provide a little more detail on each step in the body of the chapter.

In the graphic that follows, you will see the step-by-step process built on all the concepts, tools, philosophies, and ideas from the earlier chapters.

**Step-by-Step Process for Massively Impacting Company Value
by Leveraging Focused Pricing Strategies**

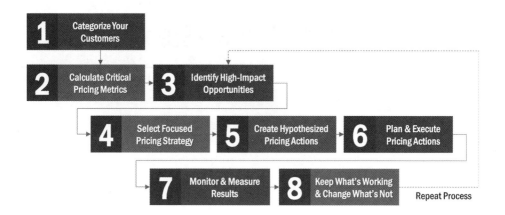

1. **Categorize your customers** to understand what type of customer they are and what stage in your customer lifecycle they occupy.
2. **Calculate critical pricing metrics** for each of your major business segments as a prerequisite to understanding the opportunities.
3. **Identify and prioritize high impact opportunities** based on their potential for increasing the value of your company.
4. **Select the most appropriate focused pricing strategy** to accomplish the desired improvement for the selected opportunity.
5. **Create hypothesized (or planned) pricing actions** along with break-even and hypothesized results, and then evaluate.
6. **Confirm, plan, and execute pricing actions** in order to set the strategy in motion.
7. **Measure and monitor results,** then validate or reject your hypothesis as soon as reasonably possible. Update your hypothesis based on what you've learned.
8. **Keep what's working and change what's not**.

That's the process. That's it. And if you do that, you will be able to impact the value of your company more than you have ever thought possible before.

You will soon see that this process can quickly produce an avalanche of value. You will want to ensure that you are communicating your strategy and expected results at all times, so others in the company can get aligned and not inadvertently sabotage the pricing results that are designed to have the biggest impact on the value of the company.

Just by reading this book, you now understand principles and concepts that others in your organization probably don't yet understand. Some things may seem counterintuitive to some of them, even some of the leaders who have managed confidently in their jobs for a long time. It's important to make sure people understand the **five sacred metrics of pricing success** and how they translate to company value. This is the core concept that will make it easier for you to communicate the rationale for your strategies and actions. You should always show the metrics you are trying to improve and how they connect to overall company value.

IMPORTANT: It is possible that after reading this book you realize there are some foundational or organizational changes that must be made inside your company before you are ready to start following a regular pricing strategy management process. While this recommended process does not specifically cover these types of changes, let me stress that you do not have to put this process on hold while you implement larger structural changes. You can do both simultaneously.

Now let's dive into each step.

# Step 1: Analyze and categorize your customers

The first step is to analyze and categorize your customers, so you can set up the framework for categorizing your revenues and profits and also see how customers are currently flowing through the different stages of the customer lifecycle. This will allow you to benchmark your current state in Step 2 when you calculate your critical pricing metrics. In this step, you will undertake three different analyses:

## Determine the Velocity of Your Business

How frequently does your typical repeat customer buy from you? Annually? Quarterly? Monthly? Weekly? Daily? Hourly?

This is important to know because this will serve as the basis for defining your customer lifecycle stages and parameters.

Determining the **velocity** of your business includes understanding the variations in the regular purchase behavior of repeat customers. You may have one set of customers that purchases once a month and another set of customers that purchases almost daily. If so, you may find the need to divide these customers into different segments, perhaps with different customer lifecycle models.

Below is an example histogram showing variations in customer purchase frequency, which is a key part of velocity analysis:

**Number of Customers by Average Purchase Interval**

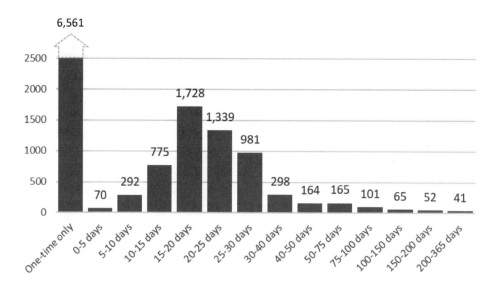

From this analysis, you will need to measure two important customer velocity metrics for repeat-purchase customers:

- **Purchase frequency**: This is the average interval between purchases over a specified time period.

- **Purchase interval uniformity**: This is a measure of how uniform the intervals are between purchases. This can be expressed with a statistic known as **coefficient of variation** (**CV**), which is the standard deviation divided by the mean.

In addition, you will need to measure two additional metrics to gauge the size of typical transactions. These metrics will help you understand when a customer is growing or moving into the **declining** customer lifecycle stage.

- **Average purchase volume**: This is the average invoice revenue of each purchase event in a specified time period.
- **Purchase value uniformity**: This is a measure of how uniform the size of each purchase is. It is typically expressed using the **coefficient of variation (CV).**

This first step forms the foundation, which serves as the basis for your customer lifecycle models and your current-state benchmarking.

## Lay out the Customer Lifecycle Model

After the key velocity metrics are calculated for each customer, you have the information needed to define the parameters of your customer lifecycle model. Most customer lifecycles for repeat-purchase businesses will have the following stages, as described in Chapter 10:

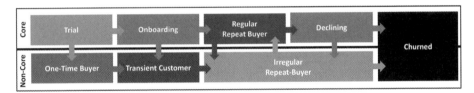

The velocity metrics will help to define the boundaries and thresholds for each customer lifecycle stage. For example, depending on the typical velocity of the business, you may have different parameters to define your customer lifecycle stages.

Below is a brief example of how the definitions can differ according to **business velocity**:

| Stage | Business Velocity | | | |
|---|---|---|---|---|
| | Daily | Weekly | Monthly | Quarterly |
| Trial | 1–2 days | 1 week | 1 month | 1 quarter |
| Onboarding | 7–10 days | 4 weeks | 4 months | 1 year |
| Regular Repeat Customer | Regular purchases 5 out of last 7 days | Regular purchases 3 out of last 4 weeks | Regular purchases 3 out of last 4 months | Regular purchases 3 out of last 4 qtrs |
| Declining | 5–10 days of significantly lower purchases | 3 weeks of significantly lower purchases | 2 months of significantly lower purchases | 2 qtrs of significantly lower purchases |
| Churned | 10 days of no purchases | 5 weeks of no purchases | 4 months of no purchases | 2–3 qtrs of no purchases |

## Solidify the Primary Customer Loyalty Profile Types

The third aspect of categorizing your customers is to solidify your customer loyalty profile types. For most repeat-purchase businesses, the following profiles should work:

- **unprofitable bottom feeders** (irregular repeat customers)
- **opportunistic customers** (irregular repeat customers)
- **light-inertia customers** (regular repeat customers)
- **heavy-inertia customers** (regular repeat customers)
- **captive or die-hard customers** (regular repeat customers)

You can revisit the detailed definitions of each of these loyalty profiles in Chapter 10 of this book. You can use those definitions as a starting point, from which you can make any necessary modifications to fit your business.

There are simple tools for profiling and categorizing your customers just by uploading your historical sales transaction data, and then checking off some recommended parameters. If you'd like to see examples of these tools, please check out the book website, PriceForGrowth.com.

Once you have done the initial analysis to categorize your customers into segments, you are ready to move onto the next step.

# Step 2: Calculate Your Critical Pricing Metrics

After you have completed the analysis to put your customers into appropriate categories, the next step is to calculate critical pricing metrics for each of your major customer or business segments. This will allow you to understand and benchmark your current state and allow you to identify the high impact opportunities to improve your business.

By defining your business velocity and your customer lifecycle stages in the previous steps, you will easily be able to calculate your most critical pricing metrics, which will include the following:

## Five Sacred Metrics of Pricing Success

1. **New customer revenue acquisition rate** (repeatable)
2. **Expansion rate of existing customer revenues** (repeatable)
3. **Revenue churn rate** (repeatable)
4. **Annualized profits** (sustainable)
5. **Present-value discount rate** (a measure of risk)

## Customer Lifecycle Conversion Rate Metric

- **lead**-to-**trial** conversion rate
- **trial**-to-**onboarding** conversion rate
- **onboarding**-to-**regular-repeat-purchaser** conversion rate
- **regular**-to-**declining** conversion rate
- **declining**-to-**churned** conversion rate

## Metrics that Define the Theoretical Value of the Company

This will include the following metrics in addition to the **five sacred metrics**:

- customer lifetime value (LTV) of existing customers (non-discounted)
- discounted customer lifetime value (CLV) (of existing customers)
- discounted net growth factor (all present and future customers)

## Additional Metrics of Pricing Success

In addition to the high-priority metrics listed above, there are often other metrics, such as the following examples, that can be useful to help companies locate opportunities and improve performance:

- gross margin %
- pocket margin %
- contribution margin %
- price variance % (percent change in prices)

Once the metrics are chosen, it is beneficial to go back and calculate the metrics each month on a rolling 12-month basis to highlight trends and irregularities in performance over time.

In earlier chapters, you saw how these critical pricing metrics can be used to identify high-value opportunities on which you can focus your improvement efforts. Keep in mind that the purpose of analyzing these metrics is to understand how the company has been performing, what the company has been doing well, and where there is room for improvement. For this reason, it is more important to try to understand what is driving the performance than it is to stay too focused on any specific number.

Most pricing software solution vendors have tools that can be configured to calculate most of these metrics. Again, you can find examples of these tools at the book website, PriceForGrowth.com.

Once all the important metrics have been calculated, you can move to the next step.

## Step 3: Identify and Prioritize High-Impact Opportunities

After the critical pricing metrics have been calculated, you are now prepared to identify and prioritize the highest-impact opportunities to increase the value of your business.

To accomplish this, you will evaluate opportunities across the improvement opportunity hierarchy illustrated below:

- Improve Value of Company via the Present Value of All Future Profits
    - o Increase new customer revenue acquisition rate
        - increase lead-to-trial conversion rate
        - increase trial-to-onboarding conversion rate
        - increase onboarding-to-regular conversion rate
        - increase irregular-to-regular conversion rate
    - o Increase existing customer revenue expansion rate
        - increase revenue per customer due to organic customer growth
        - increase revenue per customer due to wallet-share growth
    - o Decrease customer revenue churn
        - decrease conversion rate from regular to declining
        - decrease conversion rate from declining to churned
    - o Improve annualized profit percentage
        - decrease costs
        - increase net prices by removing discounts
        - increase net prices by raising prices
    - o Improve present-value discount rate (reduce risk)
        - increase consistency of business
        - reduce business risk due to overly high prices

As you review the current state of performance across all of these metrics, combined with your target/typical values for each, you will be able to easily see the highest impact areas of focus. This will be easiest to see by creating tables of opportunity, like the ones that Marta McClain used (See Appendix B). These examples are also shown in the tables that follow:

## Improvement Impact Leverage Table

*This table shows, for each metric, the relative impact a single standard increment of improvement can have on the value of the company.*

| Metric | Current Min Max | Typical Target | Standard Increment | Impact of 1 Increment on Growth or Churn | Impact of 1 Increment on Net Growth Rate | Impact of 1 Increment on Company Value |
|---|---|---|---|---|---|---|
| Lead-to- Trial Conversion Rate | 20% 0% 100% | 33% | 3.3% | 16.5% | 30% | 89% |
| Trial-to- Onboard Conversion Rate | 40% 0% 100% | 50% | 5% | 12.5% | 22.7% | 55.5% |
| Onboard- to-Regular Conversion Rate | 80% 0% 100% | 80% | 2% | 2.5% | 4.5% | 7.6% |
| Churn Rate | 9% 0% 100% | 10% | 1% | 11.1% | 5% | 16.7% |

This example table above shows that improving the **lead-to-trial** conversion rate by a standard increment can have a bigger impact on company value than any other metric because it has the highest value (89%) vs. all the other metrics. This is shown in the last column.

The next table (below) shows where there is the most room for improvement relative to a target value. This example shows that there is more room for improvement in the **lead-to-trial** conversion rate than in any other metric. This is because the current value is further away from the target value, measured in standard increments (3.9) and shown in the last column.

## Improvement Opportunity Table

*This table shows, for each metric, how much opportunity for improvement exists based on the distance between the current value and the typical value, measured in standard increments.*

| Metric | Current | Typical | Standard Increment | Standard Increments Between Current and Typical |
|---|---|---|---|---|
| Lead-to-Trial Conversion Rate | 20% | 33% | 3.3% | 3.9 |
| Trial-to-Onboard Conversion Rate | 40% | 50% | 5% | 2 |
| Onboard-to-Regular Conversion Rate | 80% | 80% | 2% | 0 |
| Churn Rate | 9% | 10% | 1% | 1 |

The table below shows how the different metric improvement opportunities rank based on the combined priorities of leverage (impact) and opportunity (room for improvement).

## Improvement Opportunity/Impact Rank Table

*This table shows the combined ranking of metrics based on which one has the biggest potential impact and the most room for improvement.*

| | Leverage Rank | Opportunity Rank | Combined Rank |
|---|---|---|---|
| Lead-to-Trial Conversion Rate | 1 | 1 | 1 |
| Trial-to-Onboard Conversion Rate | 2 | 2 | 2 |
| Churn Rate | 3 | 3 | 3 |
| Onboard-to-Regular Conversion Rate | 4 | 4 | 4 |

In the case of this example, the ranks are identical, and they unanimously show that the highest potential impact opportunity is to improve the **lead-to-trial** conversion rate.

These tables and metrics are easy to construct with your existing data, if you know how to do it. But the knowledge of how to create them is unfortunately not widely available. However, you can find examples of these tools, and potential resources on how to construct these tables yourself, at the book website, PriceForGrowth.com.

After identifying the top priority improvement area, it's now time to move to Step 4.

## Step 4: Select the Most Appropriate "Focused Strategy" to Accomplish the Desired Improvement

Once you've determined which metric you will focus on improving, you must consider the best or most appropriate method for accomplishing the improvement. I expect that, to answer this question, you will review the chapters that discuss potential strategies for your respective improvement metrics (Chapters 15–19).

For example, if you have chosen to improve your **lead-to-trial conversion rate**, what pricing strategy will you use to accomplish this? (Refer back to Chapter 15.)

- Will you offer a trial discount?
- Will you offer free services?
- Will you offer a rebate?

If you have chosen to improve your **annualized profits** by raising prices, how will you accomplish this? (Refer back to Chapter 18.)

- Will you increase all prices across the board?
- Will you increase the prices of only select products?
- Will you change the standardized discount structure?

If you have chosen to improve your **churn** metrics, how will you accomplish this? (Refer back to Chapter 17.)

- Will you offer a loyalty discount?
- Will you offer a discount program for regular participation in customer satisfaction surveys?

Once you've reviewed the potential strategies from the respective chapters, you can start putting together a strategy structure that you believe will be effective for your company based on your industry and customer base. It's okay if it's not perfect the first time because this will be a continuous learning process to arrive at something that works really well in accomplishing your desired improvements with minimal costs or disruptions.

## Consider Potential Negative Effects

As you consider the alternatives, you should also keep in mind that changing one metric for the better may also lead to a decline in another important metric. For example, raising prices may help you expand margins, but at the same time, it may lead to an increase in customer churn. You should make note of any metric you think might be negatively impacted by your strategy and include it in the hypothesis you will create in the next step.

# Step 5: Create Hypothesized Pricing Actions

Once you've determined your chosen strategy, you will create a hypothesis with three elements:

1. Your hypothesized action
2. The break-even outcome
3. The hypothesized outcome

## 1. Hypothesized Action

The hypothesized action is simply the structure and magnitude of the action you will take. For example, if you have decided to increase the trial incentive from a 10% discount to a 30% discount, your hypothesized action is just that: increasing the trial discount by 20%, from 10% to 30%.

## 2. Break-Even Outcome

There are three different types of break-even calculations you can use. I recommend using all three simultaneously.

- **Profit break-even**: What has to happen to keep the actions and results profit neutral over a 12-month period?

- **ROI (Return on Investment) break-even**: What outcomes are required to achieve a positive ROI investment?

- **Company valuation-based break-even**: What outcomes are required keep the company valuation neutral (requires a company value calculator)?

An example of a break-even table that includes all three break-even values is shown in the table below:

| Break-Even Calculation | Incremental Cost (foregone profits) | Unitary Benefit (per incremental customer) | Break-Even Units (new customers) | Hypothesized Incremental Units |
|---|---|---|---|---|
| Profit Break-Even | $10,000 | $450 | 22.2 → 23/mo | 100/mo |
| ROI Break-Even | $10,000 | $3,000 | 3.3 → 4/mo | 100/mo |
| | Annualized Cost | Incremental Valuation (per new customer) | Break-Even Units (new customers) | Hypothesized Incremental Units |
| Valuation-Based Break-Even | $120,000 | $66,600 | 1.8 → 2/yr  Less than 1 per month | 1200/yr |

The table above also includes a column with the hypothesized outcome, which will be discussed next.

The break-even outcome is helpful in that it provides a quick benchmark for considering the likelihood of success with the strategy. If, looking at the break-even outcome, you feel confident that you will easily exceed that benchmark, you should take that as a green light to proceed with your strategy. If not, you may want to pause, and potentially consider a different strategy.

## 3. The Hypothesized Outcome

The hypothesized outcome is a best guess of what you believe will happen as a result of the strategy or action. It does not need to be a precise forecast. In some cases, it can be the same as one of the break-even values. The key point is that the hypothesized outcome is the value you will test against, in order to further your base of knowledge.

Why is the hypothesized outcome important? Because it gives an initial expectation and a beneficial checkpoint in the learning process. Forcing yourself to put a best guess out there gives you the opportunity to test your gut instincts. Record your hypothesis and then see if the results are statistically in the range of your hypothesis, so you can accept or reject it. If you accept the hypothesis after the results come in, then your gut feeling was good. If you reject it, you have a learning opportunity—this is very important in the growth mindset. Everything should be a learning opportunity to help you get smarter about your business.

You can find examples of tools that will allow you to easily calculate break-even outcomes and record hypothesized outcomes. Tools can also allow you to easily compare the results against the hypothesized outcomes to determine if the new results are statistically different than the hypothesis, and by how much.

For examples of tools to accomplish this, check out the book website, PriceForGrowth.com.

Once you have recorded the amounts, the break-even outcome, and the hypothesized outcome, you are ready to move to Step 6.

## Step 6: Confirm, Plan, and Execute Pricing Actions

The next step is to confirm, plan, and execute pricing actions. While it sounds straightforward, this step should not be taken lightly. To be effective, some pricing actions require planning, education, enablement, communication, and time for people to adjust.

### Confirm

Once a pricing action is decided, many calculations may need to be made. It's important to take the time needed to double check and confirm that the desired prices have been correctly calculated and assigned to the appropriate segments of the business. This is a critical step.

### Plan

It's important to plan all the necessary aspects of a pricing action before executing it, most importantly the communication plan. How and when will you communicate the appropriate messages to your customers, to your salespeople, and to your digital channels and partners. The plan must allow for the appropriate timing to ensure things happen not only in the right sequence, but with appropriate time for customers and other stakeholders to adapt. You always want to come off as being fair to your customers.

Part of the planning needs to include a target time horizon for how long the experiment should last before forcing a decision to confirm or reject your hypothesis.

Part of the plan needs to include what you will do if the experiment is not successful. Will you return to the old way of doing things? Will you try a different approach? Or will you stay with the new approach anyway? This should be planned out ahead of time, so you don't have to waste time evaluating and planning at the end of the experiment. It will enable you to move more quickly, having already thought through different potential scenarios.

## Execute

Executing means actually doing the work and making the changes—making sure that all the changes have been made in all the appropriate systems to ensure that advertisements, quotes, and invoices all have the correct pricing information. And they should all be instantiated (i.e., made effective) at the same time.

There are many different tools for calculating new prices. This can include everything from Excel to very advanced price calculation engines. A pricing system with integrated analytics can make it easier to verify that the right prices are being charged and invoiced.

Don't forget that execution includes the entire plan, including adequate communication to ensure your strategy has a chance to be successful. And you may have to communicate your message multiple times over several months to ensure your customers understand what you're doing and how they will be affected.

Once you've successfully planned and executed your pricing action, you are ready to move to Step 7.

# Step 7: Measure and Monitor Results

Once you have executed a pricing action, you'll want to quickly verify whether or not your hypothesized outcome is being achieved. Although it may take several months to determine the entire impact of your pricing action, you will likely get much earlier signs indicating whether or not you are directionally in the ballpark of your hypothesized outcome, especially if you see results which are either significantly higher or significantly lower than you expected. You will always want to validate or reject your hypothesis as soon as you have sufficient data to do so.

Keep in mind that, even though you may have an excellent communication plan and program, it may take customers several days, weeks, or even months to understand what is happening, especially if they don't purchase very frequently. You'll need to allow plenty of time to let the customers absorb the new information at their own pace and decide how they will let it affect them.

During the planning period, you should determine the expected time horizon needed for the new action to have its full effect. Measuring and monitoring should continue until the end of that pre-determined **evaluation time**. Once that time has been reached, you need to make an assessment of the effectiveness of the new strategy or action with the data that you have. Can you say with statistical certainty one way or the other that the hypothesis should be either accepted or rejected? If not, then it was probably not a very well-constructed experiment, and you should consider that in the experiments that follow.

It is also possible that the results are so definitive, one way or the other, that you know early on whether or not the hypothesis will be accepted or rejected, and you don't need to wait for the planned **evaluation time**. If that happens, it is perfectly fine to stop the experiment and either make the change a permanent move or retract the move—or create an altogether different action that might elicit a more desirable response from the customers.

You may also decide to update the hypothesis based on the learnings. That will allow you to accept or reject with more certainty and create better hypotheses for similar experiments in the future. For example, you may have an original hypothesis that conversion rates will improve by 50%. However, as the results come in, you may not have enough data to statistically confirm that 50% was achieved, as the limited data seems to point to 45%. You may decide to update the hypothesis to say conversion rates will improve by 35%, as that is more than sufficient to justify the move, and it allows you to immediately confirm the hypothesis of >35% as true. Now you can declare victory and move on to the next improvement opportunity.

Finally, the analysis should continue beyond the end of the experiment horizon. Keep in mind that the further away you get from the change, the harder it is to attribute results to that specific change.

The whole idea of Step 7 is to analyze results and draw conclusions as soon as the data is sufficient to support them. On to Step 8.

## Step 8: Keep What's Working and Change What's Not—Document Your Decision and Move On

After you get to the point where you can either accept or reject your hypothesis with some reasonable level of certainty, it's time to move on to the next opportunity. Before moving on, you will decide to either stay the course and roll with the new changes or revert back and do something different. When you are in the planning stage, you will have already determined ahead of time what steps you plan to take depending on the outcome, so this step will mostly be confirmation and validation of which path you ended up on.

## If There's a Victory, Recognize It

At this point in the process, if the action proved to be beneficial, you would want to pause to reflect on the value you have just created for the company. You will want to document the before and after of both the key metric you sought to improve and the resultant impact on the overall value of the company.

If you found a way to improve conversion rates by 10%, and that translates to a 4% increase in net growth rate, which translates to a 25% increase in company value, that is huge. It will be something you will want to share with other interested stakeholders in the company. And you'll want to do it for the following reasons:

1. You'll want to make people feel positive about the changes in the company and committed to the new, improved way.

2. You'll want to reinforce the chain of metrics that has high leverage on the value of the company. The more the rest of the company understands this, the more they will value the strategy changes you propose. It helps when they understand how relatively small changes in metrics that compound on themselves can lead to massive changes in company value.

3. If you have a team working on these changes, it will be nice to give them a chance to receive recognition for the big impact they are helping to make to the value of the company.

You will want to document this achievement and compare it to the original baseline state. Once you achieve a significant result that should be sustainable, you'll want to continue to measure it to ensure you don't see a backslide. This will also help you keep a running log of all the ways your actions are increasing the value of the company.

Recognition is very important. But perhaps equally important are the collection of facts and the process of learning. When the facts change, it's an opportunity to learn. Why did they change? If you have an improvement metric that holds a high value for several months, and then starts to backslide, it's important to find out why. Is it because competitors started responding with their own actions? Is it because sales reps stopped doing something they were doing before? Is it because something else has changed in the market? Whatever the case, it's important to know if the new strategy is still working or if it needs to be changed.

## Final Call, and Then Move On

Once the appropriate analysis has created a good understanding of the effectiveness of any new pricing strategies or actions, and once it's clear what path to take, it's time to make a decision, document it, and move on. At this point, you can return to Step 3 to revisit the new list of high-impact opportunities, so you can get started on the next area of potential impact.

# Chapter Summary

There is an easy, step-by-step process to use all the concepts, tools, and philosophies in this book to drive massive impact to the value of your company through focused pricing strategies.

1. **Categorize your customers** to understand what type of customers they are, along with their current stage in your customer lifecycle.

2. **Calculate your critical pricing metrics** for each of your major business segments as a prerequisite to understanding opportunities.

3. **Identify and prioritize your high impact opportunities** based on the potential to have the largest impact to the value of your company.

4. **Select the most appropriate focused pricing strategy** to accomplish the desired improvement for the selected opportunity.

5. **Create hypothesized (or planned) pricing actions** along with break-even and hypothesized results, and then evaluate.

6. **Confirm, plan, and execute pricing actions**.

7. **Measure and monitor results, then update your hypothesis**; validate or reject your hypothesis as soon as reasonably possible; update your hypothesis based on learnings.

8. **Keep what's working and change what's not**.

This process will allow you to identify the highest-impact opportunities from your own data and create pricing strategies that will impact the value of your company more than you ever imagined.

---

*Next chapter preview: In the next chapter, we will cover the final case parable about TransformaCo and their longtime CFO, Bill Burley, which gives a nice overview of the process and shows how a company that is fairly set in their ways can change their strategies in order to accomplish outcomes that would have never been possible with their previously existing mentality.*

## CHAPTER 21

# TransformaCo's Step-By-Step Journey

**Case Parable 5: TransformaCo and Long-time CFO Bill Burley**

*This is the story of TransformaCo, a $182-million manufacturer and distributor of exercise equipment. The company served a broad range of commercial facilities, and was publicly traded on the NYSE. Even though the company had seen moderate success over the years, they had never been able to drive the higher level of accelerated growth that would really spur improvements to the stock price. Longtime CFO Bill Burley was determined to drive a change using principles he'd learned in* **Price for Growth**, *a book he'd read a few days earlier. This is the story of TransformaCo's journey.*

As the raindrops rolled down Bill's office window, he was reminded of the rainy morning 10 years earlier, when he'd first joined TransformaCo. In the early days, he'd had such high hopes for the growing fitness company. Now, 10 years later, he still felt hopeful that the company would finally find a way to achieve the illusive growth that they had promised to Wall Street many years ago.

Even though Bill had accomplished a few major successes over his 10-year run as CFO, the recent back-office chatter had steadily gotten louder regarding the company's inability to achieve meaningful growth. Bill and his fellow executives had, for years, said growth rates of 20% or more were easily achievable, but the company had never exceeded 10%.

Behind closed doors, some employees questioned whether or not the current executive team was fit to continue to lead the company. Bill was well aware of the chatter, which now seemed to be more frequent. Though typically mild-mannered, Bill was starting to display a visible sense of urgency to make whatever changes were needed to achieve the higher growth everyone had been expecting.

His frustration turned to hope when a close friend gave him a copy of the book, *Price for Growth, A Revolutionary Step-by-Step Approach to Massively Increase the Value of Your Company by Leveraging Focused Pricing Strategies*. He consumed it in just three days, and he was captivated by the concepts and messages. He realized his company was missing out on their desired growth results due to practices and decisions that could easily be changed. He realized that even with their recent innovations, their focus on margins was distracting them from the growth-focused pricing strategies that could drive the changes they were seeking. With renewed hope and optimism, he began to plan a different approach using the prescribed steps in the book.

## Previous Changes in Pricing Strategy

Five years before, Bill Burley decided to make a major change in TransformaCo's revenue and pricing model, switching from up-front equipment sales to monthly subscriptions for each piece of equipment, which included unlimited support and service. He felt like this would be more appealing to their customers who were mostly commercial facilities, such as fitness centers, hotels, apartment buildings, schools, and corporate office buildings. This new approach would remove the requirement for a large, up-front cash outlay and allow customers to fully equip their facilities for a reasonable monthly charge.

This change resulted in an initial surge of sales, which partially offset the massive, one-time revenues hit from the change in collections and revenue recognition. Once revenues stabilized, though, they were back to the same 10% growth they had experienced before. Only now, their revenues were much more stable and predictable, and they delivered five straight years of 10% growth and 8% profitability.

Despite this major change to the sales, billing, and revenue model, TransformaCo's stock price barely moved. For five years, their stock price grew at a slower rate than their revenues—not a good sign of investor confidence in the company's future.

## Potential for Change—the Book and the Meeting

After reading the book *Price for Growth* and reflecting on his own profit-protecting pricing strategies, Bill wondered if his company would be able to improve growth by relaxing profits enough to enable some growth-focused pricing strategies. But he didn't want to act alone. He shared the book with his VP of Pricing, who in turn, bought copies of the book for the entire Pricing team. All were challenged to read the book over the next few days, after which they would come together and discuss what changes they should consider for TransformaCo's pricing strategies.

A few days later, the meeting happened. What came out of it would change the company forever. After reading the book, they all had a renewed appreciation for the compounding effects of growth and how that translates to increases in the company value. As the team discussed the strategies they'd been using for the last few years, it became apparent to all that their previous strategies were holding back the company's growth. So, they decided to use the prescribed **step-by-step approach** in the book to see if they could make it work for them.

# Step 1: Understanding and Categorizing Customers

As prescribed, the first step was to understand the velocity of their business. Following the directions in the book, they analyzed the last three years of their data to learn key insights about their business, including the following:

- Their business velocity was monthly, which came as no surprise because most customers were billed on a monthly basis.

- One-time purchasers made up 29% of their customers, but only 4.5% of their revenues.

- Repeat-purchase customers made up 71% of their customers, but 95.5% of their revenues. Clearly this was the principal area of focus and leverage.

Based on the analysis, they set their Customer Lifecycle Model as follows, with **regular-repeat status** achieved after three months of regular purchases.

### TransformaCo Customer Lifecycle Model

| Lifecycle Stage | Stage Length |
|---|---|
| Trial | 1 month |
| Onboarding | 2 months |
| Regular Repeat Customer | Regular purchases three out of last four months |
| Churned | 4 months of no purchases |

With their new customer lifecycle definitions in place, they looked at their current customer lifecycle segments along with the respective revenues from the previous year for each segment. The breakdown of their customers is shown in the table below.

### TransformaCo Snapshot of Current Customer Lifecycle Segments

| Lifecycle Stage | Percent of Customers | Percent of Annualized Revenues |
|---|---|---|
| Trial | 1.7% | 3.1% |
| Onboarding | 1.7% | 3.1% |
| Regular Repeat Purchasers | 38.7% | 71.5% |
| Irregular Repeat Purchasers | 29.0% | 17.9% |
| One-time Purchasers | 29.0% | 4.5% |
| Total | 100.0% | 100.0% |

From this analysis, it was clear that the majority of their revenues were in the **regular-repeat-purchasers** segment, and it would do them well to find ways to move more customers into this customer lifecycle segment.

## Step 2: Calculating Their Critical Pricing Metrics

After Bill and his Pricing team had a good understanding of their customer segments, they turned their attention to their critical metrics. Using the tools they had acquired, they started with the **five sacred metrics of pricing success**, shown in the table below.

### The Five Sacred Metrics of Pricing Success

| Metric | Value (Last 12 months) |
|---|---|
| New Customer Revenue Acquisition Rate | 24% |
| Existing Customer Revenue Expansion Rate | 2% |
| Existing Customer Revenue Churn Rate | 16% |
| Profit Expansion Rate | 0% |
| Present-Value Discount Rate (calculated from stock price) | 17.5% |

From their company market value of $194.8 million, they used the company value calculator to determine the present-value discount rate was 17.5%.

They also recorded average values of other critical metrics in the table below:

### Other Critical Pricing Success Metrics

| Metric | Value (Last 12 months) |
|---|---|
| Net Growth Rate | 10% |
| Profit Margin Percentage | 8% |
| Current Company Market Value (from stock price) | $194.8 million |
| Lead-to-Trial Conversion Rate | 20% |
| Trial-to-Onboarding Conversion Rate | 60% |
| Onboarding-to-Regular Conversion Rate | 90% |
| Lead-to-Regular Conversion Rate | 10.8% |
| Trial-to-Regular Conversion Rate | 54% |

## Step 3: Identifying and Prioritizing High-Impact Opportunities

After Bill and his Pricing team had reviewed the critical Pricing metrics, they were ready to start reviewing and prioritizing potentially high-impact opportunities.

To do this they used one of their acquired tools to create the table below, listing six candidates for improvement objectives.

### TransformaCo Improvement Impact Table

| Metric | Current Min Max | Typical Target | Standard Increment | Impact of 1 Increment on Growth or Churn | Impact of 1 Increment on Net Growth Rate | Impact of 1 Increment on Company Value |
|---|---|---|---|---|---|---|
| Lead-to-Trial Conversion Rate | 20% 0% 100% | 33% | 3.3% | 16.65% | 39.96% | 114% |
| Trial-to-Onboard Conversion Rate | 60% 0% 100% | 60% | 4% | 6.67% | 16% | 27.1% |
| Onboard-to-Regular Conversion Rate | 90% 0% 100% | 90% | 1% | 1.1% | 2.64% | 3.65% |
| Churn Rate | 16% 0% 100% | 10% | 1% | 10% | 10% | 15.38% |
| Margin Expansion Rate | 0% 0% +2% | 2% | 0.2% | 0.25% | .01% | 0.13% |
| Annualized Profits | 8% 0% +20% | 10% | 1% | n/a | n/a | 12.5% |

From the table, it was clear that improving their **lead-to-trial** conversion rate would have the biggest impact on overall company value. Improving that rate from 20% to 23.3% would increase theoretical company value by 114%. The next highest leverage opportunity was improving their trial-to-onboarding conversion rate. Increasing this rate from 60% to 64% would increase theoretical company value by 27.1%.

Next, they wanted to judge the attractiveness of these opportunities by seeing how far their current performance in each metric was from the defined target. The thinking was that the further away they were, the easier it would be to achieve a single standard increment of improvement in that area.

The results of this analysis are shown in the table below:

### TransformaCo Improvement Opportunity Table

| Metric | Rank | Current Min Max | Typical Target | Standard Increment | Number of Increments between Current and Target |
|---|---|---|---|---|---|
| Lead-to-Trial Conversion Rate | 3 | 20% | 33% | 3.3% | 3.9 |
| Trial-to-Onboard Conversion Rate | 5 | 60% | 60% | 4% | 0 |
| Onboard-to-Regular Conversion Rate | 5 | 90% | 90% | 1% | 0 |
| Churn Rate | 2 | 16% | 10% | 1% | 6 |
| Margin Expansion Rate | 1 | 0% | 2% | 0.2% | 10 |
| Annualized Profits | 4 | 8% | 10% | 1% | 2 |

From this table, it seemed that they were furthest away from their target in terms of **margin expansion rate**, which the previous analysis showed would have the smallest impact on overall company value. The next biggest opportunity was to improve the **churn rate**, followed by the **lead-to-trial** conversion rate. But in order to evaluate the most attractive opportunities for focusing their improvement efforts, they needed to look at the combined rankings from both tables. This is shown below:

### TransformaCo Improvement Opportunity/Impact Rank Table

| Metric | Leverage Rank | Opportunity Rank | Combined Average Rank |
|---|---|---|---|
| Lead-to-Trial Conversion Rate | 1 | 3 | 2 |
| Churn Rate | 3 | 2 | 2.5 |
| Trial-to-Onboard Conversion Rate | 2 | 5 | 3.5 |
| Margin Expansion Rate | 6 | 1 | 3.5 |
| Annualized Profits | 4 | 4 | 4 |
| Onboard-to-Regular Conversion Rate | 5 | 5 | 5 |

From this analysis, Bill and his pricing team collectively decided to focus first on improving their **lead-to-trial** conversion rate because it had the highest combined ranking of all the potential metrics they evaluated.

## Step 4: Select the Most Appropriate Focused Strategy to Accomplish the Desired Improvement

### Improving Lead-to-Trial Conversion Rates

For the previous few years, TransformaCo had generated leads by running ads in both print and online publications, offering 50% off the first month of equipment subscriptions with the option to cancel at any time. As an additional incentive, they gave all new customers a 15% discount on all remaining months of the first year.

The trial customers were required to pay a delivery and setup fee equal to 60% of the monthly service fee. And so, even though the customers were getting 50% off the fee, they still were required to pay a total fee equivalent to 110% of the monthly fee, and the delivery and setup fee was not refundable if the customer canceled. TransformaCo charged this fee to prevent people from calling in and ordering a trial if they were not serious customers.

Anyone who responded to the ad was deemed a lead, as long as they fit the profile of a potential customer. Approximately 20% of the people who responded to the ad ended up agreeing to a one-month trial within 30 days of first contact—that's the 20% conversion rate.

Bill and his team had a brainstorming session on how they might increase trial conversion rates, and they came up with three different ideas that seemed worth further discussion:

1. Increase the discount off the first-month fees (currently 50% off).

2. Remove or reduce the delivery and set up fee.

3. Make the set-up fee refundable if the customer decided not to continue after the first month.

In further discussions, they all seemed to agree that the delivery and set up fee was taking the "punch" out of the 50% discount. They felt that the only customers doing the trial were customers who had mostly already decided to do business with them, and they weren't really changing anyone's behavior with the incentive. Furthermore, they didn't feel like they were getting maximum output out of their sales and marketing costs converting only 20% of their leads.

They felt that now was the time to try something more extreme, to see if they could make a difference. This led them to offer a 100% rebate of both the first month's fees and the delivery and set up fee to make it a true risk-free trial. They decided it was important to offer it as a rebate instead of a discount because they wanted the customer to set up their automatic billing to remove that friction from later in the process. In order to pay for some of the discount, they decided to reduce the first-year discount from 15% to only 10%. They felt this was justifiable because they were already hitting their target conversion rates to both **onboarding** and **regular-repeat-purchase** customers.

They felt that this new 100%-risk-free-trial rebate would make a significant impact on their conversion rates. Given the fact that they were spending $36 million per year on sales and marketing already, they felt that this strategy might help them get more out of their sales and marketing budgets.

So, they decided to move forward with the new trial incentive.

# Step 5: Create Hypothesized and Break-Even Results

The more Bill and his team thought about it, the more they became excited about the possibilities.

## The Hypothesized Outcome

They believed that because they were increasing the value of their trial incentive by 220%, they might see very significant increases in lead-to-trial conversion rates. Some of the team members thought the conversion rate could grow from 20% to rates as high as 40% or maybe even 50%. But for their official documented hypothesis, they decided to be much more conservative because they wanted the strategy to be deemed successful. And so, **they hypothesized that the conversion rate would grow from 20% to 25%**. This would translate to a 25% increase in the new customer revenue acquisition rate, transforming it from 24% to 30%. And this would increase the net growth rate by 60%, from 10% to 16%, which would have tremendously positive effects on the company valuation. As a public company, a 60% increase in the company growth rate would be huge, even with the decrease in profits caused by the need to pay for the new rebate incentive.

## Break-Even Outcome

The new incentive would cost the company approximately $3.65 million in additional annualized incentives, equal to approximately 25% of the annual expected profits, if they continued the program for a whole year. From a profitability perspective, they would have to increase their total revenues by 33% (at the new lower profit percentage) just to make up for the lost profits. This was not very likely, and that's probably why they hadn't done it before.

Here's another way to look at it. Each new customer provided an average of
$1,440 profit per year after their trial and onboarding periods. From a profit
perspective, they would need to convert approximately 2,535 additional
customers to break even and make up for the $3.65 million incentive expense.
This would mean their new customer growth rate would have to go from 24%
to 49%, meaning their lead-to-trial conversion rate would have to more than
double from 20% to approximately 41%.

The **profit break-even** calculation is shown in the first row of the break-even
table below:

| Break-Even Calculation | Incremental Cost (foregone profits) | Unitary Benefit (profit per incremental customer) | Break-Even Incremental Units (new customers) |
|---|---|---|---|
| Profit Break-Even | $3,650,000 | $1,440 | 2,535/yr (25% New Customer Growth) |
| ROI Break-Even | $3,650,000 | $9,000 | 406/yr (4% New Customer Growth) |
| | Valuation lost from profit decrease | Incremental company valuation per new incremental customer | Break-Even Incremental Units (new customers) |
| Valuation-Based Break-Even | $48,718,400 | $240,000 | 203/yr (2% New Customer Growth) |

For the ROI investment break-even value, they calculated the average customer
lifetime value by dividing the average customer profits ($1,440) per year by
the churn rate (16%) to get an estimate of all the profits TransformaCo would
receive over the lifetime of each customer ($9,000). By dividing the cost ($3.65
million) by the average customer LTV ($9,000), they determined that the **ROI-
based break-even** value was 406 new customers per year, which would equate
to 4% added to their existing new customer growth rate of 24%, bringing it
to 28% total. This would mean the lead-to-trial conversion rate would need to
increase to 23.3% from 20%, a 17% improvement. This is shown in the second
row of the table above.

Finally, the **company-valuation-based break-even** showed that the $3.65 million
in added cost would reduce the company profits by 25%, resulting in a $48.7
million decrease in company valuation, from the company value calculator.
That represented the cost of the investment in valuation terms. But they also

calculated that, based on the average customer values, increasing new customer acquisition by 203 customers per year would increase the new customer growth rate from 24% to 26%, and the net growth/churn rate from 10% to 12%, which would more than make up for the loss in profits. Essentially, each new customer was worth another $240,000 to the valuation of the company, assuming identical continuity of the both the investment and the new growth rates. To achieve this would require increasing the lead-to-trial conversion rate from 20% to 21.7%, an 8.5% improvement.

Using the **company-valuation-based break-even** number, since they were planning to more than triple the value of the trial incentive, and they knew they needed only an 8.5% improvement in the conversion rate to break even, everyone on the team thought this was very achievable. They realized they were willing to try such a drastic move only because they were looking at how much their actions would impact the value of the company, something they hadn't done in the past because their primary focus had been on profit dollars.

# Step 6: Confirm, Plan, and Execute Pricing Actions

In order to execute this new **trial incentive**, they realized they needed 60 days to prepare because they needed to change the ads that were going out in print media. So, they decided to plan the launch date 60 days in the future.

## Confirming the New Promotion Internally

They confirmed with all of the relevant internal stakeholders that they would be offering a 100% rebate on both the first month's service fee and the delivery and setup fees, which would be paid 30 days after the end of the 30-day trial. They made sure that Accounting, Accounts Receivable, Accounts Payable, Marketing, Customer Service, Sales, and all company managers were aware of the new promotion.

In order to avoid upsetting recently signed new customers, Bill and his team decided to make the promotion retroactive for customers who started a trial promotion in the 90 days prior to the launch of this promotion.

They decided they would run it on a trial basis for 90 days, and if they liked the results, they would continue to run it each quarter for the rest of the year. The decision about whether or not to continue the new incentive would be based on achieving an incremental **net revenue growth rate** of at least 2%, which would require a **lead-to-trial conversion rate** improvement from 20% to 21.67%. This was the **company-valuation-based break-even value**. The hypothesis was that this conversion rate would improve from 20% to 25%.

## Planning

Bill and his pricing team made a list of all the communications they needed to prepare or alter, as follows:

- Email to all channel partners outlining the new promotion and pointing them to new web content to help market the promotion (channel partner commissions wouldn't change because they got paid only after a customer moved from **trial** to **onboarding**, and when they moved from **onboarding** to **regular repeat buyer**)

- Four different email campaigns to all known prospects 30, 15, 7, and 1 days prior to the planned launch of the new campaign.

- Switching out all print ads and online ads that would be released within 30 days prior to the **launch date.**

- New automated emails from their order management system to inform all new trial customers when their payments would be due and when they would receive their rebates.

- Training classes for all Sales, Customer Service, and Channel Partners scheduled at least 30 days before launch.

### Executing the New Promotion

Because of their planning and communication, the actual promotion launch was successful and uneventful. All the physical and online ads were changed and released 30 days prior to the launch. All the system changes were made. All the training classes were conducted successfully.

## Step 7: Measure and Monitor Results

In the first few days after the promotion, there was not a noticeable increase in the number of leads converting to **trials**. This had a few people concerned. But they stayed the course. After the first two weeks running the promotion, they measured a conversion rate of 20.5%, just a 0.5% increase over historical observations and small enough to be within the statistical "noise." More people were starting to worry. After all, they were making an incredibly large investment, and they were hoping to see much more dramatic results.

Fortunately, the results in the third and fourth weeks started to trend up significantly. After the first 30 days, the TransformaCo team measured conversions at 26.3%. It was starting to look like the promotion would beat both the break-even rate and the hypothesized result.

After 90 days, the conversion rates were averaging 25.4%, so the team decided to continue for another 90 days. In addition, they found that there was no negative effect on the conversions from either **trial-to-onboarding** or from **onboarding-to-regular repeat customers**. **New customer revenue growth rate** grew from 24% to 30.48%, and the **net repeatable revenue growth rate** increased from 10% to 16.48%. After accounting for the effect of lost profits, the increased growth rate raised the theoretical value of the company by 375%. For such a simple change to the new customer trial incentive, this was considered a massive success. TransformaCo increased the theoretical value of their company by $730 million in less than one year.

As expected, the actual market value of the company did not grow by $730 million, as determined by their stock price, because investors would have to see consistent repeatability of the results for a few years before they could be sure of the new growth and profit trends. However, the 65% increase in net revenue growth rate was noticed by investors, and the stock price had grown by 90% in one year. Still, Bill and his team were confident that the stock price would continue to grow rapidly as long as they could maintain the new growth rates and profitability levels.

# Step 8: Keep What's Working and Change What's Not

Bill and his team, in their year-end strategy review meeting, decided to keep the new pricing strategy in place, as it had delivered results better than their expectations. But this was after a discussion about whether or not the strategy could be improved. After all, the 25.4% lead-to-trial conversion rates were still below their target conversion rate of 33%. But in the end, they decided to keep the new trial incentive in place for another year to promote stability and continue to verify their results.

## The Next Priority Opportunity

The next highest priority objective they wanted to attack was improvement in the 16% churn rate, so they went back to step two to recalculate their critical pricing metrics, and then to step three to update their high-impact opportunity tables to confirm the priority. Sure enough, the churn rate improvement opportunity had bubbled up to the number one priority. So, they began the planning process to see how they could improve their churn rates.

## Conclusion

In less than one year, Bill and his pricing team had found a way to break through the 10% revenue growth rates that had been constant for nearly five years. This accomplishment was enabled by a new price improvement process based on new metrics, new ideas, and a new set of tools, all of which allowed them to see which opportunities had the highest potential impact to make a difference. This resulted in higher conversion and growth rates, and while profit percentages dipped by almost 25%, the incremental 6.5% growth rate would quickly get profits back to their original levels and allow them to grow even faster in the future.

The company's stock price, which had not grown by more than 15% in any of the last 10 years, had finally grown by 90% in a single year. This was an important validation that investors preferred the higher growth rates over the foregone profitability.

Bill and his pricing team were all given additional stock options and bonuses because of their good work in driving previously unattainable results. All the discussions about the executive team had turned positive. And within a year, TransformaCo was voted by its employees as one of the best places to work. Another successful ending for a case parable company!

## Chapter Summary

The TransformaCo case parable is an example of how one fictitious company went step-by-step through the process of segmenting their customers, calculating the critical pricing metrics, identifying and prioritizing high impact opportunities, and applying a focused pricing strategy to improve the value of the company. Obviously, the story was designed to show how a company can succeed in this process. But there are other lessons we can take away from this process as well.

**Focus on one major improvement opportunity at a time**: Sometimes, the opportunity impact tables will show two or more opportunities with similarly high potential impact. It's important to focus on only one major improvement metric at a time because it will help you concentrate your efforts and improve your chances of success. In addition, working on just one opportunity at a time allows you to better isolate cause-and-effect observations, so you can better understand what is driving the results you are seeing. Most of the time, the potential impact of just one opportunity is so large, there will be plenty of value generated by that improvement opportunity alone.

**Value trade-offs and break-even relationships:** In this story, increasing one metric (growth) led to the decrease of another important metric (profits). It's important to understand not just the profit break-even, but also the company-valuation-based break-even relationship. Typically, a company would not sacrifice 25% of their profits to grow revenues by 5%. But when you consider the compounding effects of the revenue growth by looking at the trade-offs in the company value calculator, it becomes clear that increasing growth can have a much larger effect on the value of the company than the reduction in annualized profits. In the TransformaCo story, they were essentially tripling the value of the incentive, and all they needed to do to make up for the profit loss, from a company-valuation-based break-even perspective, was to increase their net growth rate by 2%. This is often difficult to see without the five sacred metrics of pricing success and a company valuation calculator.

**Delayed results**: Sometimes, as was the case in this story, it can take a few weeks to see the results start to trickle in. They don't always manifest themselves until much later than you may initially expect. In this story it was a two-week delay before they saw any difference. Sometimes it can take months before customers start exhibiting the behavior changes you are looking to find. It's important to monitor results closely from the very first day, but don't assume it's not working if you don't see the change you're looking for within the first few weeks. If you don't see what you're looking for immediately, try to see if there are explainable reasons why it might take a little longer for the results to show up in the numbers. Sometimes it just requires a little patience.

While the specific details of the story can be entertaining, and even on the edge of realistic, the main lesson from this story is simply to illustrate the sequence of steps that should be taken to identify high-value opportunities and create focused pricing strategy changes to improve the objective metrics of those opportunities. Without the steps, it's easy to get lost or feel overwhelmed, but everything is manageable if you simply follow the steps, identify the break-even values of any potential strategy you are considering, and monitor the results after you execute any change, so you can know if it's working as expected or required.

Using pricing to make big changes to the value of your company is very doable if you focus on the right metrics and follow the steps.

---

*Next chapter preview: The next chapter includes important information that will help you move forward to take action at your own company. It will include tips on how to prepare, what to expect, how to mitigate resistance to change, and how to drive success both for your company and for your own career.*

## CHAPTER 22

# Moving Forward and Taking Action

*If you can't fly then run, if you can't run then walk, if you can't walk then crawl, but whatever you do, you have to keep moving forward.*

—Dr. Martin Luther King Jr.

This is the last chapter. In the preceding chapters, I've laid out a revolutionary approach for creating focused pricing strategies to massively impact the value of your company. I call it revolutionary because it is so different than the majority of the pricing solutions I've seen marketed, sold, and implemented over the last two decades. Most other pricing experts would agree that this approach is different than what is being discussed at pricing conferences. Of the many books I've seen written on the subject of pricing, I have yet to see anyone talking about this approach along with the tools I describe in this book. In this sense, the approach is revolutionary.

## Revolutionary, Yet Consistent with Common Sense

But if you reflect on what I've covered, nearly everything I have said is consistent with the leading and modern thinking on the subject of pricing. Most of what I've put forth is really not very controversial. My suggestions are largely a collection of common-sense approaches for growing your business.

Think about the major points I've put forth.

- Sales-driven profit growth is more sustainable than price-increase-based profit growth.

- The value of a company is based on the present value of future profits.

- Maximizing the value of a company means maximizing the present value of future profits.

- Due to the compounding nature of growth vs. profit harvesting, increasing growth rates typically has a much larger effect on future profits than increasing prices.

- Higher growth and lower churn are achieved by creating stronger value propositions and relationships with your customers.

- Customers have a better experience when the price is fair, rational, and transparent.

- Contrary to popular belief, discretionary discounting does not improve the overall customer experience because it creates more work for the customer, and it leads to unfair prices.

- Different pricing strategies and actions will have different levels of impact on the value of your company, and you'll get more out of your pricing efforts if you focus on the highest impact opportunities first.

- Because growth rates have taken a back seat to margins in pricing and finance for so long, it's likely that strategies to improve net growth rates will be the highest impact focus areas for most companies.

- An open mind and a growth mindset will allow you make faster improvements to your pricing strategies.

That's it. That's the revolutionary approach. Is there anything I said in that summary that defies common sense? I don't think so.

## If It's Common Sense, Why Aren't More Companies Doing It?

So why aren't more companies utilizing this approach?

I will share with you my candid observations. I've had a few people disagree with me on these observations over the course of my career, but my continued experience has only reinforced them. I offer them for your consideration, and I will let you make your own judgments on why more companies aren't taking advantage of growth-based pricing strategies.

1. **It is happening, but people don't see it**: Actually, many companies are pricing for growth. It's just not happening in very many Pricing departments. It's typically happening in Marketing or Sales.

2. **It's easier to measure and attribute margins to pricing**: Most finance and pricing people are disproportionately focused on margin growth vs. sales growth. After all, *why do I need to pay a full-time salary to someone to lower prices? Can't I get that from my salespeople?* And so, Finance and Pricing get thrust into the role of margin protector, and most of the time, they don't even consider that pricing should maybe be left unchanged or even lowered. Furthermore, Finance and Pricing can credibly take credit for price-based profit increases, but they almost never get any credit for sales growth, even if it was primarily driven by customer-friendly pricing that was initiated from the Pricing department.

3. **Solutions are too focused on short-term impact**: Solution providers have gotten into the habit of justifying their value by measuring profit margin improvement, as it is easier to understand and easier to measure. Because most pricing solutions are so expensive, companies are looking for quick and measurable benefits to justify their expense. As a result, pricing solutions have gradually evolved to focus primarily on measurable gains from margin improvement.

4. **Seeing immediate results from raising prices is easier than seeing results from lowering them**: Lowering prices to grow volume often requires additional Sales and Marketing support. After all, what good is a lower price if customers don't know about it. This additional support creates unwanted complexity. On the other hand, raising prices can often be done with no additional Sales or Marketing support. For this reason, pricing organizations have found it much easier to justify their existence by raising prices rather than lowering them or holding them steady.

5. **Pricing for growth is not well understood**: Unfortunately, pricing and elasticity are complex concepts that most people don't understand very well. It can take years of focused study and firsthand experience to gain the level of understanding needed to really comprehend what's going on with a company's pricing and associated business outcomes. Most fast-moving executives want simplicity and easy-to-understand solutions. It's much easier to understand the connection between pricing and margins than it is to understand the connection between pricing and growth. That's a big reason why executives tend to focus on the margin impact of pricing. (It's also a reason why visibility to the five sacred metrics of pricing success dashboard is so important.)

For the reasons listed above, I strongly believe that pricing will succeed in growth initiatives only as Pricing becomes the poster child for revenue growth. This book, *Price for Growth*, is your first tool to drive this transformation.

# Pricing Leaders Must Become Growth Leaders

As long as **pricing** is synonymous with **margins**, Pricing will never have the ability to massively drive increases in the value of the company. Pricing needs to become synonymous with sales growth. The Pricing department needs to be seen as the enabler of growth, not the protector of margins. Their objective metric should be to maximize the theoretical value of the company. This single change will reorient the Pricing department to be focused on enabling growth.

## Pricing Job Titles Should Change to Include Growth

Anyone who has responsibility over Pricing needs to have "Growth" added to their title. VP of Pricing needs to become VP of Pricing and Growth. Pricing Analyst needs to become Pricing and Growth Analyst. Why? Because everyone else in the company needs to understand that Pricing is NOT the Growth Prevention department. The connection between Pricing and company growth needs to be highly visible. Otherwise, Pricing leaders might as well assume their title means stagnation or shrinkage. Would anyone want to be the VP of Pricing and Stagnation? Or VP of Pricing and Customer Shrinkage? It makes no sense, but this is often the unfortunate result of traditional margin expansion strategies. Carrying the title of Growth will result in other employees seeing you as an ally and wanting to help you.

## The Five Sacred Metrics of Pricing Success Must Be Visible

In order for Pricing to drive the focused pricing strategies that translate to growth in company value, all relevant managers and teams need to understand the five sacred metrics of pricing success and how they contribute to the theoretical value of the company.

In order to accomplish this, you'll likely need to assemble a few meetings where you can communicate your new approach to others. Everyone needs to see your presentation on why Pricing for Growth is so important. (you can download a template copy of this presentation from PriceForGrowth.com. You'll also want to show them a copy of your critical pricing metrics, so they'll know what to expect when you share your pricing dashboard with them on a regular basis (an example of the dashboard can also be downloaded). This will show how business results are translating to the theoretical valuation of the company, so people can mentally connect their actions to what's affecting the value of the company.

You'll probably need to start with small, one-on-one meetings with key executives to make sure you have the support you need in larger meetings. Then you can expand your network of internal champions.

# Prepare for Resistance

Although Pricing is a complex discipline, sitting at the intersection of customer choice, economic theory, and advanced mathematics, it can be learned by those who put in the work to study, observe, and experiment. By reading this book, you've undoubtedly increased your own knowledge and expertise on the subject. But there will be many in your company who don't share your expertise.

## Why Resistance Might Exist

Unfortunately, Pricing is a topic, where people like to weigh in as experts, even though they haven't put in the requisite study to really understand it. You are likely to run into some of these individuals as you attempt to lead your own company pricing transformation. These people can be difficult to work with because they believe they have expertise that is not there, so it is often difficult to speak a common language. For these people, I've found that it's best to stay focused on the overriding objectives and concentrate on common-sense principles—like motherhood and apple pie—principles very few people will disagree with.

Even though the concepts presented in this book are straightforward and sensible, most people, especially executives, don't like change when it is something that is done to them versus something they are doing to others. Don't let yourself become discouraged by the resistance you might face. Go back and review the chapter on the **growth mindset**. This is the time to think expansively—to consider the many infinite possibilities and pathways to solutions. Remember that you've just taken a meaningful journey, where you've invested multiple hours and over 300 pages to absorb and digest the concepts in this book. Your fellow employees likely aren't there yet. You might be hitting them with some disruptive propositions. You'll be starting from level 10, when your fellow employees may only be at level two. Be prepared to go slowly and start with the foundation at the beginning. You may find that others are impatient and want to skip the foundation to get to the answers. That's okay. It's worth it to go slowly in order to get everyone on the same page.

A few of the concepts we've covered might seem counterintuitive to individuals who are not as far along in the journey as you are. The following concepts are examples of propositions some may be inclined to resist:

- Pricing should focus on growth rates more than margins.

- Pricing should be standardized and transparent.

- Discretionary pricing and discounts must be eliminated (this could be interpreted by others as a power grab by Pricing and a diminished role for Sales).

- Theoretical valuation of the company should be the single most important objective metric for all pricing strategy decisions (which is easily accomplished with the **company valuation calculator** based on **five sacred pricing metrics of pricing success**).

## Mitigating Resistance by Managing Change

There are a few best practices for proactively dealing with resistance and starting the mitigation ahead of time.

- Focus first on common objectives.

- Show the relevant data and highlight what the data means.

- Describe the change in terms of how each individual will benefit from the change.

- Indicate that, while change may be necessary, it doesn't all have to happen immediately, and you can work at a reasonable pace.

- Explain why others will benefit from the change and identify others who are already on board.

John Kotter, a world-renown expert in change management, focuses on four major reasons people may be resistant:

1. **Self-interest vs. interest of the group**: Perhaps, they don't really care about the benefit of the group if their own personal self-interest is impaired.

2. **Different assessment of the situation**: Maybe they don't think the situation is how you've described it.

3. **Miscommunication or misunderstanding of the change:** Maybe they don't fully understand what the change is all about or what they are being asked to do.

4. **Intolerance to change itself:** Perhaps they just don't like the inconvenience of change.

My experience is that these reasons often get blurred together. For example, the root of someone's concern may be their own self-interest, but their own self-interest has caused them to create a different assessment of the situation and a misunderstanding about what outcomes are being sought. For this reason, I recommend thinking of these as intertwined causes of resistance, which are all important and all require some mitigation.

The following recommendations should help to prevent some of the difficulties that can accompany individual resistance to change:

- Focus on the self-interest of each stakeholder.
- Allow for different views of the situation.
- Try to communicate very clearly to avoid misunderstandings and miscommunication.
- Be empathetic to the negative effects and personal disruption that can come with change.

## Prosci and the ADKAR model for change

Prosci is considered the organizational standard for change management knowledge and certification around the world. For coaching on change management, I recommend Prosci as well as the books written by John Kotter. There exists a wealth of knowledge that can greatly improve the success of any change initiative.

One of the tools Prosci promotes is the ADKAR model for managing change. ADKAR stands for:

**A**wareness of the need for change
**D**esire to support the change
**K**nowledge of how to accomplish the change
**A**bility needed to make the change
**R**einforcement to ensure that the change is sustained and lasting

I've found this sequence to be a very helpful progression in working with stakeholders who will be affected by the change, and this should be a good guide for preparing for difficult conversations with individuals likely to show resistance. For further study, I recommend visiting www.prosci.com (*for reference, I am in no way affiliated with Prosci*).

There are proven ways to overcome resistance and create lasting change that will bring enormous rewards to you and your company. Never let a little resistance get in the way of your success! There is too much value for you to unlock!

## You Will Succeed!

*Price for Growth* is not just a recipe for pricing success, it is a path to massively impact the value of your company. It is not out of the question for you to literally double the value of your company in less than a year just by focusing on the right pricing strategies and improvements.

With this new knowledge, you are now armed with game-changing concepts that will help you make a huge difference in your company. Your new playing field is now the value of the whole company—the present value of all future profits. You now understand why the strength of customer relationships will be more important than ever. With the five sacred metrics of pricing success, you now have a framework to measure what's most important and how it affects the value of the company. You have a significant advantage over your competitors who are still trying to balance growth and profitability, especially those who are prioritizing margin expansion over growth. These are battles your company will easily win. And you will lead the charge.

Your ability to succeed will become greater as you incorporate the **growth mindset**, which will keep you focused on learning and discovering the infinite possibilities to solve any of the challenges you may face. Your knowledge of the **80/20 principle** will keep you focused on the opportunities that have the largest impact, allowing you to produce even more extraordinary results.

Think of this book as a starting point for new ideas that you will build upon as you learn and grow. Big companies can be bureaucratic organizations where change can be difficult to accomplish. But it's almost always worth the effort to try. In addition to the benefits that you may bring to your company, your efforts will constantly add to your own personal experience and expertise. All of this will make you more valuable in your own career.

Nothing comes without work, but I expect that by employing the concepts described in this book, your success will be inevitable. I can't wait to hear about your experiences.

## You're Not Alone

Believe it or not, if you are moved or inspired by the contents of this book, you are not alone. Many people have shared with me their wish that more people looked at pricing as a tool for growth rather than a way to pick value out of customers' pockets. Pricing has a more important role to play in improving the growth rates that ultimately drive higher company valuations.

As the millennial generation plays a bigger role in both B2B and B2C commerce, you will see the principles outlined in this book becoming more and more prevalent. Learn these principles. Internalize them. Build your own ideas on top of them. Share your thoughts with the community. And your services will always be in demand.

As most veterans of the pricing industry will tell you, pricing is a vast universe of topics, experiences, strategies, and knowledge. *Price for Growth* is meant to essentially give you the rationale to accompany your intuition.

If I could give you only one recommendation, that would be to continue your journey of learning. The key to success in life is to get smarter and smarter. There is so much knowledge out there from the minds of people who have gone before us.

You will win and achieve your objectives better than your competitors because you will get smarter faster, and smarter usually wins.

Please reach out if you'd ever like to bounce an idea off me or share an experience. I wish you the best, and I have faith you will make a difference in the world by finding ways to bring your ideas to life.

Good luck!

THE END

*If you enjoyed this book, please consider leaving a review at Amazon.com. Good reviews are incredibly helpful for authors like me, as they generally lead to more exposure and the chance of future sales to others. Thank you in advance.*

*Jeff*

# Appendix A

## Potential Valuation Concerns Regarding Inherently Greater Risks Associated with Higher Growth Rates

There are several ways to value a future stream of profits. The simplest way is to use the Gordon Growth Valuation Model, as previously illustrated. And it is generally a very reasonable model for valuing future profits.

However, some concerns may merit the use of a different, perhaps more conservative, model. The following are the typical concerns that pop up:

**1. Greater uncertainty regarding the net growth rates in years way out into the future:**

Unlike a contractual financial instrument, company growth rates are never certain. And while it may appear that the sales growth rates are easily repeatable over the near-term years, there's no guarantee that those growth rates will continue into the more distant future. This is the concern.

Typically, you would see this concern when you have a start-up that is growing at extremely high rates (like 50–100% per year) that are not expected to continue as the company gets larger. This type of concern also arises when a company is competing in a mature, highly penetrated market that is not growing nearly as fast as the company. If one of these scenarios applies to you, then you should probably think about making an adjustment.

Here are a few different suggestions to handle this issue:

- Use a higher discount rate in the years further out into the future. This is probably the most appropriate way to address this concern if the problem is really around uncertainty. An example of this might be using a 10% discount rate for years 1–5, and then using a 15% discount rate for years 6–10, and then using a 20% discount rate for years 11 and beyond.

- Another way to handle this is to reduce the valuation horizon to a finite set of years, such as 10 or 20 years, and then revert to zero expected growth beyond that horizon. This may be the easiest way to handle the situation because it allows all the expected growth to be contained in just a few years. We've already seen that further-out years don't typically have much impact on the overall value, so reducing the valuation to a finite horizon of profit growth is generally fine for comparing the effects of different pricing strategies (even though this may not give an accurate representation of overall company value).

- A third way is to manually forecast the growth rate for each future year, value each year separately, and then add them all up. This is probably the best approach if you

- have a good idea of what your future growth rates will be, and you know they are going to decline.

In any case, while these adjustments may give you a more realistic view of how growth rates will compound, they may not really be necessary for evaluating most high-value-impact opportunities as they relate to pricing strategies. Most of the value of a company is dependent on what happens in the near-term years vs. the further-out years (as you will see in the example graph below). And this becomes more pronounced as discount rates get higher, which is exactly what we expect should happen with more uncertainty. So, an easy way to deal with this is to just increase the present-value discount rate by a few points, and then stick with the Gordon Growth Formula.

One thing that should help allay any concerns is the knowledge that, for present value calculations, the further-out years have much less impact on the value than the near-term years. Below is an illustration of the value of a growing annuity of various lengths, in years.

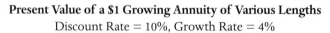

**Present Value of a $1 Growing Annuity of Various Lengths**
Discount Rate = 10%, Growth Rate = 4%

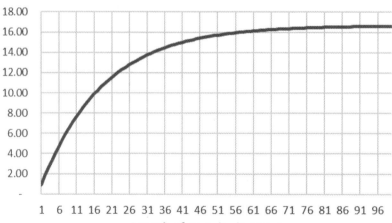

**Length of Annuity in Years**

What this chart shows is that value of a 41-year annuity, for example, is almost as high as a perpetuity—an annuity that goes on forever—even in the case where the annuity payment is growing each year.

For a growing annuity of $1 per year, growing at 4%, compounded annually, and discounted using a 10% **present-value discount rate**, the value of an endless perpetuity is $16.67. We calculate this using the Gordon Growth Formula. If we compare the value of this perpetuity to a 100-year growing annuity with the same growth and discount rates, the value is $16.61. After the first 100 years the value of the next infinity years is worth only 6 cents today. There is virtually no difference in the values of a 100-year annuity or a perpetuity. And the value of a 50-year annuity with the same rates is $15.66. That means 94% of the value of a perpetuity is from the first 50 years. The value of a

25-year annuity with the same rates is $12.57, and that ends up being about 75% of the value of the perpetuity. And it continues. The value of a 10-year annuity is $7.16, and that makes up 43% of the value of the perpetuity.

The main lesson here is that the present value of the later years of a perpetuity are exponentially less impactful than the near-term years. The first 10 years make up 43% of the total value. The remaining 57% of the value is spread out over hundreds of years, each subsequent year being less impactful than the previous.

In short, because of the lesser significance in the further-out years, it's really unnecessary to fuss over them too much.

### 2. Higher growth rates inherently embody more risk than lower growth rates

In some situations, there may be a concern that higher growth rates are fundamentally riskier than lower growth rates, and that therefore, higher growth rates should have higher present-value discount rates. This is largely a valid concern because higher sales growth is typically more difficult to achieve and repeat than lower sales growth, at least in most normal cases. The argument that discount rates, as an indicator of risk, should increase with higher growth rates is understandable. There are many people who believe that the growth rate should never be higher than the discount rate because otherwise the Gordon Growth Formula would produce company values approaching infinity and then incomprehensibility. This happens as the denominator (r - g) gets infinitesimally small and produces unreasonably large valuations.

Certainly, one way to address this problem is to simply increase the discount rate if you are planning on large growth rates. This may be acceptable for determining pricing strategies because it will give consistent relative valuations, but it doesn't necessarily solve the problem of higher growth rates leading to higher risk.

Since most people agree that higher growth companies are more valuable than lower growth companies, all else being equal, then valuation models should show higher value for higher growth, even if the discount rate is adjusted higher to reflect higher risk for higher growth rates. In other words, the discount rate should never be adjusted to the extent that it removes the value premium for a higher growth rate. To illustrate an example of this, let's say the discount rate is currently 10%, and the company is currently growing at 8%. And let's say that the company believes it can and should be growing at 12%, and they also want to raise the discount rate because of the increased risk. The previous (r - g) denominator was 2% (10% - 8%). The new denominator must end up smaller than 2% in order to reflect the increased value of the higher growth rate, so the increase in the discount rate must be less than 2%.

One could determine to, instead, increase the discount rate by only 50% of the value of the increased growth rate. In this example the discount rate would grow by only 2%, while the growth rate grows by 4%, and both values settle at 12%. This is a problem because it puts the denominator at zero, and this doesn't work.

So, we need to handle this a different way, such that the denominator always stays greater than zero and doesn't get too close to zero. The way to do this is to scale the difference (the whole denominator) instead of scaling the discount rate.

In the initial state, the (r - g) difference (the denominator) was 2% (10% - 8% = 2%). Now we are going to grow the growth rate by 50% from 8% to 12%. If we leave the discount rate at 10%, then we have a negative denominator (10% - 12% = -2%), and that doesn't make any sense. Instead, we are going to shrink the denominator by 50% because this will reflect both a higher discount rate to reflect the higher risk and it will reflect a higher company value from the higher growth rate. So, we set the denominator at: 50% x 2% = 1%. Since we know the growth rate is now 12% and (r - g) must be equal to 1%, the new present-value discount rate must be 13% (13% - 12% = 1%). What we have done is shown in the table below:

| Scenario | Annualized Profits (numerator) | Present-Value Discount Rate (r) | Net Repeatable Growth Rate (g) | Denominator | PV |
|---|---|---|---|---|---|
| Original | 1 | 10% | 8% | 2% | 50 |
| New | 1 | 13% | 12% | 1% | 100 |

We have actually built in a dampener that both accounts for higher risk associated with higher growth rates *and* keeps the growth rate from ever exceeding the discount rate. This is one way to address this issue of how to reflect increased risk associated with higher growth rates, and it usually works pretty well, so much that it is a built-in parameter option in my own value calculator. *(Disclaimer: there are a few complexities and adjustments necessary to make this work both ways—higher and lower—which I will not discuss here, but this is the general concept).*

# Appendix B

## Tools Used by Marta McClain to Identify High-Impact Opportunities in the ChangeCo Case Parable

Marta was able to locate the area of the largest potential impact by using simple technique that anyone can use. It basically starts with the five sacred metrics (or any other metric), and it looks at the current value of the metric relative to what it could or should be (the target). Then for each metric, it evaluates potential impact by estimating how a single standard unit of change would affect the overall value of the company.

As an example, let's start with the **lead-to-trial** conversion rate. When Marta arrived, the value of this metric was 20%. The theoretical minimum was 0%, and the theoretical maximum was 100%, meaning you could theoretically see a conversion rate anywhere between 0% and 100%. All Marta had to add was a typical or target conversion rate, and then everything could be calculated. Since she felt that companies should be able to convert one out of three leads to trials, she would assign the target rate of 33%. It's not critical that this value be precise. It just needs to be in the ballpark. We are going to use this value to calculate the increments of potential improvement. We are going to set the increments of potential improvement at 10% of the distance between the minimum value or maximum value (whichever is closer) and the typical value. In this case, 0% is closer to 33% than 100% is, so 3.3% will be the improvement increment: (33% - 0%) ÷ 10 = 3.3%.

The next step is to calculate the impact of one increment of improvement on either growth or churn rate.

Since a 3.3% absolute improvement would move the current value of 20% to 23.3%, a 16.5% increase, we can see that the new customer growth rate would also increase by 16.5%. This is a valuable piece of information. But what's more important is how that 3.3% increase translates to the net growth rate. Since the current net growth rate is 11%, the additional 3.3% represents a 30% increase to 14.3%. When we plug the new net growth rate into the company value calculator, we see that the value of the company increases by 89% (using an 18% discount rate). This means that a single-increment improvement in the lead-to-trial conversion rate, all else equal, translates to an 89% increase in company value.

Doing the same thing for all the metrics gives you the table below:

*(Note: If you don't want to get into the numerical complexities, no worries. Just pay attention to the last column. We want to find the highest number because that metric will have the most impact on value.)*

| Metric | Current Min Max | Typical Target | Standard Increment | Impact of 1 Increment on Growth or Churn | Impact of 1 Increment on Net Growth Rate | Impact of 1 Increment on Company Value |
|---|---|---|---|---|---|---|
| Lead-to- Trial Conversion Rate | 20% 0% 100% | 33% | 3.3% | 16.5% | 30% | 89% |
| Trial-to- Onboard Conversion Rate | 40% 0% 100% | 50% | 5% | 12.5% | 22.7% | 55.5% |
| Onboard- to-Regular Conversion Rate | 80% 0% 100% | 80% | 2% | 2.5% | 4.5% | 7.6% |
| Churn Rate | 9% 0% 100% | 10% | 1% | 11.1% | 5% | 16.7% |

And so, from the table above, Marta could tell that there was more leverage to increase company value by improving the **lead-to-trial** conversion rate first. One increment of improvement (3.3%) in that metric would improve the value of the company by 89%. The next highest-leverage metric was the **trial-to-onboarding** conversion rate, with a one-increment (5%) improvement translating to a 55.6% improvement in company value. And the third highest-leverage metric was the **churn** rate, where a one-increment (1%) improvement would translate to a 16.7% increase in company value.

The next thing Marta looked at, after leverage or impact, was room for improvement, using the hypothesis that the easiest gains would be where there was more room for improvement. This would be defined by the number of standard increments between the current value and the target value, as shown in the table below:

| Metric | Current | Typical | Standard Increment | Standard Increments Between Current and Typical |
|---|---|---|---|---|
| Lead-to-Trial Conversion Rate | 20% | 33% | 3.3% | 3.9 |
| Trial-to-Onboard Conversion Rate | 40% | 50% | 5% | 2 |
| Onboard-to-Regular Conversion Rate | 80% | 80% | 2% | 0 |
| Churn Rate | 9% | 10% | 1% | 1 |

This showed her that she had more theoretical improvement opportunity in the **lead-to-trial** conversion rate because the current metric of 20% was 3.9 standard improvement increments (of 3.3%) away from expected target of 33%. This implied that it might be easier to see benefits in that metric first, as she was further away from typical in that metric than in any of the other conversion or churn rates. In fact, the opportunity priority list ended up coming out in the same order as the leverage list (which is not typical), as shown in the table below:

| Metric | Leverage Rank | Opportunity Rank | Combined Opportunity Rank |
|---|---|---|---|
| Lead-to-Trial Conversion Rate | 1 | 1 | 1 |
| Trial-to-Onboard Conversion Rate | 2 | 2 | 2 |
| Churn Rate | 3 | 3 | 3 |
| Onboard-to-Regular Conversion Rate | 4 | 4 | 4 |

Since both the impact ranking and the opportunity ranking were identical for each metric, she decided to start with number one, and then move down the list in rank order. That's how Marta was able to focus on the highest impact opportunities first.

One clarification: Just because her current performance was zero increments from target in the onboarding-to-regular conversion rate doesn't mean there's no opportunity to improve that number. It just means that since the company is already at the typical expectation for performance in that area, but further away from typical performance in other areas, the other areas might be easier places to achieve improvement. Marta was well aware that her company could improve all four major growth and churn metrics.

There are many different ways to identify potentially high-impact opportunities to increase the value of the company via the five sacred metrics of pricing success. The tools Marta used show an easy way to identify opportunities from looking at current state metrics. You can see examples of these tools by visiting PriceForGrowth.com. At the very least, the tools described here can point to ideas about where to focus, and you can combine those ideas with any other methods to determine where you can likely have the biggest impact first.

# Appendix C

## Rescuing Angry Churned Customers Who Have No Good Place to Go

There are times when a customer becomes very upset with a company and makes an emotional decision to move to another product or another provider without any better alternative in place. When this happens, there is a strong possibility that the customer relationship can be rescued.

Emotional churn is difficult to manage because emotions can be a very strong force. However, the one thing that makes emotions what they are is that they are typically short-term in nature. It's very difficult for a person to stay angry (and I mean really angry) for a long period of time. It just takes too much energy. And so, what really happens in emotional churn is that a customer becomes angry, and while they are at the peak of their anger, they vow to never do business again with a certain company. And then they settle down a bit. But even in their settled state, they retain their resolve to not do business with the offending company. At that point, it's less about the anger, and more about their personal integrity. They said they were going to stop, so now they are going to live up to their word. And, in fact, in most situations, it is the vow to never again do business with the offending company that allows them to gain emotional closure.

Think back to experiences where you have made such a vow. Do you remember a time in your life where you made a vow to never do business with a vendor ever again, but then, later, when your anger subsided, you questioned your commitment to the vow? Perhaps you even broke the vow and started doing business with that vendor again, but maybe begrudgingly?

Looking at your own past feelings and behaviors should help bring an understanding of how others might choose to behave. We're not all that different.

So, great. Now we understand the situation. How do we use this knowledge to mitigate a potential churn event? Well, it's not easy. But it can be done.

If you think about the five stages of grief, in this context they might serve as a guide for how and when to recover a customer who has had an emotional experience with your company. First, a quick review of the five stages of grief:

### The Five Stages of Grief

Denial → Anger → Bargaining → Depression → Acceptance

If we accept this as a typical pattern in how people deal with negative emotions, we can see that the transition between **denial** and **anger** is probably the start of the most violent emotional states, and after this **anger** stage, people typically fall into a state of **bargaining**, which is a much less violent emotional state.

You see, it is in the **anger** state, that people make a vow to never do business with the company again. But then **bargaining** happens as customers start to try to figure out their next options. At this stage, they are vulnerable, and they will likely take any option that looks mildly reasonable. But they still have to deal with the fact that they have built up tremendous inertia with their existing provider, and their vow to switch is going to come with unwelcome switching costs.

They are essentially looking for a way out at this point. If there were a way to erase the negative experience they had with your company and avoid the switching costs, they'd gladly prefer that over the inconvenience of having to deal with a whole bunch of new salespeople who will likely tell them anything to try to win their business. This inconvenience is compounded by the risk that the grass may not end up being all that greener on the other side of the fence.

This realization could lead them into a mild state of depression. Things look bad from any angle. The current provider isn't working out. Getting a new provider will be a huge disruption. They are looking for any way out of this bad situation.

This is when you have your best chance of saving the relationship. But the way you have to do it is, you have to change their mind about how bad the current situation is, and you have to do something to make up for the anger you caused them. You have to do the latter first, because otherwise they don't want to listen to you.

Here's a step-by-step process to recover an angry customer.

1. **Listen to them.** They want to be heard. Have them tell you in their words what the problem is. You can't skip this step. If you do, your remedy won't be credible.

2. **Offer an apology**. This is your chance to show empathy. Some customers won't want to listen to anything you have to say until they get an apology.

3. **Ask for an opportunity to make the situation right**. This is an important step. Notice this doesn't say, "Ask for an opportunity to keep them as a customer." This step can't be about what will benefit your company. It has to be about what will benefit the customer. And if you get the customer's permission to try to make it right, you can't assume everything is okay. You've been given a gift, but you still have work to do.

4. **Offer a tangible gesture of good will.** If the customer has been injured in any way, it is often helpful to offer the customer a gesture of good will. An example might be a $50 credit, a 50%-off-next-purchase coupon, or a refund of money spent in their last purchase. The purpose of this is not to make a full recompense to make the customer whole—that's often not possible. The purpose is to make a gesture of good will—to try to reduce the bad feelings the customer experienced with you. Make sure the customer understands this.

5. **Explain how the problem will be addressed,** so the customer will know what to expect for the future. This is important because the customer needs to believe that the problem won't happen again. In cases where the problem is not something

1. that can be corrected, it's important to be honest with the customer, so they have a chance to reset their expectations. And if the problem can't be corrected, you need to offer the customer an acceptable solution for how they can effectively deal with it in the future. For example, if the service failure was a late delivery that couldn't be helped and can't realistically be prevented in the future, you need to give the customer an acceptable way to deal with it. For example: "Unfortunately, we don't always have full control over the timeliness of our deliveries, but what we can do in the future is refund your shipping if a shipment arrives late. And if it's a shipment that is critical for you to receive on time, we recommend you select Premium Overnight shipping, as that rate has built-in guarantees." However you decide to address the issue, it needs to be clear to the customer what the future will look like, and it needs to be something they are willing to live with.

2. **Arrange to follow up with the customer** after a specific period of time to ensure that things are working out better for them.

I will stress the importance of avoiding anything that conditions the customer to believe that they can get a reduced price as a result of complaining. And I will also stress the importance of avoiding exception pricing, even for special circumstances. In order to maintain a reputation of fairness and trustworthy pricing, any future pricing offers should be based on standardized pricing practices. After all, the relationship with all customers is more important than the relationship with any single customer.

# Appendix D

## Mathematical Models for Predicting Churn as a Result of Price Increases

There are defensible ways to model the expected customer response to price increases using something similar to elasticity modeling. However, rather than looking at the relationship between prices and volume, the modeling requires looking at the relationship between the magnitude of price increases and the probability of customer churn.

While these types of models can be built and beneficially utilized in the right environments, there are several challenges that prevent their effectiveness in most situations.

First of all, in the world of recurring customer purchases (so prevalent in B2B), price increases are fundamentally different than price decreases. On one hand, price increases add risk to the overall customer relationship, not just the purchase of the product in question. If prices get raised past the customer threshold of acceptability, the relationship could crumble altogether, and the customer could stop purchasing all products. Lowering prices does not do the opposite of this. Lowering prices for customers who are already purchasing at a particular price typically only moves the customer further into the zone of indifference, where they don't care what the price is. Customers typically don't get exponentially happier or more satisfied if the price decreases, and their probability of purchase certainly doesn't go higher than 100%.

Because of this fundamental difference between price increases and decreases, the expected results must be modeled differently. And although it is possible to create mathematical models, all the previously explained complexities of elasticity modeling still apply. Most importantly, there are many different factors which affect a customer's decision to purchase, and price is just one of them. But most of the time, when you're looking at transaction data, price doesn't matter at all because it's in the zone of indifference, where factors other than price are more directly responsible for the customer's purchase decision.

In the case of raising prices, the accompanying communication regarding the rationale of why the prices are being raised can be an important variable that can affect the customer's tolerance for a price increase, but it is hard to model an explanation method as a mathematical covariate. So, as with most demand and elasticity modeling exercises, the best you can do is try to hold everything else constant and test only one variable at a time. If the variable is price change magnitude, then you should ensure that the price communications are mostly identical, so you don't bias the results with a difficult-to-measure qualitative factor.

Finally, there is a problem with modeling customer acceptance to price increases of a certain magnitude because every test changes the starting point.

Let's say your product is priced 5% below the market average. You conduct an experiment where you raise prices by 4%, and you observe that 10% of your customers stop buying. Does that mean you can always assume that a 4% price increase will result in a 10% volume decrease? Of course not!

If you try to do the same thing again, you're now starting with a product price that is only 1% below market average. If you raise prices by 4% again, your resultant price will be 3% above market average. If you do it again, your resultant price will be 7% above the market average. Even though each price increase has an identical magnitude of 4%, each is from a different starting point, and there's no reason to believe that the results should be identical for all three 4% price increases.

Furthermore, if you segment your customers into those who tolerate price increases and those who don't, you'd likely have only customers in the first segment after your first price increase. The ones that are left are the ones who stayed. It would be naïve to think that just because they didn't leave after your first 4% price increase, they would all be unlikely to leave if you executed a second 4% price increase.

The last consideration is the potential for price change fatigue. If you subject a customer to multiple price increases in a relatively short period of time, you may be disrupting and eroding the customer relationship, which in and of itself could contribute to a customer's decision to stop purchasing from you, independent of the relative price level. This is another phenomenon that can be observed but is difficult to predict using mathematical models.

Statistical models depend on "random" samples which can be tested to create inferences on the whole population. Companies that have had success modeling price-based churn have found ways to run tests on random samples of the overall population. This typically requires very large numbers of customers, like those found with wireless providers, TV programming providers, and credit card companies.

In summary, while it is possible to create successful mathematical models of price-based churn for repeat-purchase customer bases, doing so successfully requires the ability to test random samples to make inferences about the rest of the population in a way that doesn't bias the samples or the tests. This is extremely difficult to do if you do not have a very large number of customers. And, even then, there are many issues to contend with, which can make the results or inferences unreliable for good decision-making.

For this reason, I recommend that companies focus on getting their prices to a "fair" level relative to the market, using the rules of thumb outlined in Chapter 18 of this book, in order to manage the risks associated with price increases.

Since modeling elasticity is quite complex, and since using a general rule of thumb to form a hypothesis is relatively simple and straightforward, I recommend this approach for estimating the outcomes of price increases. And I would attempt to minimize negative outcomes by following the prescribed process of determining the appropriate magnitude of the price increase combined with the guidelines on effective communication regarding the price increase.

In short, price increases can be successfully executed, and the process laid out should be helpful.

# Appendix E

## Tools to Complete the Journey

In this book, I've shared many important concepts and approaches for leveraging pricing strategies to help your business grow in value. In Chapter 20, I outlined the step-by-step process for how to sequence the activities to make it easy for you to get started, along with examples of how to attack each step. But to be successful, you are going to need tools.

There are 10 primary tools you will need to be successful in identifying the highest-impact opportunities and establishing focused pricing strategies to improve outcomes in each respective opportunity area. These are listed below to give you a birds-eye view, after which I will go into detail on each one:

1. Tools for customer analysis and segmentation
2. Tools to model and define your customer lifecycle stages
3. Tools to calculate critical pricing metrics
4. Business valuation calculator
5. Tools to identify high-impact opportunities
6. Tools to construct pricing and incentive strategies
7. Tools to calculate break-even and hypothesized outcomes
8. Tools to mechanically change prices in systems of record, including quoting, commerce, and invoicing systems
9. Tools to communicate price changes with customers
10. Tools to measure and monitor business results

Examples of most of these tools can be found at PriceForGrowth.com.

## 1. Tools for Customer Analysis and Segmentation

The first set of tools you will need for your journey are tools to analyze and segment your customers.

At a high level, your customer segmentation and analysis tools need to do the following:

- separate your repeat customers from your one-time-purchase customers; attribute purchases, revenues, and profits for each group
- calculate the interval between purchases for your repeat customers
- separate customers into groups based on the frequency and regularity of their purchase intervals

- calculate the age of customer relationships based on their purchase history
- create segmentation definitions based on the above metrics, along with any other critical metrics, such as size, geography, customer type, industry, product preference, etc.
- tag or label customers with their appropriate segment ID, based on the segment definition rules
- dynamically update segment assignments, based on a customer's ongoing purchase behavior

Below is an example output from **customer segmentation analysis** tools focused on average purchase interval and typical business velocity:

### Number of Customers by Average Interval Between Purchases

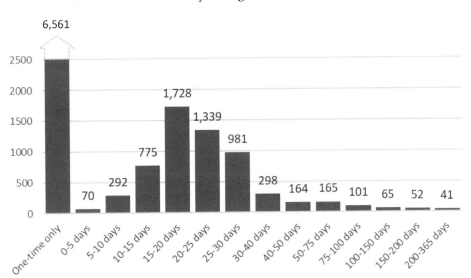

## 2. Tools to Model Customer Lifecycle

After the initial customer analysis, you should have clear visibility of how your customers are distributed across your customer segments, along with timing parameters such as length of customer relationship and interval since last purchase. This will give you the information you need to lay out and validate your customer lifecycle model.

Your customer lifecycle model should define discrete classifications for stages of maturity in your customer relationships. I recommend at least a three-stage model which includes:

1. New customers
2. Regular/onboarded customers
3. Churned customers

You will need to define the parameters of each group.

If you have the data, you may consider creating a more complex model which includes:

1. Leads/prospects
2. Trial customers
3. Onboarding customers
4. Regular repeat customers
5. One-time customers
6. Transient repeat customers
7. Irregular repeat customers
8. Declining customers
9. Churned customers

This will help you measure more granular movements inside your customer lifecycle model to help you better understand what is contributing to your overall growth and churn.

Your customer lifecycle modeling tools should at a minimum do the following:

- manually set parameters to define each stage in the customer lifecycle, which includes a catch-all stage (this will help you ensure your definitions are comprehensive)

- show the number of customers in each lifecycle stage, along with their associated purchases, revenues, and profits

- show how customers are moving through the different customer lifecycle stages over time—this is important since it will form a baseline history of conversion rates, so you can more easily identify opportunities

- (optional, if you collect leads or prospects as part of your customer lifecycle) collect information on leads or prospects and link them with new customer purchases to show conversion rates to first time buyers—this is extremely valuable because it can highlight one of the most important new customer acquisition metrics and allow that metric to be included in the opportunity ranking

After you have tools to model your customer lifecycle in place, you'll be ready for tools to calculate your critical pricing metrics. Below are some example output charts from **customer lifecycle analysis** tools:

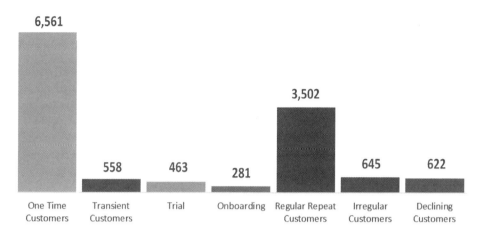

Customer Count by Customer Lifecycle Segment

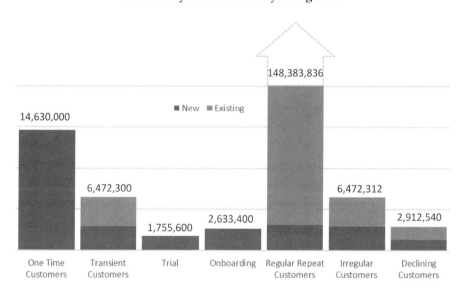

Revenue by Customer Lifecycle Segment

## 3. Tools to Calculate Critical Pricing Metrics

The key to managing any critical business decision is having visibility to the key data metrics that correlate with or impact the desired business outcome. You will need tools to automatically calculate all the critical pricing metrics for your business, including the **five sacred metrics of pricing success**, the **discounted net growth factor**, the **customer lifetime value factor**, and other key metrics related to pricing. This will include all the customer lifecycle stage conversion rates along with profit margins and customer pricing incentives.

Although almost any good BI (Business Intelligence) system could be programmed to calculate most of these metrics, it's much easier to have a system that calculates them all for you automatically.

You should be able to view metrics in dashboards and reports that can be filtered by time period and by business scope, from the lowest level of detail all the way up to the entire business. It will be important that these reports and dashboards are easy to read and understand, as they will be key to communicating opportunities, results, and strategies to other stakeholders in the organization. It should be easy to clip a chart or table and put it in a PowerPoint slide for support in a presentation or meeting with other internal stakeholders.

Below are example outputs from a **critical pricing metric calculation tool**:

### The Five Sacred Metrics of Pricing Success

| Metric | Value (Last 12 months) |
|---|---|
| New Customer Revenue Acquisition Rate | 24% |
| Existing Customer Revenue Expansion Rate | 2% |
| Existing Customer Revenue Churn Rate | 16% |
| Profit Expansion Rate | 0% |
| Present-Value Discount Rate (calculated from stock price) | 17.5% |

### Other Critical Pricing Success Metrics

| Metric | Value (Last 12 months) |
|---|---|
| Net Growth Rate | 10% |
| Profit Margin Percentage | 8% |
| Current Company Market Value (from stock price) | $194.8 million |
| Lead-to-Trial Conversion Rate | 20% |
| Trial-to-Onboarding Conversion Rate | 60% |
| Onboarding-to-Regular Conversion Rate | 90% |
| Lead-to-Regular Conversion Rate | 10.8% |
| Trial-to-Regular Conversion Rate | 54% |

## 4. Business Valuation Calculator

Since the primary objective of your pricing strategies will be to increase the value of the company, it will be critical to have some representative business valuation calculator which essentially calculates the present value of future profits based on recent growth, churn, and profitability metrics. Once baseline metrics are initialized and confirmed using the best estimate for actual company value, this will be a valuable tool for evaluating the impact of prospective strategies on the theoretical value of the company. Even though the valuation calculation will be theoretical value vs. actual market value, it will give accurate directional confirmation of various value strategies, and it should be expected that actual market value will follow in the same direction, and eventually the same magnitude, as the market absorbs the new growth and profit metrics.

This tool is critical for communicating the importance of certain strategies and decisions, and so this should not be overlooked or minimized. An example of a business value calculator is shown in the illustration below:

**Business Valuation Calculator with the Five Sacred Metrics**

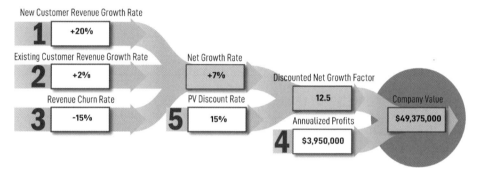

This tool will be more valuable if it can automatically take all the important pricing and conversion metrics and dynamically calculate how the theoretical value of the company has changed since the initial baseline metrics, so you can see all the different factors that have contributed to the value of the company over time. This is also an important way to measure the value of business outcomes from the pricing strategy decisions, both individually and cumulatively. This is where most companies fall short in their evaluation of not only pricing decisions, but also sales and marketing decisions. They don't have a way to track how their decisions impact the value of the company. Having a trustworthy tool in this area is a minimum requirement for a good pricing toolset.

As with all of the tools outlined in this chapter, it will save a lot of time and effort if all these tools are already integrated and can pass data back and forth.

## 5. Tools to Identify High-Impact Opportunities

After business valuation is enabled through a company value calculator, you can leverage that calculator to analyze and rank improvement opportunities based on both the amount of leverage each opportunity has on the value of the company and the theoretical ease of accomplishment based on how far current performance is from target.

This tool should automatically analyze the data and tell you which pricing metric improvement will have the largest impact on the value of the company. This will allow you to decide where to focus your first round of improvement strategies. This tool will need to look across all the growth and conversion metrics, the churn metrics, and the profitability metrics, and rank them based on where it looks like you can realize the biggest impact. An example output of this tool is shown in the table below:

**Improvement Opportunities Ranked by Potential Impact**

| Metric | Leverage Rank | Opportunity Rank | Combined Average Rank |
|---|---|---|---|
| Lead-to-Trial Conversion Rate | 1 | 3 | 2 |
| Churn Rate | 3 | 2 | 2.5 |
| Trial-to-Onboard Conversion Rate | 2 | 5 | 3.5 |
| Margin Expansion Rate | 6 | 1 | 3.5 |
| Annualized Profits | 4 | 4 | 4 |
| Onboard-to-Regular Conversion Rate | 5 | 5 | 5 |

While this may seem relatively straightforward, and while it can be done manually in spreadsheets, you will save a significant amount of time if you use a tool that is designed to do this automatically. This way, you don't have to worry about the technicalities of complex Excel functions and potentially getting something wrong. Instead, you can focus on the output numbers and think about strategies.

# 6. Tools to Construct Pricing and Incentive Strategies

Once you've identified the best area in which to focus your pricing strategies, you will need tools to construct potential strategies for implementation. Whether it is a one-time discount, a recurring discount, a periodic rebate, a standard list price, or some sort of free product or money-back guarantee, you will need a tool that can plan the structure, the amount, and the timing of the new strategy. The tool must also be able to define eligibility parameters for any new price incentive.

The tool must also be able to model current, existing incentives and eligible discounts, so it can integrate the new modeled pricing strategy and calculate the incremental differences. This must enable visibility of the impact to the current level of recurring profits based on likely and break-even scenarios.

Many pricing software programs can model new pricing strategies along with potential impact scenarios. Some of them require more custom configuration or coding than others, but these tools are easy to find. Most of them are fairly expensive and may take several months to implement.

The ideal tools will have prebuilt discount and incentive structures that can provide easy templates for creating new pricing and incentive scenarios without lots of custom configuration or coding.

## 7. Tools to Calculate Break-Even and Hypothesized Outcomes

Modeling break-even and hypothesized business outcomes is critical for evaluating potential pricing strategy decisions. Specifically, these tools need to do the following:

- allow users to select and validate the primary outcome variable that will be used to determine both the break-even outcome, and the hypothesized business outcome

- allow users to select the primary objective variable for break-even calculations, such as overall business valuation, total revenues, total profits, or, potentially, another variable

- automatically calculate break-even outcome based on the outcome variable and the primary objective

- simultaneously calculate multiple break-even values based on different outcome metrics, such as 12-month profits, lifetime ROI, and company valuation-based break-even values

- display key pricing and business metrics under each scenario to help users more easily understand the bigger-picture results

This is a particularly important capability because it gives you a window into the potential future under a different pricing scenario.

The tools available could vary in complexity, from a simple spreadsheet to very sophisticated programs that calculate bottom-up changes for each customer and product, then roll those up to summary metrics.

An example output of a break-even evaluation tool is shown in the table below:

### Break-Even Values for $10,000 Monthly Trial Incentive

| Break-Even Calculation | Incremental Cost (foregone profits) | Unitary Benefit (per incremental customer) | Break-Even Units (new customers) | Hypothesized Incremental Units |
|---|---|---|---|---|
| Profit Break-Even | $10,000 | $450 | 22.2 → 23/mo | 100/mo |
| ROI Break-Even | $10,000 | $3,000 | 3.3 → 4/mo | 100/mo |
| | Annualized Cost | Incremental Valuation (per new customer) | Break-Even Units (new customers) | Hypothesized Incremental Units |
| Valuation-Based Break-Even | $120,000 | $66,600 | 1.8 → 2/yr  Less than 1 per month | 1200/yr |

More complex tools are necessary if you have complex eligibility requirements for different prices, especially when those eligibility requirements change from scenario to scenario. On the other hand, if you just have list prices with no discount incentives, you can get away with less complex tools.

## 8. Tools to Mechanically Change Prices in Systems of Record, Including Quoting, Commerce, and Invoicing Systems

Once the pricing strategy and action is decided, you'll need to mechanically change the prices in your existing quoting, commerce, and invoicing systems. This could include changing list prices and enabling new discounts or rebates, whether at the product level or some other aggregated level.

Theoretically, the new prices should have already been successfully modeled prior to this step, so it should just be a matter of taking those prices and appropriately updating the respective system of record. This needs to include the appropriate effective dates.

In addition, these tools should be able to report back to confirm that prices have successfully been updated.

Unfortunately, because this involves updating prices in other systems, it often requires custom development, which can be quite expensive. These types of data-interface tools are sometimes built in-house. Depending on your company's IT strategy and capability, you'll need to figure out the most effective and economical approach to get these tools implemented.

Today, more and more companies are creating direct connections to existing ERP and e-commerce systems, and if you happen to have one of these systems where direct connection is supported, you can save some time and money. The potential downside is that you may be limited to only the pricing incentive structures supported by the underlying systems.

## 9. Tools to Communicate Price Changes with Customers

One critical process that is often overlooked by Pricing departments is effectively communicating prices to customers. This is very important because this is how customers will form opinions about the fairness of any price changes.

This should include email templates and enablement for Sales and Marketing to explain the attractiveness of any new incentives and the justification for any necessary price increases.

Since this is not something that most companies focus on, there are very few tools for doing this. However, there are many tools in the marketing automation category that offer this type of functionality. That said, it is generally advisable to get consulting help or training in the art and science of customer communication to ensure this core capability is effectively covered.

## 10. Tools to Measure and Monitor Business Results

Once new prices and incentives are successfully implemented in the market, the last important set of tools will need to effectively monitor business results to quickly diagnose whether the new strategy is working as expected—or not. Ideally these tools are integrated with the tools used to model hypothesized business results. However, this is not necessarily required.

These tools should be able to determine whether or not the observed results are statistically different than the hypothesized results. This capability will allow companies to react very quickly when something is not working as planned. However, companies must realize that there may be a delay of several weeks between the initial action and the ultimate market reaction. And so, companies must continue to measure market reaction, even after they get an initial read on whether or not the strategy seems to be working.

Many tools can monitor and report on business results, including simple BI (Business Intelligence) tools, advanced statistical reporting tools, and anything in-between. The ideal system should be integrated with the system that allows users to create hypotheses and model outcomes because then you have a more seamless workflow.

## Summary

In addition to sound pricing concepts, philosophies, and strategies, tools are critical to making things happen, and you should make sure you have the tools required for the journey. These tools can be built or patterned after the examples in this book or the expanded examples you can find at PriceForGrowth.com.

# Glossary

**80/20 Principle**: The concept that a relatively small portion of inputs (20%) are responsible for a relatively large portion of results (80%). For example, the top 20% of customers account for 80% of the profits. Implies that more productive outputs can be achieved by finding and focusing on the most productive inputs.

**Annualized**: Describes the result of taking the value of a performance metric over a selected period of time (typically less than one year) and extrapolating it to represent a full year under the same conditions. For example, $20,000 of profits over two months would be extrapolated to $120,000 of profits if annualized.

**Annualized Profits**: The result of extrapolating recent profits to a full year.

**Annuity**: An amount to be received or paid once per year for a defined period of time.

**B2B (Business to Business)**: Represents businesses selling to other businesses, as opposed to end consumers.

**B2C (Business to Consumer)**: Represents businesses who sell to end consumers.

**Bargaining Cost**: Any cost a customer or vendor must bear in the course of negotiating an acceptable price for a transaction or series of future transactions.

**Break-Even Value**: For any investment, the result required to make the investment profit neutral or ROI-neutral, sufficient to make the company as well off as they would be without making the investment. This book refers to three different break-even values, including profit break-even, ROI break-even, and company-valuation-based break-even. By calculating break-even values, companies can more easily make decisions about whether or not to move forward with a prospective pricing action or strategy change.

**Business Velocity**: The average or typical interval between the purchases of repeat customers, typically described in standard units of daily, weekly, monthly, bi-monthly, quarterly, semi-annually, or annually.

**Buyer Inertia**: The momentum of repeated actions or behaviors of repeat customers who buy in a repeat fashion.

**Buyer Types**: Refers to one of three different levels at which customers make buying decisions: (1) product level buyers, (2) cart-level buyers, and (3) relationship buyers. Most repeat-purchase customers are relationship buyers.

**Cause-and-Effect Mentality**: The belief that different results can be achieved by changing variables deemed to be the "cause." For the purpose of evaluating strategies, the cause-and-effect approach focuses on what "effects" might follow changes in the "cause," rather than focusing on the objective, and then imagining all the potential ways to achieve the objective. The criticism of the **cause-and-effect** approach is that it arbitrarily singles out one potential causal factor, when there are usually a multitude of causal factors, many of which are unknown.

**Churn**: The loss of regular customers or the loss of regular revenues and profits due to lost customers.

**Contribution Margin**: Margin metric defined as revenues minus variable costs. Considered a generally more relevant margin metric for making decisions related to pricing and sales because it looks only at the incremental costs associated with the new business, not the fixed or sunk costs that the business would bear anyway.

**Customer Churn Rate:** Refers to the percentage of customers lost over a defined time period, typically a year.

**Customer Lifecycle**: Represents the typical stages customers go through, from initial interest in purchasing, through purchasing as a regular repeat customer, through their decision to stop purchasing, and anything in-between.

**Customer Loyalty Profile**: A way to categorize customers based on their propensity to continue to buy from a particular company. This book describes a customer loyalty profile model that has five different categories, from low-margin, bottom feeder to captive, die-hard customer.

**Declining (Customer Lifecycle Stage)**: A category of regular customers who have recently reduced their purchases in comparison with previous levels; considered to be at risk of churning.

**Direct Costs**: A cost that is directly traceable to an item or service being sold. For example, the cost of the product itself, or the shipping cost to obtain the product. Conversely, an indirect cost, such as marketing, cannot be individually attributed to a specific product.

**Discount**: A reduction from a regular price; can be represented in a percentage or a specific dollar amount.

**Discount Rate**: A percentage used to adjust the value of money to be received in the future; like an interest rate.

**EBITDA (Earnings Before Interest Taxes Depreciation and Amortization)**: A key profit metric used by investors to value companies.

**Elasticity**: In general, the concept that there is an inverted relationship between price and quantity sold. The official term Price Elasticity of Demand is used to quantify this relationship, and it is calculated by dividing the percentage change in quantity by the percentage change in price. Values greater than 1 indicate that the sales of the product are highly responsive to price. Values less than 1 indicate that sales of the product are not very responsive to price. One of the criticisms of elasticity is that it implies that price is the fundamental driver of purchase decisions, and therefore it overstates the impact of price in buyer behavior.

**Evaluation Costs**: A cost customers must bear to research, learn about, compare, and evaluate potential purchases, potential suppliers, or potential products. This includes both monetary costs and nonmonetary costs, such as time and effort.

**Five Sacred Metrics of Pricing Success**: Five different price-influenced metrics that ultimately combine to calculate the theoretical value of the company. They include: (1) New Customer Revenue Acquisition Rate, (2) Existing Customer Revenue Expansion Rate, (3) Customer Revenue Churn Rate, (4) Annualized Profits, and (5) Present-Value Discount Rate.

**Friction in the Buying Process** (also known as **Market Friction**): Anything that makes commerce more difficult, including evaluation costs, bargaining costs, fulfillment costs, transaction costs; also includes anything that causes a customer more effort in a present or future transaction or commercial relationship, such as breach of trust, poor experiences, or price uncertainty.

**Gordon Growth Formula**: A mathematical formula for determining the present value of a growing perpetuity. It was originally created to value dividends from growing companies, and it was later used to value entire companies. The formula is $PV = D \div (r - g)$, where PV is the present value, D is the amount of the perpetuity (or dividend), r is the discount rate, and g is the growth rate of the perpetuity (or dividend). In this book, we use the Gordon Growth Formula to calculate the value of the company in our example company value calculator.

**Gross Margin**: Total revenue less total cost. Unit Gross Margin is price less unit cost.

**Growth Mindset**: A mindset that starts with the belief that there are infinite possibilities for solving any problem. It encourages individuals to attack problems with an open mind and a desire to help others in their quest for solutions.

**High-Impact Pricing Opportunity**: Any opportunity to significantly improve the value of one of the sacred pricing metrics, such that it will have a relatively high impact on the theoretical value of the company (as calculated by the company value calculator).

**Indirect Costs**: Costs that are not directly attributable to a sold product or service, such as marketing costs. Typically, indirect costs are allocated to sold products based on some cost driver metric, such as dollars, units, or even direct costs.

**Irregular Repeat Buyer (Customer Lifecycle Stage):** Refers to customers who have purchased multiple times, but without any consistent pattern or frequency.

**Learning Incentive**: Some sort of monetary incentive for a customer to learn about a product or service. An example might be a 20% off coupon code that is given at the end of a five-minute YouTube video on a new product or service.

**Margin Expansion Pricing Strategy**: Any pricing strategy that seeks to increase profits or margins through the mechanism of increased prices; typically not a sustainable way to grow profits over time, as there are clear limits to how much a price can be raised before customers stop buying.

**Market Friction**: (See Friction in the Buying Process above).

**Negotiated Pricing**: A pricing strategy which allows customers to negotiate customer-specific prices. Negotiated pricing is often based on nothing more than sales rep discretion or negotiating skills. Negotiated pricing inevitably leads to unfair prices among customers, and this book strongly discourages this practice for repeat-purchase customers who buy standard products or services.

**Negotiating Costs**: These are the costs in time, effort, and money to negotiate a mutually acceptable price prior to a transaction. It is a type of market friction that some customers have to face in order to make a purchase from some vendors.

**Net Repeatable Revenue Growth Rate**: A key metric used to value the company. It represents the "g" in the Gordon Growth Formula. It is calculated by adding the first three sacred pricing metrics: (1) new customer revenue acquisition rate, (2) existing customer revenue expansion rate, and (3) customer revenue churn rate (as a negative number).

**Objective-Driven Approach to Pricing Strategy**: This is an approach to pricing that starts with the objective the company wants to accomplish. After defining the objective, the stakeholders brainstorm the best possible ways to achieve the objective. This approach differs from the cause-and-effect approach, which starts by determining the "cause" and then seeks to estimate the impact of changing the cause. The objective-driven approach is a more open-minded approach because it does not require focus on any single "cause."

**Onboarding (Customer Lifecycle Stage)**: The stage in the customer lifecycle in which the customer is making repeat purchases, but they may still face some buying friction because they have not purchased for long enough to create entrenched habits. For this reason, companies should give these customers extra care and attention—and potentially continued incentives—to help ease them into the regular-repeat-buyer stage. The onboarding stage typically follows the trial stage.

**Onboarding Incentive**: Any pricing incentive designed to make it easier for new customers to make repeat purchases for long enough to develop regular purchase habits. The incentives typically take the form of post-purchase rebates, so the customer can build the habits around regular purchase processes and prices.

**One-Time Purchaser (Customer Lifecycle Stage):** Refers to customers who have made only one purchase with the company in recent history.

**Overhead**: All the indirect costs of running a business, including executive salaries. Overhead often includes many fixed costs; however, some costs can be scaled according to need and budget.

**Perpetuity**: An annuity that goes on forever.

**Pocket Margin**: The resultant margin when all costs associated with a transaction, including both direct and indirect costs, are subtracted from the price.

**Pocket Price**: The net price charged after adjusting for all surcharges, discounts, rebates, or any other price reduction mechanism.

**Present Value**: Today's value of money that will be received at some time in the future. To calculate the present value, a discount rate is used, and the future value is reduced by that discount rate for each year in the future until the money is received.

**Price Communication**: Any communication to customers about price changes, especially the compelling rationale for any type of large-scale price increase. As a general rule, price communication should be used to notify customers of the magnitude and rationale of any price increase the customer is not already expecting.

**Price Fairness**: The assurance that prices show no favoritism, partiality, or discrimination, and that they are generally in line with the value delivered to the customer. Price fairness also suggests that prices are generally in line with competitive market prices, do not result in unreasonably high profit margins, exhibit stability over time, and are consistent with what the company has previously advertised.

**Price Integrity**: The principle of keeping prices "incorruptible" and adherent to a stated strategy or policy determined by a repeatable process that generates consistent and defensible price outputs. It means prices are stable, justifiable, and can be trusted by customers.

**Price Manipulation**: An attempt to get a customer to pay a higher price than other regular customers by means of communicating selective or misleading information or withholding information that would cause the customer to reject the higher price.

**Price Rationality**: The principle of ensuring that prices are intentionally and logically positioned relative to each other in a way that makes sense according to implied value or customer expectations of value. For example, large versions of the same product may have intentionally higher prices than smaller versions, and equivalent products are priced the same. Rationality is the absence of logical discrepancies in prices. Rationality is important for building and maintaining trust with customers.

**Price Transparency**: Where prices are visible so all customers can see them, and there are no secret prices or pricing arrangements. Price transparency leads to improved customer trust and better customer relationships as long as the company adheres to price fairness, price rationality, and price integrity.

**Pricing Strategy**: A purposeful use of price to achieve a defined objective, such as solidifying customer relationships, expanding margins, or growing sales.

**Pricing Tug-o-War**: The situation that occurs when customers believe prices are up for discussion, where they will constantly try to find ways to get lower prices, while the company constantly tries to get prices higher. The pricing tug-o-war is an artifact of negotiated pricing practices, and it usually leads to customer dissatisfaction.

**Rebate**: A monetary payment to customers for making a purchase. It usually requires the customer to submit a rebate claim form. Rebates are usually intended to incentivize customers to make a purchase by lessening the financial burden of doing so.

**Regular Repeat Buyer (Customer Lifecycle Stage)**: Refers to customers who have been making repeat purchases for long enough to have developed consistent buying habits and inertia such that they will continue making purchases as long as their inertia is not disrupted.

**Revenue Churn**: Revenues that are lost period-over-period due to the loss of customers in that period.

**Scientific Method**: A method of learning and establishing new theories through the following steps: analyze the situation, formulate questions, develop hypotheses, conduct tests, observe results, draw conclusions, and repeat the process with revised hypotheses.

**Service Failure**: Any problem with the products or service that a customer has purchased. Examples include things like delivery delays, bungled shipments, product problems, billing issues, missed service calls, or failure to solve problems with an order.

**Switching Costs**: Includes all costs customers must bear in order to switch to another vendor, including evaluation costs, bargaining costs, transactions costs, fulfillment costs, the cost to learn new products or processes, the cost of retooling, or the cost of training internal employees or external agents. Switching costs are the driving force behind most customer loyalty.

**Theoretical Company Value**: The resultant value calculated in a company value calculator which derives the company value from the five sacred pricing metrics. It should be relatively close to the actual market value of a company as long as the calculator is initially calibrated by an actual company market value in order to get the appropriate present-value discount rate, although it should be expected that actual market value will lag behind theoretical company value as investors become comfortable with the changes in the input metrics.

**Trial (Customer Lifecycle Stage)**: The first stage of the customer lifecycle after the customer has made a first purchase. This stage should include enough time after the purchase for the customer to determine if they like the product and purchase experience enough to purchase again.

**Trial Incentive**: A monetary incentive intended to reduce a customer's monetary burden to try a new product or buying experience. This incentive might also be larger than the original price of the product, and it is meant to compensate a customer for the inconvenience of trying the product or buying experience.

**Value Pricing** (Also **Value-Based Pricing**): Pricing strategy that attempts to set prices based on the value customers place on differential features, both positive and negative. It typically starts with the price of a reference product that is well known in the market.

**Value Selling**: Selling approach that involves highlighting how a product's differential features save the customer pain or money (described in monetary terms) in an attempt to show that the price is attractive given the benefits. Value pricing often requires value selling in order to educate the customers on the value of the differences.

**Variable Costs**: Costs that increase or decrease with commensurate increases or decreases in production or sales volumes.

**Zero-Exception Pricing**: A pricing policy that insures no preferential treatment for any single customer. It is used to ensure that pricing is fair for all customers. All discounts and incentives are based on standard programs and are available to all customers who objectively qualify.

# Index